Need One!

A Lunatic's Attempt to Attend 365 Games in 365 Days

Jamie Reidy

For Michelle,

My dear friend who, in an all-time upset, became a sports fan late in the game.

Published 2017 by HumorOutcasts Press
Printed in the United States of America

ISBN: 0-9980899-4-X
EAN-13: 978-0-9980899-4-2

Cover art and design by

Angela Lewis-Akers

Prologue

The streak was dead. Even I, the Duke of Self Delusion, had to admit that.

Time of death: 9:00 a.m. on Day Twenty-One, or, as normal adults would call it, September 25, 2013. "Sports Year," my simultaneously inspired and idiotic project during which I'd attend a sporting event every day for three-hundred and sixty-five days in all fifty states, had come to a halt in Decatur, Georgia. Thanks to the fatal combination of religion and rain, the streak stopped eleven months and one week *early*. That's the equivalent of Joey Chestnut puking after just four hot dogs in the Nathan's July 4th eating contest.

I'd always known that this trip was, uh, ambitious, and that the odds were against my completing the goal. Before embarking on this unprecedented journey, my imagination conjured up innumerable doomsday scenarios that could bring the streak to a premature end – stranded by an October blizzard in South Dakota, delayed after rescuing a family from their burning minivan in Illinois, mistakenly arrested for the murder of a convenience store clerk in Alabama. In none of them, it is important to note, was I wearing only my boxer briefs.

My forehead – with its rapidly receding hairline – did not provide sufficient room for the giant "L" tattoo I deserved. I couldn't even complete three *weeks* of consecutive games in a row? And I had actually believed I could accomplish my goal of 365 in 365? That seemed laughable now, just as my jeering buddies had predicted.

Up until that moment, my life had largely been filled with cheers. Not much to complain about when your biggest disappointment was not getting into Duke. In sixth grade I was elected class president (Admittedly, though, there *was* some impeachment talk a few months later, due to my lack of action on key issues I'd campaigned on). I had a successful high school experience academically and athletically (alas, not romantically). At Notre Dame I earned an Army ROTC scholarship to help my parents pay for college and walked onto the wrestling team and earned a varsity letter. As a lieutenant stationed in Japan, I managed to avoid burning down my HQ building while safely serving in the era between Iraq wars. In pharmaceutical sales, I finished the year ranked #1 in the country at both Pfizer and Eli Lilly. As a first-time author, I miraculously got published without an agent; then I cyber-stalked Malcolm Gladwell, which led directly to my book serving as the basis for the feature film *Love and Other Drugs*. Good times.

But on September 25, 2013, winning seemed as unfamiliar to me as gelling my hair. The rain rattling the roof of my brother and sister-in-law's home bludgeoned my confidence like meat hammers. Tears welled in my eyes as I sat despairing at the dining-room table. Enveloped in a fog of my own stale body odor, I had on just the underwear I'd worn all day yesterday and slept in. (Sorry, Clare!) Only three years earlier, Jake Gyllenhaal had played a Viagra salesman named "Jamie" on the big screen. Normally, when it came to self-introspection I proved as elusive as Barry Sanders. But, now, I found myself unable to avoid this question: What the hell happened to me?

For starters, I ignored good advice. My agent was a twenty-year Hollywood veteran who sells the movie rights to books by titans like Don DeLillo and Dennis Lehane. Based on my upbeat personality and constant brainstorming, she suggested in 2005 that my professional writing future rested in television sitcoms. She offered to introduce me to several TV show runners. This woman got paid only if I got paid, so she clearly had our best interests at heart. An entertainment industry newbie like me should have dutifully followed her guidance. Instead, I declined her offer, saying, "Why would I want to go to work every day?" HAHAHAHAHAHA! Wasn't that a riot?

I'd like to go back in time and spike that cocky know-it-all's iced mocha with antifreeze. Instead of cranking out sitcom scripts, I focused on feature-film comedy screenplays, all of which were liked, none of which were loved. I stubbornly refused to get a day job, yet did not curtail my spending. You don't hear a lot of financial planners recommending that course of action.

Finally, my movie money ran out in late 2012. How'd I pay the bills after that? By racking up more of them. I took advantage of the absurdly high credit limits on my myriad cards, eventually running up $75,000 in debt. In early 2013 I cancelled my health insurance, happy to be spared the monthly payment. Right now you might be screaming, "Jamie, why not just get a job with, you know, benefits and stuff?!" Fair question.

But, puh-lease. Traditional employment appealed to me less than attending Sunday Mass the morning after a bachelor party. For a guy who didn't write horror-movie scripts, I sure had created a monster.

Get a 9-to-5 job? Negative, Ghost Rider. I was a *writer*. Never again would I don my sales hat, or seek any occupation that did not feature my skills as a wordsmith.

Except, of course, that day when I applied to work at Starbucks.

Strictly for research purposes, I told myself. I was writing *Vanilla Latte*, a sitcom in which a white guy goes to work at a coffee chain in the hood. See, he desperately needs health insurance, but he's too embarrassed for anyone he knows to see him sporting the green apron. So, he takes a job at a Starbucks located in a place he'll never run into anyone.

I applied online for positions at several franchises in Crenshaw and Compton, offering to work at any time of day, any days of the week. I never got a response. Then, I spent a morning at all three franchises, hoping to apply in person. After placing my order, I asked, "Are you guys hiring?" Each time, the barista replied, "Yep! But everything is done online. So just go to Starbucks.com and fill out the application…" My parents were super proud that their Notre Dame grad/decorated Army officer son could not get an interview, let alone hired, at freaking Starbucks.

Although I had shared few details of my impending financial doom with friends or family, unsolicited vocational advice arrived with unsettling frequency. This sparked a painful internal dialogue. *Dude, it's time to do the grown up thing: press pause on your writing "career" and get a job job. (And stop saying "Dude," already! You're forty-three years old.)*

So, I did the opposite, hatching the concept for Sports Year. *365 Games in 365 Days.* My brain latched onto the catchiness of that slogan and gripped it tightly like a quarterback taking the snap in "victory" formation. I assured myself that the book I'd write about the journey would appeal to countless people languishing in their day-to-day lives. Plus, the story would lend itself easily to movie adaptation. Ka-ching.

By any measure – scope and cost, duration and distance – Sports Year was the most ambitious idea I'd ever conjured up. This would be an *undertaking.* An internet search for similar projects proved brief; I couldn't find anybody who had ever attempted such a crazy road trip. I'd be the first! As a kid, I read a lot about Daniel Boone; being a trailblazer held great appeal for me.

Daniella, the woman I'd been dating for nearly a year, did not share my enthusiasm for Sports Year. Fabulous enough that some of my friends suggested I marry her, she cheered my writing efforts while gently nudging my return to a sales career. On cue, a buddy offered me a lucrative position hawking insurance plans to HMOs. Boom! I'd be able to pay off my debts and get serious about Daniella.

But self-doubts popped up overnight like teenage acne. In addition to my long string of unsold scripts, my last two non-fiction books had fizzled, too. Now, I panicked that Sports Year was my last good idea. That fear spread like sepsis, paralyzing me as I sat at my desk trying to update my resume. I began questioning whether I even wanted to get married and have kids, something I thought for sure I'd figured out after years of waffling.

Once again, my pride did me in; I refused to slink back into the real world and put on my sales hat without giving the writing one final shot. On July 1st I coldly broke up with Daniella and immediately began poring over pro and college teams' schedules so I could plot Sports Year. Two months later I embarked on my unfinanced, poorly planned odyssey.

Which is how I came to be a middle-aged, unemployed and lonely bachelor wallowing in self-pity and ripe underwear as I sat at my little brother's dining room table, mourning the end of my dream.

Did you know that most towns throughout the deep South and Bible Belt shut down on Wednesday nights for church activities? Me, neither. (See: earlier "poorly planned" comment.) Even *public* schools and youth athletic leagues don't schedule recitals or games on Wednesday evenings. Sports Year's Day Twenty-One fell on a Hump Day.

Staying near Atlanta, I whiffed in my attempts to find a scholastic sporting event. As a result, I planned on seeing Major League Baseball's Braves play that evening. Unfortunately, the morning brought rain hard enough to scare Noah. The weather reports predicted precipitation all day and night, meaning the ballgame could be cancelled. Local universities had no athletic contests scheduled. My streak was dead. Outside, the pounding on the roof sounded to me like mocking applause.

In pitches to publishers and TV producers, I had described the project as "a search for Americana in its bleachers." But, really, I'd be searching for me.

So, if the streak was dead, where did that leave the searcher?

CHAPTER ONE

"Definitely The Worst Idea You've Ever Had"

Ah, to be young and stupid again.

My first semester at Notre Dame coincided with the Fighting Irish returning to the top of the college football world. In 1988 Lou Holtz's squad beat two #1 teams (Miami and USC) en route to finishing the regular season with an unblemished record. This lofty achievement made me something of a celebrity among my friends when I got home for winter break. (By "celebrity," I mean "That Guy" who annoyed everyone with his incessant chatter about the Irish and "our" first undefeated season in ages.) In mid-December, my parents surprised me with an early Christmas gift: round-trip airfare to Phoenix and three nights hotel for the Fiesta Bowl, in which ND would be playing West Virginia for the national championship.

Rich and Loretta Reidy were not known for prompting their eldest child to take impromptu trips, let alone paying for them. I knew that a similar opportunity was as unlikely as my graduating cum laude. Naturally, I passed.

"We're gonna go to *plenty* of national championship games over the next ten years," I explained to my parents, who gaped at me as if I'd turned down a full-body massage offer from Cindy Crawford. "Mom and Dad, I'd rather you pay for me to go on Spring Break to South Padre Island." Of all the myriad things that still upset me about this story, what pisses me off the most is the fact that I could not do simple math: $0 < 3$, with zero representing the number of national championship games to which Notre Dame was guaranteed to return over the rest of my college career, and three representing the minimum number of spring breaks I was guaranteed to have an opportunity to attend. (Interesting fact: zero also happened to represent the number of girls I had sex with during that week in South Padre Island.)

You probably know how that Fiesta Bowl turned out: the Irish stomped the Mountaineers. My classmates who went to the game still talk about the experience in tones so reverential that you'd think the Pope stopped by their tailgater and personally blessed their cases of Natty Light. In '89, Holtz's team ran off ten more wins before losing to Miami in the last week of the season, scuttling my plans to go to the bowl game with the national championship at stake. In '90, we were ranked #1 but lost the season finale to Penn State, blowing another shot at the title. In my senior year, Irish fans' dreams of a championship ended in early November.

My decision to turn down the Fiesta Bowl haunted me. Having missed the biggest event of my college career, I pledged that *under no circumstances* would I attend a national championship game until Notre Dame was playing in it. I had a long wait. (True to my word, I turned down a ticket to the "Vince Young game," a.k.a. Texas-USC at the Rose Bowl in 2006. Clearly, I need psychiatric help.)

So, when Coach Brian Kelly's boys ran the table in 2012, you know damn well I booked a flight to Miami to watch the Irish in "our" first national title game since my freshman year. Unfortunately, Alabama also showed up. When people ask me about the carnage, I say, "For sixty-eight hours, the trip was a lot of fun." Sure, the Crimson Tide embarrassed us, but simply *being there* and reveling in the atmosphere reminded me just how thrilling it can be to see a big game.

I made a list of the big ones I'd seen. Two World Series games. Orange Bowl. Redskins at Cowboys in Texas Stadium. The first "Bowden Bowl" at Clemson's Death Valley in '99. The inaugural Opening Day in 2000 at whatever-they-call-it-now-where-the-S.F.-Giants-play. I'd been to eight of the past ten Kentucky Derbies. NYC

Marathon. US Open tennis. As for famous venues, I'd been to Madison Square Garden (for hockey, not hoops), the Rose Bowl, Yankee Stadium, the Big House, Pauley Pavilion, Fenway Park, Wrigley Field, and Soldier Field.

But *that* got me to thinking about all the huge sporting events I had not yet experienced: Super Bowl, The Masters, Final Four, "World's Largest Outdoor Cocktail Party," Daytona 500, Little League World Series, Army-Navy, Friday Night Lights game in Texas, Spring Training, Boston Marathon, McKinley-Massillon in Ohio HS football, MLB All-Star game, any SEC rivalry, Oklahoma-Texas, Michigan-Ohio State.

What about stadiums and arenas I'd missed? Lambeau Field. LSU's Death Valley. Cameron Indoor Arena. Texas Memorial Stadium. Ohio Stadium. Camden Yards. Talladega Superspeedway. Carrier Dome. Mile High Stadium. Joe Louis Arena. Allen Fieldhouse. The Swamp. Rupp Arena.

Those two lists bummed me out. But they also prompted questions. When the hell was I gonna find the time to check off all those items?! *Likely never.* Was it even possible for a non-sports writer to do all that in one lifetime?! *Maybe.* What were the biggest obstacles to completing those lists? *Three big ones: marriage, kids, job.*

It occurred to me, then, that I was not married. (This occurred to my mother more frequently.) I also didn't have kids. (See: previous "mother" comment.) And, according to an ex-girlfriend, as a writer I didn't have a "*real* job."

Which is when I got The Idea. The best idea I've ever had. Or the worst. Probably both: I'd get in the car and start driving to see an athletic contest every day for one year, hitting all fifty states. I'd have the greatest year in the history of sports fandom. Then I'd write a book about it.

But an adventure like that deserved an inspiring moniker conveying all of its ambition and grandeur. So I ideated for days. Finally, drawing on every ounce of my authorial creativity, I dubbed this undertaking in which I'd see sports every day for a year... SPORTS YEAR.

One night over many drinks with some married buddies, I asked if they thought Sports Year was possible. Their answers varied in profanities, but not themes: a) I lacked brain cells and b) I'd never do it. (In my defense, these same guys had also told me I was on dope when I expressed unwavering certainty that my little book about a Viagra salesman would someday be turned into a movie.) Their negativity was discouraging to hear, but I did sense some envy that I could even *consider* such a fun project. With some trepidation, I called my folks to share my plan.

By way of comparison, "I'm gonna drive cross country for a year to watch games" would make "I'm gonna be an English major" look like a parental wet dream. After the requisite thirty seconds of Dad trying to figure out how to put me on speakerphone, I dropped the idea on them. When Rich and Loretta both responded with, "Definitely the worst idea you've ever had!" I knew I had a winner.

Game. On!

CHAPER TWO

"The Playbook"

This story would sweat Americana: small towns, midlife crisis, road trip, sports. Additionally, I'd be trying to answer pressing questions: Are parents in Texas crazier than those in Maine? Which stadium boasts the best hot dog? Why am I still single?

My trip would kick off on September 5, 2013 in Denver with the NFL's opening game between the Broncos and Ravens. Interestingly, that was neither the date on which nor the city in which I thought I'd be starting. Up until mid-August, I assumed I'd begin in Tuscaloosa, Alabama, where the defending champion Crimson Tide was hosting Virginia Tech. My confusion was entirely the fault of the Baltimore Orioles' owner. But before I can explain *that*, I need to describe some recent NFL tradition.

In 2002, the league began launching its season with a Thursday night primetime game featuring a juicy matchup. Two years after that, the NFL rewarded the defending Super Bowl champion with the distinction of hosting the first game of the season. That's why I planned on beginning Sports Year sorta near the east coast – the Ravens had won the Super Bowl in February. I figured I'd hit the ground running with an inaugural week featuring a number of firsts for me: first visit to Alabama's famed Bryant-Denny Stadium, opening NFL game, first game featuring traditionally black colleges (Howard vs. Morehouse at RFK Stadium) and first Monday Night Football game (Eagles at Redskins). Nice start, right?!

Just three weeks prior to my departure for Alabama, though, a sports-media magnate set me straight. David Katz, the founder of ThePostGame.com, explained that when the NFL execs were assembling the 2013 schedule, they realized they had a conflict with the very first contest featuring the Ravens: the Baltimore Orioles already had a home game on Thursday night September 5th. This was problematic because both pro teams' stadiums share nearby parking lots. So, NFL Commissioner Roger Goodell called the Orioles owner Peter Angelos and asked him to reschedule the baseball game. But Angelos – a well-known asshole – refused. The NFL promptly gave the Charm City the finger, moving what should have been a deliriously happy Ravens' home opener to Denver. Had David Katz not clued me in, I very likely would have driven from California to Alabama and missed the NFL's opening game of Sports Year. (Sheesh. That last sentence pretty much says all you need to know about the quality of my planning.)

Schedule-wise, I intended to hit "Tentpole" events both professional (Super Bowl, Daytona 500, The Masters, Kentucky Derby, Indianapolis 500) and amateur (Little League World Series, Army-Navy football; LSU football game at Death Valley; the "World's Largest Outdoor Cocktail Party," a.k.a Florida-Georgia football). I was going to run the gamut from chi chi (pro tennis in Newport, Rhode Island) to tacky (Lingerie Football League in Baltimore). And I'd watch midnight baseball in Alaska and surfing championships in Hawaii.

Here's the tentative itinerary, emphasis on "tentative":

September
5 – Ravens v. Broncos in Denver
7 – So Miss v. Nebraska in Lincoln, NE
9 – Giants v. Cowboys in Dallas
13 – Air Force v. Boise St in Boise
14 – Tennessee v. Oregon in Eugene
15 – 49ers v. Seahawks in Seattle
19 – Bass Master fishing Open in Muskogee, OK
21 – Auburn v. LSU football in Baton Rouge, LA
22 – Cardinals v. Saints in New Orleans
28 – Wisconsin v. Ohio State – Columbus, OH
29 – Bears v. Lions in Detroit (Possibly MLB Pit – Cin)

October
2 - D-III field hockey Stevens at Montclair State, NJ
5 – Regatta in Annapolis, MD
6 – Maryland v. North Carolina women's soccer in Chapel Hill
MLB playoffs TBD
12 – Ole Miss v. Texas A&M in Oxford, MI
19 – Notre Dame v. USC in South Bend, IN
20 – Broncos v. Colts in Indianapolis
26 – St. Joe's Regional v. Paramus Catholic (NJ high school football)
31 – Bengals v. Dolphins in Miami

November
2 – "World's Largest Outdoor Cocktail Party" aka FLA v. UGA in Jacksonville
9 – BYU v. Wisconsin in Madison
10 – Eagles at Packers in Green Bay
16 – Oklahoma State v. Texas in Austin
23 – Cal v. Stanford in Palo Alto
24 – Titans v. Raiders in Oakland

December
1 – Dolphins v. Jets in NJ
6 – NCAA women's soccer championship in NC
7 – Big Ten championship football game in Indy
13 – NCAA men's soccer championships in Philly
14 – Army v. Navy in Philadelphia
15 – Seahawks v. Giants in NJ
21 – Bowl Game TBD
25 – NBA game TBD

January
Bowl games TBD
5 – US Figure Skating championships in Boston
NBA, NHL and college sports
NFL playoffs TBD

January
18 – Trailblazers v. Mavericks in Dallas
23 – Winter X-Games in Aspen, CO
29 – NY Rangers v. NY Islanders outdoor hockey at Yankee Stadium

February
2 – Super Bowl in NYC
9 – Michigan v. Iowa wrestling in Iowa City
23 – Daytona 500 in, uh, Daytona

March
19 – College Synchronized Swimming national championships in Oxford, OH
March
21 - Women's Hockey Final Four in Connecticut
Baseball spring training in FL and AZ
Big East men's basketball tournament in NYC

April
MLB Opening Day
5 - Men's NCAA Basketball Final Four in Dallas
8 - Women's NCAA basketball Final Four - Nashville, TN
10–13 – The Masters in Augusta, GA
Northwestern Women's lacrosse – Evanston, IL
21 – Boston Marathon

May
4 – Kentucky Derby
Women's wrestling national championships
Frog Jumping Championships in Calaveras County
25 – Indianapolis 500

June
NCAA Rugby Championships

June
Sturgis Wild West Days (rodeo) – South Dakota
College baseball World Series – Omaha
22 – US Open Golf men's and women's Pinehurst, NC
Midnight baseball in Fairbanks, Alaska
Water skiing championships

July
8 – Tennis Hall of Fame championships in Newport, RI
12 – Lingerie Football League game in Baltimore
13 – Major League Lacrosse All-Star game
15 – MLB All Star Game in Minneapolis
21 – Pro Bowlers Association tournament in Columbus, OH
22 – Ragbrai bike race across Iowa
24 – Frontier Days (rodeo) in Cheyenne, WY.
28 – Women's Tennis Association in Stanford, CA

August
WNBA TBD (But Sue Bird and/or Skylar Diggins will definitely be involved.)
12 – US Amateur Golf Championship – Brookline, MA
14 – Little League World Series, Williamsport, PA
18 – LPGA's The Solheim Cup – Parker, CO
19 – Amgen Tour bicycle race in CO
AVP beach volleyball TBD

August
22 - Women's Longboard Surf Championships in Oahu
CFB Kickoff Weekend

September
4 - NFL Kickoff Game
5 - Sofa City

But those big deals would only fill about two months' worth of games; I still needed to fill in the other 300 days of Sports Year. To do so, I'd mainly be catching smaller contests, from college's Division III to adult leagues to youth sports.

However, not just any game would count. Initially, Sports Year had no regulations beyond seeing some kind of athletic contest every day. But, then a friend happily commented, "And when you're home visiting your parents, you and your Dad can go play golf and then that'll count as that day's event!" I tilted my head at him and furrowed my brow. No.

My old man and me playing golf is *not* a sporting event; it's an assault on innocent flora and – on one, distressing occasion – fauna. On Saturday February 23, 2008 I inadvertently killed a waterfowl with a straight, but extremely low tee shot on the 10th hole at El Dorado Golf Club in Long Beach, California. Yes, I am a burderer. (Here's the truly regrettable part about that incident: thanks to my first drive, which did the geometrically impossible by finding a small pond five-degrees to the right of the tee box, I had to hit a second ball, which proved to be the kill shot.)

Unwilling to let suspect events jeopardize the validity of an endeavor that did not exist until I'd invented it, I set a rule for Sports Year. In order to qualify as "official," a sporting event required an umpire, referee or judge. (The latter was a nod to the inclusion of gymnastics and figure skating, helping me to reach my goal of attending a minimum of 45% female sports.) Ten NBA stars running full court in a summertime pickup game at UCLA's Pauley Pavilion and calling their own fouls? Didn't count. Half-drunk adults playing kickball on a weed-infested public park in a game overseen by an umpire? Counted.

The smalltime nature of the games lent itself to equally sparse crowds, which I figured would make it a lot easier to meet locals. I looked forward to strangers in Mississippi inviting me home for a catfish dinner. That would've been a life-affirming experience. Or, those people might have turned out to be certifiably insane.

Either way, it would make for a great chapter in the book that would become a bestseller and serve as the basis for a major motion picture. (Note: when it's somebody else's project, it's a "movie." When it's yours, it's a "major motion picture"). The sale of all those books and the film rights would get me back in the black.

Speaking of money… just how was I gonna pay for all the gas and hotels and food and beer and game tickets?

CHAPTER THREE

"Now Accepting Donations..."

As I mentioned earlier, I was already $75K in debt; obviously, then, I would not be personally bankrolling my trip. So, I needed to find funding.

To me, Sports Year presented lots of obvious sponsorship opportunities, from automotive to fast food to apparel. Plus, the fact that I was a total shameless whore could only help my chances. If Fiat was willing to pay me thousands of dollars to drive a hot pink 500, Bon Giorgno! If Taco Bell wanted me to eat tres Dorito tacos every day for lunch, I'd risk the drag on travel time due to late afternoon bathroom stops.

But I also saw a bigger play: multi-media. Both NBC and Fox had recently launched 24-hour sports networks that desperately needed content. With Sports Year, I could provide them with a daily blog about covering the sporting event (and possibly other updates if goofy shit happened) and videos of me interacting with fans at tailgaters and in the stands, or parents at youth soccer games, etc. At bigger events, the network could establish a "Where's Waldo?" type of contests in which people could find me in stadiums and post my picture to win prizes or whatever. Interactive opportunities abounded.

I bounced the concept off my friend Allan, a fellow bachelor and a former Coordinating Producer at Fox Sports. Unlike our married buddies, he thought I could actually pull off Sports Year. But before he approached anyone at Fox on my behalf, he wanted me to determine two important things: the project's costs and what I should charge a network.

Allan pointed out that I'd actually be doing three jobs. "You'll be the writer and you'll be the producer, but on top of that you'll also be your own cameraman a lot of the time."

"Yeah, but it's just shooting with my iPhone, so, does that count?" His stare and arched eyebrow told me I had a lot to learn.

"Yeah, so, you really need to get paid for all three roles. I've got a guy for you to talk to."

Allan arranged a meeting for me with Mark Mayer, a successful freelance sports producer/director who had overseen projects for Fox, ESPN, Showtime and many other networks, handling talent as diverse as Alec Trebek and Dick Vitale.

Mark and I sat down for breakfast at a locals' joint in Hermosa Beach, where, before assessing my plan, he assessed my sanity. "You don't *look* crazy." I had to laugh; nobody had put it just that way yet.

He agreed with Allan's point that I should be paid for writing, producing, and video shooting. He quickly jotted down some napkin calculations based on my staying at a good hotel every night and eating better than fast food for each meal. "Salary and expenses… you should ask for at least $300,000." *Excuse me?* The thought that I could actually make a lot of money during Sports Year had never entered my brain. "But," he added, "*I'd* ask for 400 grand. That's a lot of freaking work you'll be doing." I thanked Mark for his time and happily paid for breakfast.

Armed with some actual facts, I told Allan I was ready to meet with Fox Sports. He forwarded my pitch document to a former colleague, who totally dug it. *That guy* put me in contact with "Joe," a sales manager. I didn't understand that move; I mean, wouldn't the producers be the ones to green light a project? Uh, no.

Fox Sports wasn't willing to pay for the project, so it would be up to the sales department to get sponsors to pay the network, which would then pay me. I did some LinkedIn-ing and learned that Joe had graduated from Ole Miss.

After we got on the phone and had exchanged pleasantries, I asked, "Will you be joining me in Oxford on October 12th?" That was the day the Rebels were hosting Heisman Trophy winner Johnny Manziel and Texas A&M. The sales guy didn't hesitate in his response. "Believe me, I would. But with four young kids, that's not happening. But let me know if you need help with tickets or a tailgater. I've got guys who will take care of you." I liked him immediately.

Joe asked me for my "number," meaning the amount of money I wanted. Despite what Mark the freelance producer had suggested, I simply could not utter the words four-hundred-thousand-dollars. I grimaced as I said "300K," then closed my eyes and hoped. My trepidation proved unwarranted, as Fox's sales manager simply said, "Yeah, that's about what I was thinking. Of course, I'll charge the sponsor $500,000." I punched my thigh, furious with myself for not having followed my new mentor's advice.

Joe explained that he needed to sit down with members of his sales team, but that off the bat he saw a natural fit with an American automaker that might pick up the whole tab. If not, he felt confident they'd find other options for a patchwork deal.

Unfortunately, potential sponsors did not share his vision. The car company responded to the pitch with, "But who's the audience?" The sales guy explained that it was everybody: men, women, children – fans of all sports. But that only confused the auto guy and other subsequent sponsors, who were accustomed to ads specifically targeting, say, NFL fans. The idea that I'd be at an NFL game on Sunday, an MLB game on Monday and a U8 soccer game on Tuesday just didn't compute. Sadly, the Fox sales staff struck out in their attempts. I truly appreciated their efforts and wish we had been able to make something happen.

Unfortunately, I was out of media outlets. I'd already emailed a big-time producer at ESPN – we'd been groomsmen in the same wedding party the previous year – with the pitch. He responded, "I freaking love this," which sent my arms rocketing skyward like my kicker just nailed the game-winning FG. Then I read the rest of the sentence, "But I don't think we'd ever do something like this," which hit me like the realization that the opposing coach had called a timeout just prior to that kick. Unfortunately, I had zero contacts at the fledgling NBC Sports Network. I sent a Hail Mary tweet at one of The Dan Patrick Show's Dannettes, Seton O'Connor. No surprise that I didn't hear back.

Friends in high places pitched potential sponsors at Bank of America, Red Bull, StubHub, Under Armour and Subway, and emerged with interest but no offers.

My deflated spirits got a lift after my pal Jodi Lederman, an LA-based PR guru and Baltimore Ravens fanatic, heard my pitch and immediately asked if she could share it with a friend of hers. Within twenty minutes, I got an email from the aforementioned David Katz.

Anyone who has ever used a sports website owes David a debt of gratitude; in the late 90s, he convinced the execs at CBS that the network needed a standalone sports presence online. After CBS Sportsline's success stunned the entertainment industry, ESPN.com and Yahoo! Sports followed suit. In his latest role, he founded ThePostGame.com, a site hosted by Yahoo and dedicated to everything *but* the scores and highlights.

David instantly connected with the Sports Year concept, and invited me to lunch the very next day in Hollywood to discuss my partnering with ThePostGame. I liked David immediately. He resembles David Blatt, the ex-Cleveland Cavaliers' head coach, which is somewhat fitting given that Katz played backup point guard at the University of Pennsylvania.

(Having walked-on to the Notre Dame wrestling team, I love hearing other non-scholarship athletes' stories. David has a classic. During his senior season, he played garbage time minutes in several contests, but did not attempt a shot, make an assist, grab a rebound, block a shot or commit a foul; as the result, he had no statistics. Before his final home game, desperate to finally get his name into the box score, he promised himself he would shoot the first time he touched the ball. He entered the game in the last minute. Off an inbound pass, he turned and found himself 30-feet from the bucket. *Screw it; a promise is a promise.* He let it fly. Swish. "And that," he said with charming self-satisfaction, "is how I came to be permanently tied for the career three-point shooting percentage record in Division I.")

ThePostGame sent me a contract that I was prepared to sign. But then my lawyer – a close friend – explained that the terms were really bad for me. I wouldn't even own the brand Sports Year. Since I was interested in expanding the concept internationally, that was a major problem. Faced with my last option, I waffled like Brett Favre in August. Ultimately, I followed the legal advice and turned down the deal, a decision I still regret.

In one of my last conversations with David, he impressed upon me the need for Sports Year to be about something bigger than just a bachelor enjoying the greatest road trip ever. In short, I needed a cause. Immediately, I knew which one I'd pick.

For the previous seven years, I had volunteered weekly at a Los Angeles family shelter for abused women and their children. Did you know that one out of four American women suffer abuse in their lifetimes? I had no clue about that distressing statistic until I'd begun volunteering there. That lack of knowledge isn't surprising, since Domestic Violence is an uncomfortable topic for people. One out of nine women will get breast cancer, and the entire NFL wears pink for all of October; yet nobody wants to talk about Domestic Violence?

I pictured myself speaking to teams at middle schools and high schools about Domestic Violence and explaining why it's not okay for men to abuse the women in their lives. While acknowledging the worthiness of that cause, David suggested I pick something more embraceable from a sponsorship perspective. Basically, nobody in corporate America would want to be associated in any way with abuse of women, even if I'd be working to stop such behaviors. Going against my gut, I dropped DV and took up the cause of bringing Wounded Warriors to sporting events on their Bucket Lists. As a former Army officer, this was still a mission close to my heart.

Armed with a cause but no financial backing, I turned to complete strangers for support. Hello, 2013 sensation: Crowdfunding!

Here's my Kickstarter campaign, cut and pasted from the site (with some deletions due to my already covered them in this book):

Why I Want to Do This: When asked why he wanted to climb Mount Everest, George Mallory famously responded, "Because it's there." I think we can all kinda relate to wanting a challenge like that. (I'd love to climb Everest someday. Only, I'm afraid of heights. And I get really cold when it's really cold. Oh, and I'm pretty lazy. Aside from those things, though, I'm all in.) One more motivator: my buddies told me I could never do it. Giddy. Up.

I want to do Sports Year because I'm an avid sports fan looking to chronicle an adventure that's never before been undertaken. This story will sweat pure Americana: small towns, midlife crisis, road trip, sports. Additionally, I will be trying to answer some questions: what makes Americans so damn competitive? Are people in the south crazier about their teams than the rest of the country is? How many hot dogs will I eat this year?

Most importantly, though, I want to use Sports Year as a way to give back to some of the servicemen and women who suffered injuries in Afghanistan and Iraq. I served in the Army as a personnel officer at a sleepy post during peacetime; my gravest danger came in the form of paper cuts. **In honor of the sacrifices Wounded Warriors have made for our country, I want to bring some of them to the events on their sports Bucket Lists.** It's the least I can do. I ask those heroes or people close to them to tweet at me (@Sports_Year) or email me (sports.year.jamie@gmail.com) to let me know what contests they'd like to attend. Then we can compare schedules and see when and where we can link up. I can't wait to make that happen week in and week out.

Thank you for your time and consideration of this project. I hope to see you at a game during my Sports Year!

- Jamie

Risks and challenges:

Initially, I figured that getting tickets to the Super Bowl and other big sporting events would be my highest hurdle in completing Sports Year.
But guys who know about this sorta stuff assure me that Mother Nature will be my toughest opponent.

In the spring, summer and fall, outdoor sports can get rained out or lightning-ed out. That could leave me scrambling to find a different event to attend without enough time to get there. In the fall and winter, snow and ice could force the cancellation of events, or simply leave me stranded like Steve Martin and John Candy. ("Those aren't pillows!")

Let's shift gears to "Sabrina," my second biggest challenge. No, she's not my road trip partner. Sabrina is my 10-year old Saab. (SABrina. Get it? This is the kind of world class wit you can expect from me every day.) The rust water stains she sports on the roof are the least of her worries. The driver's side window doesn't work, which makes for a fun time at toll booths and stadium parking garages ("Move it, jackhole!").

Two other windows go all the way up, but they don't STAY all the way up, which can be problematic. Additionally, Sabrina is a standard transmission. I mean, what could possibly go wrong with a ten-year old clutch that has never been replaced??? And it's not like the Saab motor company went out of business in 2011, making the parts hard to get. Oh, wait...

I don't anticipate any problem finding sporting events to attend. (My new friends on social media will help me with that.) But I do predict lots of problems LOCATING those events. You see, my sense of direction is non-existent; I think that wherever I'm looking is "north." So, I'll be in big trouble if my GPS goes out when I'm in areas of poor AT&T cell coverage (insert joke, here).

And then there's the matter of that Super Bowl ticket...

Pledge $10 or more

"FAN": For being a normal get happy/get angry kinda athletic supporter - not a cup! - you get the official Sports Year drink koozie.

Estimated delivery: Oct 2013

Pledge $25 or more

"PUDDY": You're a face-painter. Not that there's anything

wrong with that. You get the DRM-free version of the book + the official Sports Year drink koozie (delivered October 2013). This is the fastest and cheapest way to get the book!

Estimated delivery: May 2015

Pledge $50 or more

"FANATIC": You have broken things - walls, promises, relationships - over a loss. For your pain, you get a signed copy of book + DRM-free version of the book + the official Sports Year drink koozie (delivered October 2013).

Estimated delivery: May 2015

Pledge $100 or more

"Bethpage Black": For being batty enough to sleep in your car for a tee time, you get your name listed in the book's acknowledgments section + signed copy of book + DRM-free version + the official Sports Year drink koozie (delivered October 2013)

Estimated delivery: May 2015

Pledge $200 or more

"Krzyzewskiville": For being kooky enough to sleep in a tent for a college hoops game, you get 6 post cards from the road + your name listed in the book's acknowledgments section + signed copy of book + DRM-free version + the official Sports Year drink koozie (delivered October 2013)

Estimated delivery: May 2015

Pledge $300 or more

"Shirtless in Seattle": For pretending to enjoy hypothermia at a football game, you get 12 post cards from the road + your name listed in the book's acknowledgments section + signed copy of book + DRM-free version + the official Sports Year drink koozie (delivered October 2013)

Estimated delivery: May 2015

Pledge $500 or more (Limited to 50 people)

"Score Checker at A Funeral": No, we have not ALL done that. Your level of dedication merits attending a game with me when I'm in your area. You pick the event. (If tickets are required, we'll go Dutch.) YOU GET A CHAPTER IN THE BOOK. Plus, you get 12 post cards from the road + your name listed in the book's acknowledgments section + signed copy of book + DRM-free version + the official Sports Year drink koozie (delivered October 2013) This is first come, first served, i.e. I can only go to the A&M - Ole Miss game on October 12th with one person.

Estimated delivery: May 2015

Pledge $500 or more (Limited to 50 people)

"Morganna": Ladies only. In honor of the legendary Kissing Bandit, I will join you and a friend (or 2. Or 12.) for dinner when I'm in your area. (See: earlier "going Dutch" comment.) YOU GET A CHAPTER IN THE BOOK. Plus, you'll get 12 post cards from the road + your name listed in the book's acknowledgments section + signed copy of book + DRM-free version + the official Sports Year drink koozie (delivered October 2013)

Estimated delivery: May 2015

Pledge $750 or more (Limited to 5 people)

"The Hunter S. Thompson": You might be the craziest of us all because you actually want to be a writer. For your masochism, I'll read your manuscript and then do a 60 minute Skype session with you to discuss it, offer suggestions, etc.

Estimated delivery: Aug 2014

Pledge $2,500 or more (Limited to 5 people)

"Metta World Peace": Your fandom is unusually unusual. You get to spend a week with me on the road and pick the events we attend. (See: earlier "going Dutch" comment.) YOU GET A CHAPTER IN THE BOOK. Plus, you'll get 12 post cards from the road + your name listed in the book's acknowledgments section + signed copy of book + DRM-free version + the official Sports Year drink koozie (delivered October 2013)

Estimated delivery: Aug 2014

Pledge $5,000 or more (Limited to 10 people)

"Brett Fav-ruh": You want to be an actor, but you shouldn't be. If the book gets turned into a major motion picture (not a documentary), you will be a "featured extra." Plus, you'll get 12 post cards from the road + your name listed in the book's acknowledgments section + signed copy of book + DRM-free version + the official Sports Year drink koozie (delivered October 2013)

Estimated delivery: Aug 2018

Pledge $10,000 or more (Limited to 3 people)

"Kareem Abdul-Jabbar": In honor of the Hall of Famer's legendary performance as Roger Murdock in "Airplane," if the book gets turned into a major motion picture (not a documentary), you will receive one line in the movie. Plus, you'll get 12 post cards from the road + your name listed in the book's acknowledgments section + signed copy of book + DRM-free version + the official Sports Year drink koozie (delivered October 2013)

Estimated delivery: Aug 2018

Today, I could write an e-book on how to screw up a Kickstarter campaign. For, uh, starters, when asking people for money, don't send the email on a Friday afternoon. Especially a Friday afternoon in *late August*, when pretty much everybody in America is enjoying their last vacation of summer. (Pro tip: I've since learned that the best time to send an important email is Tuesday morning at 10:00.)

Also, don't set a ridiculous goal of, say, $100,000. If you think you may not actually reach your goal, don't use Kickstarter, which is an all-or-nothing proposition; if you fall short, you don't get *any* of the money you raised. Aware of this, a friend strongly suggested that I use Indiegogo, because that site gives you whatever money you raised, minus a penalty for failing to reach your goal. I, however, chose not to heed that sage advice, because the name Indiegogo bugged me, and I didn't want to have to say it for the rest of my life when explaining how I had funded Sports Year. (In case you were wondering, no hedge fund has ever wooed me for my razor sharp business acumen.)

I did not arbitrarily choose $100K; I simply took Mark Mayer's calculation of $300,000 and divided by three. The total still sounded crazy to me, though not as much as the original amount. But the new goal obviously sounded insane to regular people. One of my non-donating buddies told me, "I wish somebody would give *me* a hundred grand to drive around and have fun, Reidy!" Yeah, point taken.

Along those lines, I'd considered just setting the goal at $30K, both to avoid the "Are you freaking kidding me?!" sticker shock while also providing a reachable amount. Thirty grand would at least have kept me on the road for several months, and just maybe the success of the Kickstarter campaign would have prompted more social media coverage that I could have parlayed into a brand sponsorship or two that would have provided enough money for me to complete the entire year.

But, just prior to typing $30,000 in the amount space of the Kickstarter website, I made the mistake of Googling "Kickstarter lawsuits." Reading about donors who had sued people who failed to deliver on their projects, I panicked. Suddenly, the "active imagination" for which I was praised in my first grade report card ran amok. *What if I ask for $30K and raise $30K, but I never get any sponsors and I run out of money? Will some asshole sue me because I didn't complete Sports Year?* (Once again, simply typing that sentence makes me feel like such a moron.)

So, I went with $100K. Despite garnering mention in a few online blogs about interesting crowdfunding projects, my campaign earned less than a fifth of that: $19,600. Several friends confided that they were going to donate, but didn't because "What's the point?" After all, whatever they contributed – whether $100 or even $1000 – wasn't going to get me anywhere near my goal. People like to be associated with a winner, and I had proven to be the Matt Millen of crowdfunding GMs.

With my Kickstarter tail tucked between my legs, I resorted to Indiegogo. I emailed the 110 kind souls who'd donated to my Kickstarter, explaining the failure and asking them to support the new project. But my ineptness continued, as many donors either got annoyed by the hassle or confused by the new project; 57 people didn't contribute. My Indiegogo raised only $9,000.

Fortunately, I was able to beat my buddies to the inevitable George Costanza jokes – getting less money than I could have gotten thanks to my own ignorance and stubbornness.

CHAPTER FOUR

"Setting Out"

Tuesday, September 3rd. Manhattan Beach, California.

How do you pack for a yearlong road trip? Very slowly, apparently.

To say that I had a "lousy plan" would be an insult to lousy plans. Free advice: if you ever start a yearlong road trip, don't spend the day prior to departure drinking at an outdoor beer garden while listening to an 80s cover band. Actually, the music is irrelevant in that PSA; don't get loaded the day before, unless you've packed already. Which I had not.

I also hadn't unpacked my car's trunk, which had been serving as a de facto storage unit for a lot of crap I'd forgotten I even owned, like a deflated basketball, a Compaq Presario (two laptops ago) and a copy of the book by Dennis Prince, *Get Rich with Twitter* (which I obviously never read). Buh-bye, forty-five precious minutes.

Packing list:

Blue Suit (In case a stranger invited me to a wedding. Or late night TV interview. Or, God forbid, a job interview)

Sports Jacket

Tuxedo (Because you never know)

Leather Jacket

Pea Coat

Ski Jacket (Since I didn't plan on returning to California until late November, I had to pack way in advance of bad weather.)

Jeans – 3

Flat front khakis – 1

T-shirts – 8 (5 good, 3 "play clothes")

Sweaters – 2

Dress shirt – 2

Collared shirts – 5

Workout clothes, underwear, socks

Shoes – 3

Hair clippers – 1 (Every 7-10 days)

The drive from Manhattan Beach to Denver would be 1035 miles, or roughly 17 hours. Splitting it in two, I set a first day goal of nine hours, which would put me someplace in southeastern Utah.

I departed 3.5 hours later than scheduled.

That turned out to be poor timing, as only two miles from home, the Saab came to a an unexpected halt in a traffic jam on the highway's *on ramp* – an apt metaphor for the project. Took me half an hour to get out of my town, not exactly the omen I was looking for as I stared down the barrel of 365 days on the road. I covered 19 miles in my first hour.

Near Barstow, California, a town halfway between L.A. and Las Vegas, I made my initial pit stop. One of my major concerns with this adventure was gaining fifty pounds due to all the fast food I'd grab on the road combined with all the hot dogs and crap I'd scarf down at games. Obesity, heart disease and diabetes run in my family – partially because nobody *runs* in my family – so I needed to be vigilant about my diet. (Besides, I was already pale and bald; I didn't need to complete the trifecta with fat, too.) Stopping at *McDonald's*, then, was an odd first choice.

Fear not, Mom! I skipped the Quarter Pounder with cheese combo in favor of two grilled chicken wraps – hold the Ranch. In another departure from the norm, I ordered an iced tea instead of a Diet Coke. I did this not because I prefer the blah of iced tea to the tingle of carbonated caffeine, but because of all the scientific data my friends Jeremy and Angie have bombarded me with showing that Diet Coke melts rats' brains or something.

Twenty minutes later, I further regretted the iced tea call because the formerly hot liquid had melted all the ice. That was problematic because I love me some cubes of frozen water, a trait inherited from my father, who requests extra glasses of ice at restaurants. I required ice for two OCD reasons: I'm a chewer (much to my orthodontist's dismay) and I'm a swirler. Anyways, I decided I'd be switching back to Diet Coke, brain of Swiss cheese be damned.

Outside of Vegas, storm clouds filled the sky. I rolled down the windows to catch the smell of rain in the desert. Intoxicating. Minutes later, my iPod shuffled to Springsteen. As the song ended, I wanted to get out of shuffle and into Bruce's catalog. But I fumbled with the iPod, allowing the next song to come on: The Who's "Love Reign O'er Me." Such perfect timing as the rain pounded my windshield. I couldn't have planned that if I tried.

Sometimes it's a good thing when a plan doesn't come together. Except when you end up at this high security motel:

Need One

Fortunately, I MacGyver-ed a solution:

35

CHAPTER FIVE

"T-minus 1"

Wednesday, Sept 4th. Cedar City, Utah

Two good things happened this morning: I awoke and I awoke with both my kidneys and all my stuff. Victory. But I overslept by two hours. Defeat.

Even worse, over the course of the night I acquired a sore throat, which I hoped was simply the result of motel mold rather than an actual illness. I'd never rooted for mold before. I'd like to not make a habit of that.

Southern Utah boasted absolutely gorgeous country, full of ranges and rolling hills. It made for one of the better drives I've experienced. Of course, it would have been even more enjoyable if not for the temperature in the high 90s

You might be wondering why I could feel the oppressive heat when inside my car I had the AC on. That would be a perfectly rational thing to wonder. I should preface the following explanation with an admission: I know dick about cars. The logic I am about to share could be as f'ed up as a football bat.

Here goes: I was worried about my 10-year old Saab making it through the yearlong journey, especially through mountainous terrain. So worried, in fact, that I tried to give her a break any way I could, like keeping the cruise control set at 80 or below. Additionally, to ease the strain on the engine I utilized a variation of what my Uncle Gerald once called "460 air conditioning" – keep the AC off, roll down four windows and do 60 MPH. My version was 380 Air Conditioning, in which I rolled down the three windows that could be, uh, rolled down.

My uninformed 80 MPH personal speed limit turned out to be ideal, because it was the actual speed limit for long stretches of highway in Utah! That speed confused me: this is the state that insisted on limiting the alcohol content of beer. They trusted us to be adults on the road, but not in the bars? I'd trade the ability to be a speed racer for the chance to drink a Racer-5, any day.

Refueling at a rest stop, I spotted a well-used Jeep Wrangler sporting the bumper sticker, "Save The Peel." Instantly, I surmised that religious zealot local politicians had stuck their noses into a woman's right to choose... her facial treatments. As I waited for the gas pump to finish, I decided to Google the phrase. I'd been pretty close.

"Save The Peel" was an environmental movement focused on keeping the Canadian Yukon's Peel River Watershed clean. At that point, it occurred to me that maybe twelve years in the Los Angeles area had permanently warped my perspective.

Later on the drive, I called a college friend who'd become a big Broncos fan since moving to Denver a decade earlier. I figured Pete might also be at the game tomorrow night. Yes and no.

"I've got a ticket, from Sarah's friend's father. Kind of a Dad and daughter double date." Sounds good! "But we may not go, because Sarah is worried that she's not going to be able to handle the homework in 7th grade, so she doesn't want to spend the time at the game."

"Didn't school just start, like, last week?"

"That's what I said!" Pete yelled. I cracked up.

"Quite a dilemma for a dad: you're psyched that you raised this girl who takes her studies seriously, but now it's—"

"—It's freaking killing me!" Pete promised to keep me posted on whether or not he proved able to talk his 12-year old daughter into blowing off her homework.

In Denver, my ticket to the NFL opener was waiting for me at the Ravens' team hotel downtown. Jenn Redman, a close friend from junior high, and her husband Mark had generously arranged it for me. George Kokinis, Mark's brother-in-law and an executive with the Baltimore Ravens, liked the idea of Sports Year so much that he invited me for a beer at the hotel bar, rather than just having a staffer drop the ticket at stadium Will Call.

I showed up to find him hanging out with several team scouts and a prominent agent. George introduced me around and the guys expressed both encouragement and disbelief upon hearing about Sports Year. One gentleman took a particular interest in my story.

"Are you gonna hit Army-Navy?" he asked.

"You mean the game in Philly on December 14th?" I responded.

He laughed and introduced himself. Over a beer, I learned that Phil Hoffman, a Naval Academy graduate and former SEAL, served as the team photographer for both the Ravens and the Midshipmen. After retiring from the Navy, he'd turned his hobby into his dream job. Phil gave me his card and told me to reach out to him in the weeks before the Army-Navy game because he had something special for the wounded warrior I'd be bringing to the game. Aye, aye, sir!

What a blast I had, drinking a local IPA and listening to these pro football experts swap stories. George Kokinis has an inspiring backstory, a testament to unrelenting determination. After playing football at D-III Hobart College in upstate New York, he hustled for a gofer job with the Cleveland Browns, and started grinding his way up the NFL ladder, moving to Baltimore when the Ravens relocated. Now, he's the right-hand man for Hall of Famer and General Manager

Ozzie Newsome, serving as Director of Pro Personnel. Following the Ravens victory over the 49ers in the Super Bowl, my friends Jenn and Mark and their two sons got to join George for the celebration on the field in the Superdome.

But for a modest, humble guy, George has a bit of deviousness to him. I noticed it when I first approached him at the bar. With a twinkle in his eye, he handed me a sealed Ravens envelope. *Something's up.* Then he handed me a plastic bag from the Ravens' team store in Baltimore. "This is from Mark and Jenn." *Awww, that's so nice of them! I mean, they already arranged for my ticket and now...* The thought froze as my hand squeezed the bag and instantly recognized its contents: a team jersey. Panic washed over me and George couldn't help giggling. "It was all their idea, I swear!"

There was no need to tell me that; I already knew what had gone terribly wrong. On the night before I'd set out from Manhattan Beach, I'd spoken to Jenn on the phone. She had called to wish me luck, and then happily informed me that they had been able to get George to give me a ticket. Drunk with gratitude – and from the aforementioned daytime beers – I blurted, "I'll wear whatever team clothing you want me to wear!" It was a throw away line into which I'd put no thought whatsoever. Apparently, Jenn did.

Standing in the hotel bar with my new friend George, I looked down at the Ravens' store bag in my hand. *Gulp.* I pulled out the black jersey and held it up with both hands to check out. The situation was even worse than I had originally thought: an official #5 with "Flacco" imprinted on the back.

As I mentioned earlier, this game was being played in Denver despite the fact that the Ravens were the defending champs. They'd gotten to the Super Bowl by beating the Broncos on the road in overtime in the conference title game, thanks largely to the heroics of Baltimore's quarterback Joe Flacco. As part of its publicity campaign to hype the 2013 season opener, the NFL hung a huge banner of Joe Flacco on the *outside of Mile High Stadium*. As you might imagine, the locals did not share the league's enthusiasm for these marketing efforts.

So, now, thanks to a completely insincere promise to my clearly sadistic longtime friends, tomorrow I would be donning the uniform of Public Enemy Number One, er, Five.

.

DAY ONE

Thursday, September 5th. Denver, Colorado.

My host Kevin, a college roommate, left me an inspiring note on the dining room table:

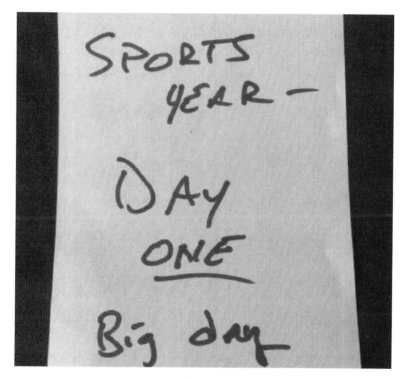

A "big day," indeed. Today I would launch what I hoped to be an incredible journey for me, personally, and, good memories for the wounded warriors I'd be bringing to games on their Bucket Lists.

Despite my buzzing excitement and a mid-morning coffee buzz, I found myself unable to keep my eyes open, and had to take a nap after lunch. I woke up disoriented, proof I'd slept too long. *Great f'ing start, Jamo!* My energy level distressingly low, I headed to

41

Starbucks for a second iced mocha, a personal first. As I sat journaling my Day One thoughts, my iPhone rang with a 407 area code. Orlando. Who do I know in Orlando? At first I worried it was a creditor. But then I realized the caller could be from the Wounded Warrior Project!

On August 28th 2013, I cold emailed a man named Louis, an "Alumni Manager" at WWP, whose name was given to me by an Army buddy of mine who had done some National Guard training with him. In the message, I explained what I was attempting to do and why:

> When I was a lieutenant (92-95), I was fortunate to serve during peacetime and get stationed at Camp Zama, Japan, the safest post on Earth. There is no comparison between my service and that of the people you represent.
>
> I'd like to bring a little joy to the lives of those heroes, which is why I am emailing you.
>
> I reached out to WWP through the website but haven't heard back yet.
>
> Would you like to help me connect with Wounded Warriors who'd want to see their favorite team play for the first time or make their initial visit to an iconic stadium?
>
> I want to give back to those who sacrificed so much in these wars. Hopefully, you see the benefit - however brief - that Sports Year can give them.

I had yet to hear back from Louis. But a phone call could only mean good things, right? Nobody responds to a stranger's unsolicited request for help by calling to say, "Thanks, but no thanks." That bad news is either not delivered at all, or it's sent via email, so as to avoid an awkward conversation.

A pleasant woman named Brea introduced herself. Within seconds she said, "This is a great thing you're doing for wounded warriors, but we can't help you." My throat tightened as if strep had instantly spread to every cell. I have no idea what she said next, because I was focused on the Starbucks floor; specifically, not puking on it. *With no help from the Wounded Warrior Project... how the hell am I gonna find any wounded warriors to bring to games?*

Finally, I snapped back to the conversation. Brea explained that although my mission was admirable, my being a solo operation made WWP sponsorship impossible. Basically, they only dealt with much bigger and more legit operations. "But I'm not looking for sponsorship," I said, undoubtedly sounding desperate. "I really just want you to put the word out that I'm looking for wounded warriors to bring to games. You know, post the link to my Facebook page on your website, so the wounded warriors or their family members and friends can reach out to me."

That was a no-go, too. "We don't put anybody on our website, not even Bank of America, one of our biggest sponsors." She thanked me again for my effort and wished me the best of luck. We hung up. I hadn't even attended a game yet, and already I felt like Sports Year was a total failure. Committing suicide by stabbing myself in the jugular with a coffee straw didn't seem like such an unreasonable option.

Which is pretty much what I was about to accomplish, anyway, by wearing Joe Flacco's #5 to the game.

My hosts lived in Denver's Washington Park neighborhood, and Kevin explained that the light rail would take me directly to the stadium. As I waited on the platform, I couldn't shake my cloud of negativity. When the train's doors opened, a raucous crowd of orange-clad riders ceased their merriment and glared at me in my black jersey. Improbably, my negative thoughts increased. I almost didn't climb the steps.

On board, the tension was palpable. After nervously clearing my throat, I said to no one in particular, "I'm not really a Ravens fan." A large man, who appeared to be well ahead of schedule in meeting his pre-game goal of intoxication, barked, "Whatever you need to tell yourself, pal!" For the remainder of the ride I avoided eye contact like it caused cancer.

The walk from the light rail stop to the stadium was only a half-mile. Yet it seemed never ending. Walking the parking lot solo, my physical wellbeing was definitely in jeopardy. Never in my life had I felt as isolated and intimidated. One of the nicer things a Denver fan said to me was, "Flacco, you're a homo!" Pre-trip, I was sure I'd never let myself get into a fight during my year on the road. Now? I felt certain I'd be fighting back after getting punched before the first quarter of the first game.

Eventually, though, I realized that I *wasn't* alone; there were hundreds of other people wearing black or purple. *They* didn't know I wasn't a true fan. All they knew was that I was wearing a Joe Flacco jersey in enemy territory with no wingmen to get my back. Emboldened, I offered a high five to the next purple-clad guy I saw. SMACK! Ditto a fist bump to a woman with a Ravens hat. Within minutes of my possibly lifesaving realization, I was enjoying a cold beer courtesy of Kyle and Mike, two brothers who'd traveled from Baltimore to root on their team – tribe members. They wore matching purple and white camouflage cargo shorts.

"You're rolling solo in a Flacco jersey?!" one of the guys asked. "That's *balls*." Feeling a bit guilty over my charade, I told them about Sports Year. Thankfully, they loved the concept and didn't even care that I wasn't a true Ravens fan. We stood united as Bronco fans walked past cursing at us. Kyle and Mike even gave me another beer for the walk to the stadium. Good lesson in life: act like you belong, and you will.

Inside Invesco Field at Mile High, I immediately began searching for dinner; apparently, all that fear of bodily harm had worked up an appetite. I was psyched to find a concession stand devoted to foods "created" by Bronco legends. I ordered The Mecklenburger, a cheeseburger with sautéed mushrooms named in honor of Karl Mecklenburg, a star defensive lineman from the 80s whose name lends itself to a stadium food better than any other pro athlete-inspired product I had ever heard of. One problem: they were out of the mushrooms. The game hadn't even started yet! Is there no training camp for concessions operators? This was a failure ranking with the Broncos' two Super Bowl performances in the 1980s. Annoyed, I cancelled my Mecklenburger order, settling for a Polish dog.

My seat was in the official Ravens section – nosebleeds in a corner. It was a strange experience to be surrounded by such passionate fans while I only wanted to see a good game. And stay dry; the rain started falling prior to kickoff.

At halftime, I met up with Pete, my friend whose daughter had managed to complete all her homework. "I'm a triple winner!" he smiled over a fresh draft beer. "My wife and I are raising a great daughter, I made it to the game, and the Broncos are kicking ass!" Yes they were.

Day One of Sports Year made me a witness to history, as Peyton Manning tossed seven touchdown passes, tying the NFL record. Well, I should say I witnessed him set *some* of the record.

It hurts to type the following words: I left my first game of Sports Year early. Like, "mid-third quarter" early. Shortly after I met up with Pete, my energy level crashed again. I felt achy and had chills. (It should be noted that those are all common side effects of hanging out with Pete.)

I weighed my options: sitting by myself among strangers or getting some much needed sleep back at Kevin's house. I made the decision faster than #16 could say, "Omaha."

DAY TWO

Friday, September 6th*. Denver, Colorado to Lincoln, Nebraska*

Yet another late start. If this kept up I was going to have to fire myself.

Today I ran tardy because I could *not* find my flip-flops. After packing, I looked all over Kevin and Fran's guest room, as well as the entire first floor of the house save the master bedroom. No joy. After twenty minutes of increasingly frustrated searching, I snapped. *Screw it. I'll just buy some in Lincoln.* I furiously yanked my garment bag off the floor… to reveal the flip-flops perfectly aligned on the carpet. Some super genius must have dropped the bag on top of them. #CurseWords.

More profanities followed thirty minutes later on I-76 east when I realized I'd be losing an hour due to the time change from Denver (mountain) to Lincoln (central). (See: earlier "firing" comment.) I would now most certainly miss the start of my Day Two event, which was, somewhat alarmingly, still TBD.

After I decided to plan Sports Year around the pro and college football schedules, I reached out to friends in those cities and along the route for places to bunk. In some areas, though, I didn't know any locals. That might stop a normal person from attempting to freeload, but not me. Hotels loomed as my biggest financial drain. I'd risk crashing with Freddie Krueger, as long as he had Wi-Fi.

David Martin, a producer at the new Al-Jazeera network, was the only person I knew who lived in Lincoln, Nebraska. We'd met in 2007 when, in his role as a producer of Dr. Sanjay Gupta's show at CNN, he asked me to do an on-camera interview for an hour-long special on the pharmaceutical industry. The plan didn't call for me to actually meet the host, however. David wanted me to drive to the network's studio in Hollywood where I'd be filmed as I answered questions asked by an off-camera staffer. Later, David would shoot Sanjay in NYC asking the same questions. An editor would then intercut the two reels, making it look like I'd been in the same room with Sanjay. I asked if CNN could fly me to New York, but the project didn't have the budget.

Unwilling to pass up a chance to meet one of the most famous physicians in America, somebody who might end up Surgeon General someday, I offered to fly myself to NYC. We all ended up happy that I did. Prior to the interview, I Googled Sanjay and learned that he did undergrad at Michigan, a few years ahead of me. Naturally, I busted his balls about the "Rocket game," the epic 1989 ND-UM contest in which Head Coach Bo Schembechler idiotically kicked off to Raghib Ismail after my classmate had already taken one to the house in the Big House. Dr. Gupta was clearly not accustomed to his interviewees taunting him with painful memories, but he flashed a quick smile. Then he mentioned the "Desmond Howard game" from 1991, in which that season's Heisman winner singlehandedly killed the Irish. Oooompf. I liked Sanjay right away.

We sat across from each other, about three feet apart. My inquisitor had not read my book, so David the producer handed him a long list of questions on a yellow legal pad. Sanjay asked the first two, but then ignored the rest as we got into a free flowing and occasionally argumentative conversation. As a neurosurgeon, he had little exposure to drug reps; the main sales people he saw were the device reps. So, Dr. Gupta had no experience to go off of, and simply could not believe that other physicians would listen to somebody like me with absolutely no medical or scientific background. Our session lasted close to an hour, and as David walked me out he said, "That was terrific. This is going to be the best segment of the show." I practically skipped down 6th Avenue, my brain calculating the book sales I'd get from a featured spot in Dr. Sanjay Gupta's controversial look at the pharmaceutical industry.

Only, CNN killed the show. David wasn't allowed to explain why. I might still be hungover from the ensuing drowning of my sorrows. He and I stayed in touch, though. In fact, after suffering a severe back injury that looked as if it would require surgery, I emailed him with the relatively unreasonable request of asking Sanjay what neurosurgeon *he* would go to in LA if he needed spinal surgery. David wrote back twenty minutes later with a name, a direct phone number and an instruction to "Tell him Sanjay sent you." How freaking cool was that? (Thankfully, I didn't end up needing an operation.)

As a big fan of college football, I'd always wanted to attend a game at Nebraska. So, before starting Sports Year, I emailed David for the first time in a few years to see if he had a couch on which I could crash. Unfortunately, he wasn't going to be in town that weekend. But he asked, "Would you like a tour guide on Friday night?"

And that's how I met Scott, a lifelong Cornhusker, who helped me find my Day 2 event: a high school JV boys' tennis match. On the phone, we also made plans to grab a beer later on that night, with him picking me up at my hotel at 7:00. But, thanks to my getting on the road late and forgetting about the time change, I was definitely going to miss that target. *Way to make a first impression and show your appreciation, Jamie!*

My crankiness was not helped by the realization that I was definitely sick. The tennis balls in my neck where there used to be lymph nodes proved that it wasn't the motel mold in Utah that had made my throat hurt. At least, I should say, the mold wasn't the only cause. My throat hurt as if I'd swallowed rusty barbed wire. Even though I'd only been awake a few hours, I already needed a nap. But I couldn't park at a rest stop and catch some z's, thanks to my ridiculous lateness.

I saw the roadside sign for the Pony Express museum, but sadly didn't have time to stop and take the tour. This felt like a mule kick to my heart. When I was six or so, my father ordered the entire Time Life series on the Old West, and I devoured it. Even now, I can still feel the slippery, brown covers of the books. 1976 Jamie would not have believed 2013 Jamie would pass up the Pony Express museum. I felt like the boy in *The Kid* yelling at Bruce Willis, "I don't even have a dog?!"

Confusing fact learned on I-80: Nebraska contains a city named Lincoln and a county named Lincoln, but the former is not located in the latter.

I arrived at the tennis match an hour late. Unfortunately, it took place at a city park, not the home team's high school, but that information was not available in the sports section of the newspaper Scott had checked. I learned that the hard way, showing up at the school's courts to find a varsity practice in session. Through the chain link fence, I asked one of the kids for the location of the matches. He turned to look for a coach.

"This dad wants to know where the JV is playing!" *Uh, who you calling "Dad," son?!* Rarely do I remember that I am in my 40s, not 20s. That kid drove home that point with the force of a Djokovic serve.

Cursing, I sped across town and caught the last doubles matches.

I also saw an, uh, effective new way for a high school girl to meet boys. Her parents must have been so proud.

After finally reaching my hotel in downtown Lincoln, all I wanted to do was go to sleep. But I had to rally to meet Scott, my tour guide who must've lost a bet to David or something. I mean, who volunteers to show some stranger around? Rushing to be on time, I chugged a Diet Coke as I showered off the grime from nine hours of 380-AC in near 100-degree temps.

As I stood on the sidewalk, a black SUV pulled up to the curb. The window rolled down and, as I peered inside, I kinda felt like a prostitute. A guy who looked like he was from Nebraska – sandy hair, stocky build – asked, "Jamie?"

Turned out that Scott hadn't lost a bet; he was a twenty-year veteran of the pharmaceutical sales world who wanted to meet the guy who wrote *Hard Sell*! He drove us to Zip Line, a new microbrewery started by a friend of his and David's. We got two seats belly up to the bar, where we learned David had staked us to a $50 tab. Holy Husker hospitality!

Scott and I hit it off, bonding over our love of IPAs and distaste for the pharma biz. He'd recently become national sales manager for a new medical device startup company. We got along so swimmingly that he invited me to crash dinner with him and his wife. They took me to their favorite restaurant, an Indian place. *Uhhhh*. Steaks in Nebraska? Yes, please. But Indian? Naan.

But I could not have been more wrong. That would certainly not be the last time on this journey that my preconceived notions were proven narrow minded. Wow. If you're ever in Lincoln, you must go to The Oven. In fact, much of the state capital turned out to be a revelation: cobbled-stoned streets, cool bars, hip restaurants.

Did you know that legendary Memorial Stadium is located in the heart of downtown? I did not. Unsurprisingly, the city buzzed with energy as throngs of red-clad fans drank to their beloved Cornhuskers' chances in the new season.

By night's end, I crashed hard with a great buzz, a newfound appreciation for the state of Nebraska and a job offer.

DAY THREE

Saturday, September 7ᵗʰ. Lincoln, Nebraska.

Personal first: woke up to a text informing me, "Your drugs are ready."

Let me back up. Prior to passing out last night, I stood in front of the bathroom mirror, opened wide and did that awkward neck thing to peer deep into my throat. I discovered several white spots the size of Mentos. Consequently, I emailed a doctor friend of mine in Indiana and asked her to call in a prescription to a downtown Lincoln pharmacy for a Z-Pak, an antibiotic. I had actually sold Z-Paks for Pfizer when I first started in pharma sales in 1995, so I knew those six pills were exactly what I needed.

It was only a ten-block walk from the hotel to CVS, but it proved quite challenging thanks to the trifecta of stifling heat, strep throat and slight hangover. I paid for my meds and a cold bottle of water and washed down the first dose outside on the sidewalk. I felt confident I'd be feeling better shortly, but that optimism quickly faded – probably wasn't a good sign that I'd required medical treatment less than 72 hours into my yearlong trek.

Sweating profusely, I hailed a taxi to the game. The women's indoor volleyball game, that is.

Sure, the fabled Nebraska Cornhuskers would be playing tackle football at Memorial Stadium, a gridiron shrine, tonight. But I'd been justifiably criticized for Sports Year's being too football-centric and too male-driven.

So, since Sports Year was supposed to be a journey of self-exploration and self-improvement, I decided to buck tradition today. Football got bumped (pun intended) for women's volleyball.

At dinner last night, Scott's wife Lori suggested that I catch the Lady Huskers in action. "It's sold out, but we can get you a ticket! Our friends have season tickets, but I know they can't go tomorrow." I didn't even try to stifle my mocking laughter, equally befuddled that a) a women's volleyball game could be sold out and b) people bought season tickets to women's volleyball. But Scott assured me that I was in for a wide awakening. Unwilling to further insult my gracious hosts with my sexist preconceived notions, I agreed to take them up on their offer of the free ticket.

Holy cow. That was F-U-N.

First of all, the Lady Huskers play volleyball in the former men's basketball arena. That fact immediately places this program and facility at the very top of the sport. Opposing coaches may bag on Lincoln as a lame farm town, but recruits *must* be impressed when they see the importance with which volleyball is treated at UN-Lincoln.

There were so damn many things to love about indoor volleyball: How the fans happily cheered the opposing lineup during intros. How the crowd chanted and clapped in unison like members of a long running musical. How the reserve players stood throughout the entire match. How everyone was diving and hustling on the court.

How the girls looked so graceful and athletic, unlike women's hoopers who often appeared slow and clumsy. How the volleyball players huddled after each play, good or bad. How they smiled often on the court; not fake cheerleader smiles, but sincere ones. Speaking of cheerleaders, there was a squad assigned to women's indoor volleyball. And there was a pep band. How the fans called the players by their first names – "C'mon, Ally!" – but never in critique.

Nebraska volleyball fans, like the football fans, all wore red t-shirts. Like, *everybody*. This was quite impressive. And intimidating. I was wearing the Zip Line brewery T-shirt I bought last night. It was light blue. #NewGuy

After thirty minutes of watching, I finally noticed that one Husker player wore a different color jersey from her teammates. It had long sleeves, unlike her teammates' sleeveless ones. Then, I saw that the *other* team had a player with a different jersey, too. Pointing to her, I asked the nice woman to my right about the reason for this. Despite being distracted from the action by the idiot she was unlucky enough to sit beside, my neighbor patiently explained that the "libero" was a defensive specialist who remained in the game at all times but could never rotate to the front row herself. Sure enough, she never did. Knowledge!

In between the first and second game, I asked my helpful neighbor and her husband if they wanted anything from the concession stand. It was the least I could do, given their patience with my cluelessness. They politely declined, but the guy suggested that I order the "Runza." His explanation eluded me, but I gathered that it was a cabbage something. This was not a good marketing campaign. But, hey, when in Lincoln... Color me amazed that I liked Runza. Basically, it's a Midwestern calzone, with a beef and cabbage mixture inside. It even had a little kick to it. And scarfing it down made me feel like a local, which, I began to realize, was going to be a major theme of Sports Year.

The Lady Cornhuskers swept the first three games of the best-of-five series. I filed out with the other 5000 fans, elated. Many of them headed to tailgaters prior to the football game later than evening.

Me? I got in my car, seemingly the one person heading *out* of Lincoln. I had a long haul to Dallas, where I'd be seeing the Cowboys host the New York Giants tomorrow night.

Somewhere in Kansas on US-77 south, I spotted a fellow traveler in grave danger.

He was heading across two lanes of traffic toward the grassy median. So I pulled over and staged a daring rescue that saved his life. I picked him up and carried him back to the side of the road from which he came.

A few hours later, I realized that I had no right to turn that turtle around. What made me think he didn't know where he was going? He was probably walking to get laid. Or, maybe he was a *she*. What if that female turtle was heading to the spot where she always lays her eggs, but now I disrupted her timing and her babies wouldn't hatch in the right place, thus dooming the family line?

Gender aside, that turtle knew damn well where it was going. I, on the other hand, had no clue about my own direction. Sure, I had an itinerary and GPS, but in the grand scheme of things, I had no idea where I was going in life.

Maybe that turtle should have turned *me* around.

DAY FOUR

Sunday, September 8th. Arlington, Texas.

In a lot of areas of my life, I am an adult by age standards only. Fantasy football is one of the big culprits.

I'd been in the same league for seventeen years; the core five guys have remained the same as others dropped out due to wives' wishes or their inability to attend the annual draft. (We do an auction. It's so supremely superior to a snake draft that I will not even tolerate an argument.) To me, the purpose of fantasy football is twofold: keep in touch with buddies and make you feel better about yourself by belittling said buddies' draft and lineup mistakes. As a two-time champion, I can admit that few joys surpass the feeling when signing off emails to the league with, "The Champ." And few things annoy me more than when one of my best friends Mike Pearl – a *three*-time champ – ends his emails that same way. The first full slate of pro football games normally held a place of importance just shy of Christmas Day.

But not this year. Thanks to Sports Year, today FFL was the third string quarterback.

Sunday September 5th was huge for me because I finally met my goal of bringing a wounded veteran to the game of his choice. He was a former Marine. My father also served in The Corps, so it felt special to bring one of his brethren as my first guest.

Oscar, a former gunnery sergeant who served three combat tours in Iraq and was wounded twice, was a lifelong Cowboys fan. But he hadn't yet been to the new AT&T Stadium, built in 2009. I felt honored to be able to bring him to the season opener against their divisional rival New York Giants.

I was not as enthused, however, to be wearing a dark blue Tony Romo #8 jersey. I grew up outside NYC and attended high school in New Jersey. In my formative years, the Giants went from pushovers to punishers; led by Lawrence Taylor, their games were on CBS every Sunday, seemingly all of them called by the iconic broadcast duo of Pat Summerall and John Madden.

Admittedly, thanks to the devil's combo of fantasy football and gambling, I no longer rooted for the G-Men. But, still, I would not have chosen to wear a freaking Cowboys jersey into Jerry Jones' shrine to himself. Like in Denver, though, I didn't have a choice. This time, my attire was forced on me, ahem, *provided by* the person who got me the tickets. Unlike at Mile High Stadium, though, at least this QB's jersey wouldn't nearly get me punched in the face.

My benefactor in Dallas was also gracious enough to open his home to me for three nights. Greg Hendry, a college classmate and fellow Army ROTC cadet, gave me quite a welcome to the Lone Star State. In fact, he even arranged for Sports Year to bring Oscar to this game.

Greg volunteers with Folds of Honor, a foundation that has been providing educational funds to spouses and children of America's fallen and wounded since 2007. He put the word out to his fellow volunteers that I was looking for a very specific individual: a wounded veteran and Cowboy fan who had not yet attended a game at the new stadium. Fortunately, somebody knew of just the person. Adding to the fun, a church friend of Greg's worked security at AT&T Stadium and had tentatively arranged for a special treat: Oscar and me down on the field prior to the game. A number of variables had to fall perfectly into place, though, so it was far from a lock.

Greg arranged for us to meet Oscar at a Starbucks a few miles from the stadium. I was sweating, and not simply because it was a dreadfully hot and humid day. It was one thing to *talk about* bringing a wounded veteran to the game of his choice, but my anxiety told me it would be something else entirely to actually do so. Oscar wore a crisp white polo shirt with the Cowboys star on his left chest. It contrasted with his jet black hair and late summer tan. He declined my offer of riding shotgun, instead climbing in back. He kept his sunglasses on for the drive and didn't bite much on the hooks I cast into the conversational pond. My twisting around in the passenger seat so I could look at him while we made small talk only added to the awkwardness.

Finally, I remembered a topic that most people in Texas could agree upon: Jerry Jones is a selfish egomaniac who was singlehandedly ruining the Cowboys. Approaching the massive parking lots, we also bonded over our mutual view that $50 for parking was plumb crazy, no matter how close to the stadium the spot was. The price dropped the further away we got. "You guys up for humping it?" Greg asked, invoking the infantry term for walking. Oscar nodded without hesitation.

Nothing like a quarter-mile stroll in 104 degrees to bring strangers together! Trying to keep the mood light, I busted Greg's balls for the color jersey he'd forced upon me. "A road jersey? Couldn't find me a home one?!" Oscar laughed and shined his knuckles on his white polo with a smile. By the time we stopped in front of the stadium to pose for a picture of the two of us, I was sweating through the dark blue polyester. But not Oscar. "I grew up in this, man," he smiled at me. A worker handed us little white terry cloth towels to wave wildly during the game. I used mine for a quick wipe of my sweaty dome.

As we entered through the double doors, the three of us could not believe how cold it was inside AT&T Stadium. A wall of frigid air hit us immediately. I made a mental note to finding out how much the monthly AC bill was for this architectural marvel. (The total, according to kgbanswers.com, is roughly $200,000 per month.)

I hadn't said anything to Oscar about the field visit that possibly awaited us, for fear of jinxing it. But, now, Greg smiled and waved to a clean-cut fortysomething wearing a blue blazer and carrying a walkie-talkie. *We were a go.* But, because we had no credentials, this would have to be a covert, high speed, low drag mission.

Whoosh! Greg's friend escorted us to a private elevator. Before we could even fully explain it all to Oscar, we were on the field during pre-game warm ups. "You guys just missed Giuliani," the security manager lamented, referring to the former New York City Mayor. Oscar didn't care about that; he was star struck seeing NBC color commentator Cris Collinsworth standing in a roped off area near the Sunday Night Football set. (I was kinda star stuck, too.) We quickly got a strategic picture taken.

On the sideline, Oscar spun in slow-motion circles, neck craned upwards and mouth agape as he took in the spectacle of the cavernous stadium. He and I shared a "Can you f'ing believe this?!" grin.

The security manager's walkie-talkie squawked, turning us into pigskin pumpkins. He led us off the sideline and back inside. He shook our hands, thanked Oscar for his service and pointed us in the direction of the escalator. When we got there, none of the security guards knew what to do with us because our tickets were for the uppermost level and yet we were on the bottom level. There was a lot of, "And how'd you guys get down here...?" Not wanting to get Greg's buddy in trouble for the favor, we just played dumb. They didn't let us get on. Which meant we were stranded in Rich Town.

So, we aimlessly wandered the corridor flanked by the high priced shops – it was like the mall inside Caesar's Palace. "Who buys normal stuff at a football game?" I wondered. Oscar just shrugged. Outside Juicy, a company with whose merchandise we were both familiar but whose store we'd never entered, hot young women handed out samples to female passerby. I hustled over, and told them Oscar was a wounded veteran. I hope he's still got the picture of himself surrounded by four Amazonians.

In Iraq, Oscar suffered a traumatic brain injury when his Humvee ran over an improvised explosive device. Inside AT&T Stadium, his tan helped a bit in diminishing the jagged scar that runs from his forehead past his right eye, almost reaching the bridge of his nose before hooking down into his eye socket. Other than that telltale sign, though, I had no sense that he was still plagued by the lingering effects of his injuries.

Eventually, we took advantage of distracted security guards and "escaped" to the upper deck, which cost $109 per seat. We stopped at the nicest low-rent concession stand I'd ever patronized, where we grabbed draft beers and hot dogs. After a stop at the condiment stand, we merged into foot traffic en route to our section. Somehow, the topic of live music came up.

Oscar smiled brightly. "Man, I love concerts! And the louder, the better." Reading my arched brow, he said, "You'd think that from the explosion, I'd hate all that noise, right?" I nodded sheepishly. He smiled. "It's the opposite. At those shows, I like to get close to the speakers and just, like, feel it. When it's *quiet*, that's when I get..." His voice trailed off, the explanation unnecessary.

That casual acknowledgement of his Post Traumatic Stress Disorder caught me completely off guard. I'd never met anyone with a combat-related traumatic brain injury (TBI). The wars in Iraq and Afghanistan saw vast improvements in the medical treatments administered on the battlefield and the evacuation time from it, enabling thousands more soldiers and marines to survive injuries that would have proven fatal in prior wars. On paper, that was a good thing. But the lasting effects many of those survivors must endure were not.

Eager to steer the conversation away from PTSD, I mentioned having recently attended Pearl Jam's first ever concert at Wrigley Field. But as the words left my mouth, I wondered if Oscar – a Latino from southwest Texas – had ever even heard of a grunge band from Seattle. His face brightened. "Pearl Jam?! I'd love to see those guys!" I couldn't hide my surprise. Once again, he read my thoughts.

"I know. Weird, right? The guys in my unit couldn't believe it, either. Mexican guy from Texas, and all. Yeah, man, I dig Pearl Jam, and Nirvana, but you know who I *really* like?" As we walked, I shook my head, excitedly awaiting the answer.

It took me a few strides to realize that Oscar was no longer next to me. I looked around, confused. Finally, I looked back to see him standing frozen, his face still turned toward his right, where I had been alongside him. Impossibly, he looked both focused and lost. Dozens of people seamlessly streamed around. I hurried back to him and waited. Seconds passed. "Good place for a rest stop!" an annoyed passerby drawled. Others echoed that sentiment. I grew uneasy, concerned that the comments would soon be replaced with shoves or worse. Finally, Oscar shook his head like he'd just received smelling salts. Disappointment flashed across his face and he pointed to the scar on his forehead. "Sometimes I can't remember stuff," he said. I wanted to give him a hug. But I didn't.

Instead, I tried to be Mr. Upbeat Guy, a rodeo clown determined to distract from the menace at hand. "Don't worry, brother! We'll think of the band name! No problem!" Still standing in the path of oncoming fans, I began rattling off the names of other grunge bands – Soundgarden, Stone Temple Pilots, Mud Honey, Puddle of Mudd. But none of them were *them.* We eventually resumed walking toward our seats, an air of defeat hovering above us. I nearly suggested we stop for another beer, but then didn't. *Sure, Jamie, just go ahead and get the guy with the TBI shit-faced. Great freaking idea.*

We reached our row, which had an incredible view of the… video screen. But that was just fine by us, since, from the third tier, the players on the field resembled miniature action figures, anyway. Plus, the video screen just happened to be among the biggest in the world and featured a higher quality-picture than my TV at home. Unfortunately, the product on the field in the first half of play – both teams committed multiple turnovers and costly penalties – did not match the setting. At halftime, we made small talk with Greg.

Out of nowhere, Oscar turned to me and blurted out, "Alice in Chains!" Greg's confusion was obvious as I leapt to my feet. Oscar stood, too, and we exchanged a particularly dorky double high five. The former marine's face alternated between ebullience and utter relief at having remembered the band that had flummoxed him.

From there, the night only got better. The second half turned into a high-octane shootout. Oscar's favorite player, Cowboys tight end Jason Witten, caught two touchdowns, leading the home team to victory over their rivals. Despite my New York background, I cheered along with Oscar and the rest of the Dallas faithful on our way out of the stadium. "How 'bout them Cowboys?!" I bellowed with my arm around him. "Loud and proud!" he shouted.

Greg and I dropped Oscar at the Starbucks where we'd picked him up six hours earlier. It was close to midnight, and he had to get up early to work at the auto body shop he ran with his brother. He thanked us for bringing him to AT&T Stadium for the first time. We exchanged promises to keep in touch.

Later, Greg's large house was quiet, but I struggled to fall asleep. At first, I wrote it off to simply being amped up by Oscar's happiness over his Cowboys' thrilling victory. But I finally realized that wasn't it. No, I simply couldn't stop thinking about Oscar's brain injury. Its impact on his daily life – preventing him from doing, and, even thinking normal things – stunned me. These veterans come home from war, but still have to battle for the rest of their lives to reclaim the people they were before deployment. Can they ever do that?

My experience with Oscar reinforced my determination to bring wounded veterans to the events on their sports Bucket Lists, to help more servicewomen and men enjoy a brief respite from their troubles like Oscar did.

I hope he remembers the day fondly.

DAY FIVE

Monday, September 9th. Arlington, Texas

Today was the first day I actually sat down and wrote something about the trip.

If not for leaning down to scratch indecipherable notes on a note pad pressed against the passenger seat while driving on highways, or occasionally utilizing the voice recording feature of my iPhone to narrate an anecdote, I would not have had any chronicle of my trip so far.

I was frustrated to learn I had far less time to write than I'd expected, thanks to the combination of driving and video editing. First, I did myself no favors with my ambitious event schedule. The fewest number of miles I'd driven in a day so far was 240. On the rare occasion when I did have a few hours to sit and collect my thoughts before logging them into my Mac Book, my road-weary brain failed to answer the bell.

That lack of cranial concentration also hurt me in my newfound role of video editor. Back when I was in negotiations with David Katz from ThePostGame.com, he repeatedly emphasized how valuable it would be to me to have his editors cut and post the raw video footage I'd be shooting daily. I ignorantly scoffed at that. In just four days, though, I'd already learned how right David had been. Trying to learn how to operate iMovie left me bewildered.

But, on Saturday night I had no excuses. I'd pulled off the road at a Motel 6 early enough in the evening that I napped, edited and uploaded my video, ate dinner and showered. Refreshed, I could have done some quality writing. Instead, I prioritized watching the Notre Dame-Michigan game in my room. The Irish lost.

So did my book. "Need One"? A clue would be nice.

DAY SIX

Tuesday, September 10th. Flower Mound, Texas (a.k.a. Dallas).

Wracking my brain, I couldn't remember the last time I'd been a spectator in a high school gymnasium.

Since the answer probably resided in the 25-year range, I cut short the mental exercise. Regardless, I was beyond thrilled to hear the once-familiar squeaking of sneakers on the gym floor. When my nose informed me that all high school gyms smelled alike, no matter the geographic area or time of year, I got a warm sense of contentment.

Which was needed, since geographic differences stressed me out majorly earlier in the day. The cause? I discovered the hard way that Sunbelt high schools and junior high schools do not play all the same sports that their counterparts in the northeast and Midwest do. For instance, Texas didn't have field hockey. Additionally, the southern schools had different seasonal sports, i.e. girls played soccer in the spring down here, whereas it was a fall sport elsewhere. I'd blindly assumed the seasonal schedules would be the same as I was used to.

Sitting at Greg's dining room table, a sense of doom settled over me as I realized it would be a lot harder than I expected to find amateur sporting events to see each day. Fortunately, the local high school's girls' volleyball team had a home match. While the level of play fell far short of the Nebraska women's volleyball I saw on Saturday, the same camaraderie and enthusiasm abounded. It was official: I loved this sport.

Flower Mound High's squad boasted Lauren Cox, a sophomore who starred on the basketball court, as well. In fact, she played on the USA-16 national team. Kim Mulkey, Baylor's Hall of Fame basketball coach, and two of her assistants made the two-hour drive from Waco just to watch Lauren play volleyball. And a Tennessee assistant coach *flew to* Dallas for the match, too. College coaches are not allowed to speak with the players or their families, so they merely wanted to show their faces and school colors and let the recruit know they supported her. (Update: After the 2016 season, Lauren was named the #1 high school player in America and signed with Coach Mulkey and Baylor.)

I left the gym impressed with the concession stand hot dogs, but depressed that no college coaches ever wooed me when I was in high school. Only one wrestling coach, the guy at LaSalle University in Philadelphia, even sent me a recruiting letter.

He misspelled my last name.

<u>DAY SEVEN</u>

Tuesday, September 10th. Dallas en route to Austin.

Was it possible to pick up a southern accent from singing along to the radio for four hours?

My 2003 Saab might have been the last car ever made without an AUX jack. This meant if I wanted to listen to my iPod, I had to use headphones. Already affected by a lifelong hearing problem in my right ear, I didn't want to run the safety risk. So, I simply listened to FM – that's right, I didn't even have Sirius XM.

With four hours in the car, I was either going to learn Spanish or pick up a southern accent. I chose the latter. Lots of twangy tunes in Texas. I got pretty good at hitting the Scan button.

There's a saying about country music, "You're either Crying, Loving, or Leaving." At times I felt like crying over the fact that I'd left. Daniela, the woman I abandoned to do Sports Year, weighed heavy on my mind.

Was I in love with her? No. Rationally, I knew that I was not. She'd hardly occupied my thoughts during the two months between when I'd broken up with her and today. I must have just been lonely, and listening to a lot of breakup music didn't help.

Mexican music sure did feature a lot more accordions than I realized.

DAY NINE

Friday, September 13th. Austin, Texas.

My virgin visit into Friday Night Lights territory. I was more than a little excited for this matchup of teams in Texas's largest class: 5A. The McCallum High Knights hosted Hutto High's Hustlin' Hippos. (Sitting in the stands, I Googled "Hustlin' Hippos" just to make sure I wasn't seeing things. I wasn't. As an English major, I adored the alliteration.)

When I arrived twenty minutes before kickoff, the parking lot did not have room for me. As the result, I was forced to park in an unofficial area ¼ mile away; this involved making an illegal stop in the right hand lane of a two-lane road, *backing up over* a curb and onto a grass lot next to a highway overpass. After pulling off that maneuver, I felt manlier than I had since graduating from Airborne School at Ft. Benning.

It cost $7 to get into the game, or a buck more than it cost me on StubHub to see the Texas Rangers play on Monday. To repeat: it was more expensive to attend an early season high school football game than it was to attend a late season major league baseball game with playoff implications.

Despite being the visiting team, Hutto used a corner of the field to inflate a huge brown and white helmet, out of which the players sprinted during pre-game introductions. Both school bands boasted six tuba players. That seemed excessive to my untrained eye. Each school had dance squads featuring dozens of girls in sparkly cowboy hats. Hutto's were called the High Steppers, McCallum's the Blue Brigade.

McCallum actually had a student mascot dressed in full-length knight garb, which, on a 95-degree night, must have alarmed the EMT on site. But this kid gave it his all. Hopefully, a Guinevere in the band appreciated his effort.

In the stands, the parental, uh, enthusiasm lived up to my pre-conceived notions, which was really saying something. Even moms were yelling out play call suggestions. I had to agree, the tight end *had been* open all night.

Today I received an email that made me scream and then laugh:

Jamie,

> I hope that this finds you well. I thought I had responded to this email but I'm not seeing my response as being sent. So if this is the second time I have sent this email my apologizes. If this is the first time then sorry that it took so long for me to get back to you.
>
> This sounds like a great thing you're doing!! I want to thank you for taking this on. For something of this scale and with all the moving parts it's going to work best if we loop in a teammate of mine Brea. She is a great resource and would be able to give us a better idea of how we could make this work. I look forward to working with both of you and have a great day.
>
> **LOUIS**
> *alumni manager*
> **A Decade of Service.**
> **A Lifetime of Commitment.**
> wwp10.org
>
> Wounded Warrior Project

First, I screamed from a combination anger and frustration; I'd been close to getting the boost I needed to recruit the wounded warriors. If only Louis had noticed earlier that he hadn't actually responded, maybe things would have turned out differently.

But then I couldn't help laughing at that fact that Louis, in his zeal, CC'd Brea, the woman who'd christened Day One of Sports Year with the news that the WWP couldn't help me. I would've loved to see Brea's reaction when she read that email!

Of course, I immediately hit reply all, thanked him for his interest and said I looked forward to working together. Unfortunately, I never heard back.

I was still on my own for finding wounded veterans.

DAY TEN

Saturday, September 14th. Austin, Texas.

One of my best friends from Notre Dame had just moved here with his wife and four kids, so this was an incredibly fun visit for me. The timing synched perfectly, too, because the entire college football world focused its attention on College Station, Texas, where A&M was hosting Alabama in a rematch from the 2012 Aggie upset.

Naturally, I was focused on football in Texas, too.

8-year old flag football.

My buddy Danny would be coaching his son Austin in his first game. (How cool would it be as a kid to move to a town that has your name?!) Actually, it was a first for both of them, since father had never coached flag football and son had never played.

In fact, this was the first day. The league schedule called for an hour-long practice to be followed by the first game of the season. This arrangement lent itself to high comedic potential, which was quickly on display prior to practice as our boys repeatedly hurled their wraith-like bodies at a tackling sled. Such actions made no sense, of course, since the kids would be playing *flag* football, but it was extremely entertaining for a non-relative to watch them ricochet off the padding.

That lack of gridiron savvy reflected our inexperience level: second graders and one third grader, most of them flag football rookies. Conversely, our opponent featured third graders and just one second grader – all grizzled vets who had been playing flag football for two or three seasons. Danny met his assistant coaches that morning, right before practice. *Nice to meet you! Have you done this before? No? Me, neither!* The opposing coaching staff wore matching shirts and communicated in familiar shorthand. Just like in T-ball, coaches stand on the field of play during flag football. But, as our

73

adults struggled to line up our kids in the correct spots on defense, their grownups stood by calmly as their players flawlessly executed motion and play action.

Surprisingly, blitzing was legal, which we learned when Austin took the snap – without stumbling which, for us, was an accomplishment – and looked up to find a linebacker in his face. Danny objected loudly to the officials, only to be informed by the referee that he might want to read the rulebook.

Thank goodness we didn't keep stats, because the number of quarterback sacks would have been depressing. Of course, we could have gotten that information from the other team, which had its own statistician.

The state of Texas certainly took its football seriously. Suddenly, six tuba players in each of the high school bands last night made more sense.

<u>DAY ELEVEN</u>

Sunday, September 15th. Houston, Texas.

Today's schedule called for driving the three hours from Austin to Houston, where I'd then attend the Week 2 NFL game between the visiting Chargers and Texans.

But I called an audible, and I'm so thankful I did.

I'd already planned on staying with my friends Suzanne and David. In a voice mail, he mentioned that she, a world-class violist in the Houston Opera, had a chamber music concert that afternoon. Like the good husband he was, he'd be in attendance. Assuming I would not be, he suggested a few bars near their neighborhood and said they'd meet me after her performance.

I knew less about classical music than I did about 18th century French poetry, which was to say, nada. Figuring I would have dozens of opportunities to see a football game over the next three months, I chose the concert. But that decision forced me to scramble to find another event to replace the NFL game.

Fortunately, while driving east on I-10 in Houston, I spotted light stanchions off to the right of the highway. Athletic fields! I quickly exited at the next off ramp. Leaning forward so I could look up though the windshield like Ray Liotta in *Goodfellas* searching for the Feds' helicopter, I found my way into a public park where a Latino men's soccer league match was in progress. GOOOOOOAAAAAALLLLL!

After the team in white finished dismantling the team in red, I hustled over to David and Suzanne's house for a much-needed shower. Then we rolled to Gremillion & Company, a fine art gallery hosting the concert, which was sponsored by the River Oaks Chamber Orchestra. (For the uninitiated, like me, the aforementioned description of the location – "fine art gallery" – doesn't mean it's a *fine* art gallery. Rather, it's a gallery featuring *fine art*.)

What an ear-opening experience!

Chamber music, as I learned from Wikipedia, is a form of classical music that is composed for a small group of musicians, a group that could fit within the room of a home. Because of its intimate nature, chamber music is described as "the music of friends." I certainly felt the love: free sushi and wine! The other fifty attendees all seemed to know each other. I definitely felt out of place, certain that they could tell I didn't belong. *Dammit, I should have worn my tux.*

The concert consisted of four stringed instruments – two violins, a viola and a cello – accompanied by a world famous pianist from Thailand, Christopher Janwong McKiggan. The beautiful music did soothe the savage beast, and my eyelids drooped heavily. In Army boot camp twenty years ago, drill sergeants had instructed my fellow cadets and me that it was always better to stand in the back of the classroom than get caught asleep in our chairs. So, that's what I did: quietly stood up and positioned myself in the rear of the gallery. Back there I stayed awake and spotted several older gentlemen's chins falling into their chests. During the first intermission, I chugged two Diet Cokes and proved able to sit down and stay awake for the second act.

Late in the concert, my friend Suzanne introduced me to the audience. I beamed with pride. What an honor! Then, as people turned around to see who she was pointing at, my hostess helpfully described me as the, "The balding man in the back."

As everyone chuckled in recognition, I said, "Why not 'The man in the blue shirt'?!" Despite the fact that there were several other folic-ally challenged men in attendance, nobody came to my defense.

Suzanne, David and I laughed about it later over many drinks at their delightful home. They may have laughed more than me. The party swelled with the other musicians and some of the audience members. It was the most culturally advanced evening of my life, but there was *some* talk of fantasy football!

I woke up in the morning after my hosts had left for work. In the middle of the dining room floor a little red and white cooler awaited me. I knew that because someone had written "Sports Year" in permanent marker on one side and "Go Reidy, Go!" on the other. I opened it, stunned to find it filled with cans of apple juice and Diet-Coke on ice, along with some fresh fruit.

I simply could not get over that act of kindness. Suzanne's brother David LeFevre is one of my closest friends. As a chef, he has won a Michelin Star and now owns three distinctly different yet equally successful restaurants in Manhattan Beach. Before leaving his sister's, I emailed him to ask him why she and his brother-in-law took such great care of me.

David replied, "I think you will find that when people experience other people really living out their dreams, they want to be part of it and want to support. It's associating with greatness."

I told him I'd keep that email forever. And I hoped he was right, I hoped that I was on to something great.

DAY TWELVE

Tuesday, September 17th. Texoma, Oklahoma.

D'oh! We had our first unforced error in Sports Year planning.

I'm more of an indoors guy than an outdoors guy. During Army Basic Training, some of my platoon-mates took my disinterest in guns and/or hunting as clear proof of my homosexuality. Given my lack of *Field & Stream* experiences, it was important for me to hit some manly "red state" events during Sports Year. So, as soon as I saw a Bass Masters fishing tournament scheduled for mid-September in *Muskogee*, Oklahoma, I knew I'd landed a big one.

Only, I got the day wrong. I set up my schedule based on the competition occurring on Wednesday the 19th, when actually the fish would be swimming for their lives on *Thursday* the 19th. Commence cursing. I desperately began looking for an event somewhere along the seven-hour drive from Houston to Muskogee. A lot of online searching revealed a region on the Texas-Oklahoma border known as Texoma.

Obviously, I would be going to Texoma.

Today, for the first time since 1982, I attended a cross-country meet. On that previous occasion, I ran the race as a 7th grader. Immediately afterwards, I quit the team, declaring I never wanted to punish myself like that again. Rich and Loretta Reidy had never let me quit *anything* before, so my misery must have been too much for parents to behold. Long distance running was not for the wussy.

Today, more than eight high schools competed in the event at Fort Washita, a former United States Army post. Established in 1842, it is now a National Historic Landmark. The grounds consisted of dried out grass across acres and acres of slightly rolling hills and copses of trees. Boys and girls ran in three categories: freshmen, JV and varsity. (Suggestion: do not wait in line for the men's room prior to a cross country race, unless you adore the stench of nervous diarrhea.)

Prior to the boys' varsity event, I eavesdropped on a conversation between four freshman boys, only one of whom had won a medal in their race that had concluded half an hour earlier. They stood shuffling their feet, antsy as they ogled the JV girls ten yards away.

"*Go over* there!" one lad said, elbowing his buddy.

"Why don't *you* go over there?!" It was comforting to realize that nothing had changed in three decades conversation-wise.

Finally, one of the boys worked up some nerve. Clearly destined for sales success, he nudged the best runner and asked, "Can I borrow your medal?" I had to turn away and stifle my cackle. A father leaned into the foursome and said, "I like the way you think, kid!" Preach! The enterprising young man strutted over to the gals, who instantly reached out and examined the medal, thinking he'd earned it.

Later, I spoke with an upbeat "track mom" who volunteered at all the meets. Her pride over her senior runner of a son was palpable. How great it was, then, to see the boy finish in 7th place out of ninety competitors. I easily found his mother afterwards, as her smile could be seen from outer space. The varsity boys' race even had a photo finish – bonus!

As some competitors did their cool downs, I decided I needed to run the course in honor of the thirty-first anniversary of my last cross-country race. That turned out to be an early candidate for "Dumbest Decision in Sports Year."

Pre-run

Post-run

My initial concerns of having a heart attack on the course with nobody around to perform CPR – and no cell phone coverage to call 911 – proved unfounded. Probably thanks to the cramping in my left quad that prevented me from completing the course.

I walked the last ¾ mile, my pride dragging far behind me.

DAY FOURTEEN

Wednesday, September 18th. Durant, Oklahoma.

Today was not supposed to be book-worthy, aside from the struck-me-funny that Oklahoma has a town that shares its name with the state's most popular athlete: OKC Thunder superstar Kevin Durant. (Update: Kev ain't so popular no more.)

But then my lunch at McDonald's lasted 2.5 hours, not by choice. Unfortunately, as a Wi-Fi whore, I had no other option in Texoma to power my increasingly futile search for today's sporting event. I couldn't find a Little League game or a youth soccer match. Not one high school had anything scheduled. Every one of them held all sorts of sporting events yesterday and had them scheduled tomorrow, but none today. This discrepancy drove me crazier than the teenage girls conversing in the booth behind me.

"There's a guy who ate McDonald's every day for a month and he, like, died!"

"No, he made a movie about it."

Instantly, my mind went in two directions. First, the cafeteria scene in *Fast Times at Ridgemont High*. "Did you hear that surfer guy pulled a knife on Mr. Hand?" "No, he just called him a dick." Second, I thought of Morgan Spurlock, and wondered if the documentarian had ever heard such a disparity between two descriptions of *Super Size Me.*

Finally, after yet another Diet Coke refill, I found the website for a local men's softball league. Alas, it had no games scheduled, either. I called the number and, whimpering with frustration, asked the commissioner, "What *is the deal* with Oklahoma and no sports on Wednesday?!"

He chuckled. "Church!"

Huh? The guy explained that the entire state avoided scheduling anything on Wednesday nights because of "church activities."

I could hear my mother laughing at me, delighted that my failure to attend Mass all these years may have come back to haunt me. Fortunately, I found a coed softball league on the University of Oklahoma campus. *Three hours in the wrong direction.* So long, geographic game plan.

But The Streak continued.

DAY FIFTEEN

Thursday, September 19th. Muskogee, Oklahoma.

Finally, this day arrived, the sole reason for my trip to Oklahoma: Bass Masters Fishing Tournament!

During my drive, I felt an almost patriotic duty to download Merle Haggard's "Okie from Muskogee." I listened to it four times in a row as I pulled into town. Catchy little ditty that hasn't left my head yet. (And, I'm willing to bet, it won't leave yours for a while, either.)

I'm not sure why, but I thought Muskogee would be a lot bigger than it is. Only 38,000 people, which makes the song's provincialism make a lot more sense. That knowledge did raise the question, though, of why Bass Masters would host an event here.

A bigger question is: why would anybody attend a bass-fishing event in the first place? Bass fishing is not a spectator sport, since you can't actually see the guys out on the water. You watch teams – each boat has two guys – leave the marina and then you sit around waiting for them to come back. There is *some* suspense in that teams have to be back at the dock by a certain time, so a few boats had to haul ass to make the deadline. Once ashore, they publicly weighed their catch.

That was it.

I didn't even drink a beer because I had a three-and-a-half-hour drive to Little Rock, and I was nervous about a local cop pulling over the car with California plates. Let me repeat: I attended a freaking *fishing* tournament, yet did not enjoy a beer.

That marked the first total let down in Sports Year.

DAY SEVENTEEN

Saturday, September 21ˢᵗ. Baton Rouge, Louisiana.

There are times when it is perfectly acceptable for a grown man to wake up in a bunk bed. For instance, on a ski trip with a big group of friends in a rented house, but he arrived too late to claim one of the bedrooms with normal size beds so he had to settle for a bunk.

This was not one of those times.

Today, I awoke in the bottom bunk of a nine-year-old boy. He was not present. His Star Wars sheets, however, were. (Sorry to bump you to the floor in your sister's room, Ryan!)

You might be thinking this represented a new low for me, but that would be incorrectamundo – I didn't view it as a low at all. Some background: at a wedding in 1997, Mr. Michael Patrick Rooney, father of my best friend, declared me "America's Guest." As everyone at our reception table cracked up, I realized that nickname truly fit me. Staying in touch with people is one of my passions, and I enjoy maintaining many different circles of friends. But, thanks to Notre Dame and the Army – two national organizations representing all 50 states – a lot of my pals are spread throughout the country. That makes it difficult to see people frequently, so I like to maximize time when I can. If given the choice between staying in a hotel and crashing with friends, I will always choose the latter. Even when traveling for business, I have passed up the Hilton for a buddy's place.

During Sports Year, sure, my finances dictated that I save money by avoiding hotels. But those frugal circumstances didn't actually change behaviors for "America's Guest." That said, I couldn't recall ever sleeping in anybody's kid's bunk bed.

Another first, this one courtesy of my high-school pal Dan Casey. I dunno how many guys from northern New Jersey have matriculated at Northeast Louisiana University (now known as University of Louisiana-Monroe), married a local girl, and put down roots in Baton Rouge, but there must be fewer of them than the number of LSU fans who pray for Nick Saban's continued good health. But, somehow, Dan did just that, even managing to douse his "Joisey" accent with a splash of bayou.

Ah, yes, the bayou. Game day!

When I initially sketched out Sports Year, LSU's "Death Valley," a.k.a. Tiger Stadium, was a no-brainer Top 10 site.

Better yet, today was much more than just my spectating at a hallowed location. For the second time, I had the honor of bringing a wounded veteran to the game of his choice. Aaron, a former Army sergeant, received his medical discharge after being severely wounded in Iraq, returning to his hometown of Baton Rouge.

We connected after I got more creative in my recruiting efforts. First, I posted a message on the Facebook page for Iraq & Afghanistan Veterans of Louisiana early in the week. "As part of my Sports Year: 365 Games in 365 Days project, I'd like to bring a wounded veteran to this Saturday's Auburn-LSU game. Preferably a diehard LSU fan who has never been to Death Valley. Can you help me find a suitable person?" Next, I cold called the Veterans of Foreign Wars (VFW) in Baton Rouge and told the administrator what I wanted to do. She directed me to a member for whom I left a voice mail.

A man named Mike McNaughton called me back. Despite my poor cell phone connection, his skepticism came through loud and clear. After hearing me out, though, he mentioned having somebody in mind. (I learned later that Mike, an Army veteran, had been wounded in combat, too, losing a leg as the result. Yet, he admirably did not give himself the opportunity to attend the game for free with me.) He called Aaron, who then contacted me.

Aaron explained that he was a lifelong Tiger fan, but sheepishly admitted he had attended a home game previously. He asked if that disqualified him from coming with me. No f'ing way! I was simply happy to have a veteran to join me.

We got our tickets from an LSU celebrity: head baseball coach and 2009 national champion Paul Mainieri. I'd met his oldest son Nick in 2007, when the recent ND grad had the great misfortune of getting me as a writing mentor. I liked Nick from the start, won over by his sincere combination of humility and humor. (Update: thanks nothing to me, Nick has achieved literary notoriety, as his debut novel *The Infinite* earned widespread acclaim in the fall of 2016.)

He served as Fighting Irish football head coach Charlie Weis's personal assistant for one year, which led to a funny story. When I was back on campus for my 15-year reunion, Nick met me at the beer tents around midnight. He arrived laughing and a bit rattled. When trying to call me to coordinate, he had accidentally clicked the name directly above mine in his iPhone directory: Reid. As in, *Andy* Reid, the Philadelphia Eagles head coach. Fortunately — or not, depending on your perspective — Nick recognized his error and hung up before the other line began ringing in the middle of the night.

After Nick told his father about Sports Year, the two-time national Coach of The Year hooked me up with tickets to today's LSU-Auburn game.

Aaron and I met outside the stadium several hours before kickoff: plenty of time for us to partake in the legendary sensory overload that is SEC tailgating. Shortly after our handshake, though, I realized we would not be whooping it up. He seemed a bit shaky and avoided direct eye contact.

As we searched the parking lot for his friends' RV, making several wrong turns, Aaron revealed that he had survived several IED ambushes, "seven or maybe nine – I can't remember." Can you even imagine your memory failing to retain the exact number of occasions on which your vehicle was blown up? We had barely started our day, and I was already agog, unable to process what he had endured.

We had to swing by the baseball stadium to pick up the tickets. Fortuitously, it turned out that Aaron's family has been season ticket holders for more than 15 years. He was crazy about Tiger baseball! This transaction had to be quick, though. Nick Mainieri had warned me that it was an important recruiting weekend, meaning his father wouldn't have much time to chitchat.

Coach Mainieri was kind enough to meet with us for several minutes, during which he asked Aaron a few questions about his service. The former Army sergeant answered with heartbreakingly matter-of-fact candor, leaving both members of his audience stunned. A baseball assistant gently interrupted *twice* to remind his boss that teenaged boys and their parents were waiting for him, but Paul shook him off.

Instead, the leader of LSU's diamond dynasty led us on an impromptu tour of the facility, which was the envy of college baseball world. The Tigers averaged 14,000 fans per game, whereas the second best drawing team averaged half that. Aaron's mouth hung open the entire time, especially when we got to walk onto the field, which had the lights on.

Inside the coach's plush office, Paul invited Aaron to hoist the 2009 national championship trophy. (In a wonderful coincidence, Aaron wore an LSU baseball t-shirt that day.)

Then, the coach gave the veteran a signed baseball, saying, "As a small token of our appreciation for your service and sacrifice." *Then,* he added. "We are going to honor you this spring." During every weekend home game, LSU hosted a Soldier's Salute, at which they invited a veteran to walk out onto the field, get introduced to the crowd and receive a standing ovation. After Paul said that, it got a little dusty in the office for me. Aaron practically floated out of there.

We had one more stop prior to Tiger Stadium. My friend Anna, a New Orleans native, scored me an invite to her old friend Hunt's "must see" tailgater. On the phone earlier in the week, I asked the host for directions to his parking spot. He simply said, "Just look for the old, yellow Caddy."

Hunt conducted a clinic on southern hospitality, introducing me to my first Boudin Ball, a fried concoction of rice and pork that some people call the "King of Cajun food." Long live the king!

For years I've heard people claim, "It never rains in Death Valley." Let me assure you that those people are liars. Thankfully, Dan's wife Jeannie had provided me with a yellow poncho prior to departing their house. Thousands of people did not have wet weather gear, but that did not seem to dampen their enthusiasm any. We sat in the upper deck one section over from the student section. I tried counting how many drunken fools stood shirtless in the rain, but the task proved impossible.

Death Valley was the loudest place I've ever seen a game in any sport, college or pro. The fans left me in awe. I had expected a rowdy crowd, since it was a night game, which meant everybody had extra time to fuel up. But that alone did not account for the volume. I've attended night games at Notre Dame Stadium, USC's The Coliseum and Clemson's Death Valley – fan bases that have never been mistaken for being Mormon when it came to tailgating – and those stadiums were not as loud. Tiger fans yelled continuously from kickoff to the final whistle. At one point, I wished I'd brought earplugs. (Perhaps I should have kept track of how many times during Sports Year I felt like my father?) Most amazingly, the stands were *not* completely full, due to the rain.

Aaron left early, exhausted from all the pre-game walking and, I assumed, excitement and emotion of meeting Coach Mainieri. As we shook hands, he held on for an extra second, thanking me profusely for the day. I insisted that it was *I* who should be thanking him, but he shrugged it off. We shared a comically awkward goodbye hug inside a stadium corridor amid a throng of drunk, waterlogged fans.

Afterwards, I found Dan and Jeani in their seats. Immediately, my hostess apologized to me on behalf of all LSU Tigers. "Sorry it was so lame and quiet."

I assumed she was joking, but her face did not break into a smile. After I admitted that Death Valley's volume was nearly more than I could handle, she shook her head. "Tonight was nothing," Jeannie assured me. "Come back again." She clearly had no idea that people have lived to regret that statement.

What a day. Geaux Tigers! (LSU won somewhat easily, 35-21, handing Auburn what would be its only regular season loss en route to an appearance and near victory in the National Championship game against James Winston and Florida State.)

DAY EIGHTEEN

New Orleans, Louisiana. Sunday, September 22nd.

This should be my second time seeing a football game inside the world-famous Superdome. But it's only my first.

During my senior year, Notre Dame played Florida in the Sugar Bowl. Four buddies and I road tripped – New York to Philly to Baltimore to Atlanta – down to New Orleans. We all had game tickets that we'd bought with our student discounts, and we were sharing a room in a Day's Inn with approximately ten other classmates. You read that right: one room, two beds.

Alas, I suffered a cocktail concussion on New Year's Eve: Bourbon Street 1 – Jamie 0. My 1992 began with a purge, as I woke up with vomit in my mouth, stepping blindly over bodies in the dark on my way to the dingy bathroom. I puked throughout the morning but remained confident I'd be able to rally for the evening kickoff. But then the dry heaves started and kept up for eleven hours. I missed the game, much to the delight of a classmate who had arrived in NOLA ticket-less.

From my bed in that room filled with the stench of stale beer and fresh farts, I watched on the bolted-down television as Jerome Bettis singlehandedly dismantled the Gators with a 140-yard, 2 touchdown performance that is etched in Irish lore. That night, I met my friends at a bar on Bourbon Street. Legend has it that I got back on the beer horse, but I must confess to only sipping water.

Upon arriving home in New York, I fibbed when explaining to my parents why I missed the final football game of my collegiate experience, the one I'd driven 2000 round trip miles to attend. "I got food poisoning from bad crawfish." My mother believed my story. I guessed correctly that, as a native New Yorker who'd never been to the south, she'd believe that no problem. My father didn't question me on it, but I think he knew his eldest was completely full of shit.

A week later, my "Uncle" Gary, one of Dad's oldest friends, came to a party at our house. In the kitchen, he asked Mom how I enjoyed the Sugar Bowl. After she explained why I hadn't attended the game, he nearly choked on his cocktail, incredulous that she had fallen for that excuse. "*Loretta!* He was in *New Orleans.* He was just too hungover to get out of bed." I can still hear my mother's voice piercing the din. "JAY-MEE!" She still brings that up from time to time. Thanks, Uncle Gary!

Twenty-one years later, I didn't arrive at the Superdome armed with a ticket. Instead, I waited until the first quarter of the Saints game against the Arizona Cardinals was completed, hoping to nab a cheap ducat from a scalper tired of hanging around outside. My plan worked to perfection, as I landed a $100 ticket for $50. The gentleman in the tracksuit actually commended my negotiating technique. "I like your style!" That made me laugh; I generally suck at bargaining due to my fear of confrontation, especially with strangers.

I lucked out, seat-wise, finding myself next to two original Saints season ticket holders. These amiable men shared some good stories with me, including one about Archie Manning's first game in 1971. "Archie got hit so hard, I thought he was decapitated!"

The Superdome was loud, but not as loud as Death Valley. Part of that, I surmised, had to do with the 1:00PM start limiting the pre-game buzzes. I asked my seatmates when was the loudest they'd ever heard it. Immediately, I kicked myself for appearing clueless, because any decent football fan would have known the answer. They said in unison, "The Katrina game."

For the 2006 season, the NFL shrewdly scheduled the Saints' home opener for Monday Night Football. Just one year after

Hurricane Katrina wrecked New Orleans, an emotional and electric crowd packed the Superdome, which had housed thousands of residents in horrific conditions. On that night, fueled by deafening fans, the home team's defense forced the Atlanta Falcons to go three plays and out on their first offensive drive. Then, in a moment worthy of a sports movie, special teams ace Steve Gleason blocked the punt leading to a Saints touchdown just 90-seconds into the game. I remember getting goose bumps as I watched it from my sofa in California. As two of the original Saints fans described it to me seven years later, I got goose bumps again. The men they still shook their heads in giddy disbelief.

Both of them bring one grandchild to each home game, alternating between many kids.

(Larry and his grandson Ethan.)

All of the sudden, I wanted grandchildren. *Probably shoulda thought of that fifteen years ago, genius.*

Saints won. Who dat?!

DAY NINETEEN

Monday, September 23rd. Decatur, Georgia.

Two Sports Year firsts: seeing a girls' softball game and attending a sporting event with my 15-month old nephew Danny, a.k.a. the Christ Child, who lived in Decatur.

Continuing the good vibes, a package arrived for me at my brother's house. A few weeks beforehand, I'd swapped emails with Jeremy Brodey, then the Director of Sports + Entertainment at Under Armour. (We connected through Mike Cuccolo, an ex-founding partner at UA, who'd moved to LA to become a movie producer. Only, he didn't really know anybody in the business, so a mutual friend introduced us in the hopes I could provide him with some guidance. I doubt I did. But Mike ended up producing the 2015 comedy *Lucky Number*.)

Turned out that Under Armour worked a lot with the Wounded Warrior Project; unfortunately, Jeremy couldn't get me any traction with my white whale of an organization. He did, however, send me a box of workout shirts and shorts. My brother couldn't believe that I'd actually found a "sponsor."

Needless to say, I became a huge Under Armour fan!

DAY TWENTY-ONE

Wednesday, September 25th. Decatur, Georgia.

The day the streak died.

To recap from Page One: sad, smelly and sitting in my underwear at my brother and sister-in-law's dining room table at nine o'clock in the morning.

Ping! My MacBook Pro's email alert shattered my fog of self-loathing. Joe, a close Army buddy from my time at Camp Zama, Japan, told me he and his wife and son had enjoyed the videos I had posted on the Sports Year Facebook page. He asked me how things were going. Dripping with "woe is me," I explained I was out of options and the streak was over. (In hindsight, this makes me nauseous; Joe's father had passed away five months prior. My "problems" didn't deserve mentioning.)

At 9:35, Joe half-jokingly suggested, "People are always bowling!" Yeah, right, *bowling.* Minutes later, I heard my brother's car door slam shut on the driveway. Took me a few seconds to assess my state of dress. I lurched spastically from the dining room and sprinted for the guest room to throw on some shorts and change my shirt. No need to show him what a loser his big brother had become.

Pat tried to spitball some solutions to my rainout, but none worked. For some unknown reason, I told him about Joe's bowling joke. Instead of the smirk and eye roll combo I expected, my brother's face flashed with optimism.

"You know, bowling actually fits your rules—"

Pfft! I scoffed at the idea of beer bellies in bad shirts saving the streak. But Pat, in the ultra-patient voice he now expertly uses on his two kids, explained his logic.

"The automatic scoring ensures that nobody cheats." I'd forgotten about the universal adoption of electronic systems that counted the pins as they got knocked down. He now had my complete attention. "And the electric eye monitors foot faults, which means it's like a referee." Strike! But the good kind, like in bowling, not the bad kind, like in baseball.

Online, I quickly found a bowling alley two miles from his house. The website's schedule listed "Club 55," a league for senior citizens that met every Wednesday. Play began at 10:00AM, or five minutes earlier. Like Uma Thurman after the shot of adrenaline in *Pulp Fiction*, The Streak snapped upward, coughing to life.

I showered in less time than a seven-year old takes to brush her teeth, tore a new, black Under Armour shirt out of its plastic bag and put it on as I ran out the door. Instantly the rain soaked me. As my car hydroplaned through the streets of Decatur, I discovered that the Saab's vaunted sensory system – the one that was supposed to inform the driver that his wheels have lost contact with the road – no longer worked. *Good to know.* I made it to the alley with little time to spare (no pun intended).

Inside, I quickly introduced myself to the manager, who informed me that a guy named Bobby was bowling a perfect game. I hustled over to lane 20 just in time to witness a seventy-three year old man in dreadlocks roll his tenth strike in a row.

The stud bowler, who looked like what I imagined Larry Fitzgerald's father would look like, made the eleventh, too. But on his twelfth roll, the number four pin remained upright, prompting a loud groan from the other 77 league members who had stopped their own games to watch. (#JamieJinx.)

Despite his disappointment, Bobby graciously agreed to an on-camera interview. He told me he'd only begun bowling in 2000. I opined that that information probably annoyed other bowlers who have been doing it for much longer much less successfully. He grinned and said, "Oh, it does!" Afterwards, Bobby introduced me around and encouraged people to speak freely with me. The effect was akin to the senior quarterback high fiving a freshman in the high school cafeteria. I discovered a delightful group of seniors, some of whom liked bowling, but all of whom *loved* the weekly camaraderie.

I particularly enjoyed speaking with Lois, a vivacious woman whose Bronx accent had accompanied her south. Turned out that Bobby was her husband. In 2002, he proposed to her *at* a bowling alley. Lois also agreed to be interviewed on camera. I expected her to remove her oxygen tubes, but she did not. Rock star!

Lois

She mentioned that Bobby had previously rolled a 298, but she did not see the final ball because her nerves forced her to step outside. After I pointed out the lack of beers being consumed in this league, Lois explained, "It's too early for the seniors." (Interestingly, my father does this same thing: referring to people his age as "seniors" without acknowledging that he, too, is a senior.) But, she added, a cocktail would soon be helping her wash down lunch.

Guessing that this group included a few widows and widowers, I asked her if love ever blossomed at Club 55. Lois pointed me in the direction of a lanky black man who looked much younger than his early 60s. "Go ask him!" I did as I was told.

Larry mischievously grinned at the question and responded in a low drawl, "I met my first *two* wahves at the bowling alley." Instantly, I recognized that we had a leader in the clubhouse for Sports Year's quote of the year.

Shortly after, I returned to Lois's table, where she, as the league treasurer, invited me to pick the winning ticket for the 50-50 raffle! I couldn't remember being welcomed so warmly by strangers. I thanked her for introducing me to Larry and agreeing to be interviewed. She thanked *me* for making *her* day with my project.

"Good for you for trying something different! Look at me; I was a lawyer. Too many people just go through life doing what they're supposed to do, instead of what they *want* to do." I can still feel the strong hug she gave me before I left.

Outside, the torrential downpour had somehow increased in intensity, but it could not douse my spirits.

Sure, Sports Year was an irresponsible, ill-advised and poorly planned project. Yes, it drove me even closer to bankruptcy. But I'd tapped into something special: people's desire to chase their dreams.

I had to keep doing just that.

DAY TWENTY-TWO

Thursday, September 26th. Cincinnati, Ohio.

Another first for Sports Year: attending a game with a complete stranger.

Before I'd begun the project, I had posted the Kickstarter video on Notre Dame's LinkedIn page, which boasted 25K members. Only one person responded: Beth Naylor, an ND law school alum married to Rick, a former Irish linebacker. They raised four kids in Cincinnati, the last of whom, Avery, was a sophomore starter on Ursuline Academy's indoor volleyball team.

Avery Naylor

Beth won me over immediately with her email, which referenced my admitted cluelessness about women's sports. At its heart, her email was an invitation. But in actuality, it was an order: attend the Ursuline Academy at Mt. Notre Dame volleyball game. Since this was the first invitation/order I'd received, I would've accepted anyway. But then she threw in this kicker: the teams were the past two state champions!

Here's how Beth described it in her LinkedIn message, "They will play each other for a LEAGUE championship. Yes, that is right, all the major girls' volleyball talent is concentrated in a very small area of suburban Cincinnati – both of the all-girls Catholic schools are sister schools for Moeller and St. Xavier." (This impressed me, as the latter two are national football powerhouses.) "The boys from Moeller and St. X head directly to the game from football practice."

Beth suggested that I wear green (Ursuline colors) to the match, and forbade me from wearing blue (Mt. Notre Dame). I arrived to find the gym jam packed and tense... and that was just for the JV teams. (Coincidentally, other friends of mine had a daughter starting for the Ursuline JV squad.) Avery's grandmother skipped church choir practice to attend the match.

Beth told me her daughter played the libero position and began explaining to me what that meant. I interrupted her with a nonchalant wave of my hand. "Yeah, so Avery's a defensive specialist who stays in the game at all times but can never rotate to the front row." My hostess could not hide her surprise. (A big shout out to the nice lady at the Nebraska match who coached me up on my volleyball!)

Ursuline swept the match, three games to zero. Avery served on the winning point, causing Beth to blow out my left eardrum with a whistle that would make a traffic cop jealous. In the hallway afterwards, parents from both teams mingled; they are quite friendly as the result of the girls playing on the same AAU teams. Beth introduced me to Jeanne, a proud Mt. Notre Dame mom who assured me, "We will win when it matters: states!" For everyone, it was a foregone conclusion that these teams would meet again in a few weeks. I briefly considered jiggering the Sports Year schedule so I could be there for the rematch.

The Naylors, including the victorious Avery generously took me to dinner at a Cincinnati culinary shrine: The Montgomery Inn, a riverside spot famous for its ribs. Half a beer into the evening, I realized Rick didn't really understand how this whole thing had come together. *So, Honey, uhhhh, you just found this guy on the internet?*

When I explained that Beth's email more resembled a military order than an invitation, her husband and daughter cracked up. "Does that sound like your mom?" Rick asked Avery. She nodded vigorously, "Totally!"

Sports Year – bringing families together.

DAY TWENTY-FOUR

Saturday, September 28th. South Bend, Indiana.

Today, according to the Sports Year itinerary that I apparently wrote on an Etch-A-Sketch, I was scheduled to be in Columbus at the Wisconsin–Ohio State football game, which had an 8:00 PM kickoff. That meant I'd be able to sleep late in Cincinnati, get in a few hours of uninterrupted writing and leisurely hang out with my friend Tracy and her three adorable girls before an easy one-hour drive to the state capital. I'd "booked" a room with a college friend who practiced medicine at OSU. Another buddy, a Buckeye assistant baseball coach, had promised me a campus tour and some school swag.

But then things changed. Mike, one of my best friends from college who happened to be at Notre Dame for the Oklahoma game, called an audible. As a $500 benefactor to my crowdfunding campaign, he invoked his right to choose what game I attended. Whoosh! Suddenly, I was setting my alarm for 5:20 AM for the 4.5-hour drive from The Nati to South Bend. That didn't jive well with the extra beers I'd had at the Reds game, ticket courtesy of Tracy's brother, also named Mike.

Aside from the brutal wakeup, Mike-at-ND's changing of my plans prevented me from seeing a football game at Ohio State's "Horseshoe." I'd been looking forward to seeing if the band would dot the "I" and all that. Unfortunately, a look at the college football schedule indicated it would be impossible for me to catch an OSU home game during the remainder of Sports Year. But, those were the breaks of needing donors. And I loved my donors! I did not, however, love witnessing the Irish flop at home.

A lot of ND fans refuse to leave a game early, and Mike adhered to that rule like it was the 11th Commandment. Me? I had exited before the final whistle many times, due to disgust with the quality of play or the quality of weather. Hell, on a gorgeous October day in 2001 I didn't even *go into* the game against USC; instead, I sat in the parking lot drinking beers with Todd Norman, a former Irish offensive lineman who graduated a year behind me. He regaled me with stories about Lou Holtz and the 1989-92 teams. Damn, those beers were cold! Before we knew it, our friends had returned to the tailgater *after* the game. Which, by the way, the Irish won in decisive fashion. More than one person looked down at us in our beach chairs and said, "Are you guys f'ing kidding me?!" (I still have the unused ticket stub.) Anyway, my belabored point is: I'm not beholden to watching every play inside Notre Dame Stadium.

Today, ND trailed OU 14-0 before Mike and I had even sat down with our hot dogs and sodas. Turnovers and uninspired play sparked a lot of cursing and thigh punching. I decided to heave a Hail Mary toward my friend. "You know, man, we don't need to put up with this. We could be drinking beers at a tailgater with a shade tree…" To my utter shock, Mike made the miracle grab; we left at halftime.

I will be forever grateful we did. He's a partner in a big consulting firm that sends him to speak at conferences all around the world. Getting one-on-one time with Mike can be challenging for his wife and three kids, let alone a college buddy who lives in another city. He struggles with the dilemma facing all executives: how can I provide for everything my family needs and wants, yet still spend enough time with them? That internal debate troubles him terribly.

When I asked about his travel schedule, Mike stood up from the picnic table, ambled over to the cooler and returned with another round of beers. He explained that the previous Saturday he and Liam, his eldest, a smart and sweet ten-year old, stopped at Subway for a bite after flag football practice. Mike was happy to get that extra father-son time. Waiting for the sandwich artist to make their orders, he noticed Liam watching the store manager intently. During the meal, his son expressed his thoughts.

"Dad, I wish you were a Subway manager."

Mike chuckled. "Why's that, buddy?"

"Because then you'd be home a lot more."

Oooof. One week and two thousand miles away, that honest comment brought tears to my eyes: for Liam, for his sisters, and, for their father. I'd never cried at a Notre Dame game before, not even happy tears. And I'd certainly never been to a tailgater where a buddy had cried. This marked yet another Sports Year first.

I reached across the table and squeezed Mike's shoulder. "What did you say?" I asked, fearing the fallout. I shouldn't have fretted.

Mike sat up straighter. His face reflected calm and focus. "I told him, 'Okay, Liam, I can be a Subway manager.'" I couldn't believe this beginning and, apparently, neither could Liam.

"Really, Dad?!"

"Sure, buddy. But, if I become a Subway manager, we're going to have to change some things."

Liam was all in. "Sure! Like what?"

"First of all, you and your sisters will have to leave your school and go to public school." (They attended a private Catholic school, just a quarter mile down the street from their house. It's like *Pleasantville* the way they walk to and from school every day.)

"Why?" the boy asked.

"Because a Subway manager doesn't make as much money as I do. And private school is expensive."

"Oh. Well, that's all right."

Mike's beloved mother-in-law lived in a, uh, mother-in-law cottage on the back of his property. "And Nana's not going to be able to live with us anymore, either."

Liam did not like that. "Why not?!"

"Because our house is really big and costs a lot of money. If I'm working at Subway I won't be able to afford the mortgage payments. So, we will have to move to an apartment and it will be too small for Nana to join us."

Liam thought about this for a long while, before finally nodding. "Okay."

"And, we are going to have to make other sacrifices, too."

"Like what?"

"No more new games for the Wii or PS3…"

On the drive home, Liam said, "Dad, I don't want you to be a Subway manager."

Mike then had his first candid conversation with his eldest child about a husband and father's responsibilities: mortgage, private school, vacations, college funds. He specified some dollar amounts, drawing gapes from Liam. "I don't *want* to spend so much time away from you and mommy and your sisters. But, unfortunately, that's what I have to do sometimes." Done with telling me the story, Mike took a long pull on his beer.

I just sat there, awestruck by his adulthood. I had none of the responsibilities Mike had described to his son. Nobody depended on me for anything, aside from being available to grab a drink on a school night. Mike, on the other hand, had grown into a man his father would be proud of.

Cue those happy tears at a Notre Dame game.

DAY TWENTY-FIVE

Sunday, September 29th. South Bend, Indiana.

I found myself whistling as I got into my car today, excited to be heading to my event. Driving off, I heard a strange whistling from the back seat, as if the rear passenger window was down. But I knew it was not.

Cringing, I looked over my right shoulder and saw bits of broken glass dangling where there should have been solid glass. Vandals!

I pulled over immediately and did a physical accounting of all the stuff I'd left in the car overnight. Everything was present. That made me even angrier; the bastards hadn't found any of my things worthy of stealing. WTF? C'mon, bad guys, I've got *some* good stuff.

Internally, I eviscerated myself over a lazy decision I'd made yesterday. Prior to setting out for tailgating, I had glanced back at my car, which was unnecessarily parked at the curb. My hosts had a big driveway and it would have been easy to re-park the Saab. I briefly pondered doing so before deciding, nah, they lived in a wealthy neighborhood; the car was fine on the street.

Today, I called 911 even though I didn't really know why. It wasn't like the SBPD were likely to do anything. The cop who responded said there had been a rise in auto vandalism cases in good neighborhoods recently. "Teenagers, probably."

No auto glass shops were open in South Bend on Sunday. Not that my schedule allowed for a multi-hour glass replacement. After today's event, I had intended to haul ass east for six hours, toward D.C. Now, I'd have to make the trek with the constant howling of wind outside my makeshift Hefty trash bag "window" I had duct taped to the doorframe.

Hopefully, no nice folks heard me as I finally drove to Notre Dame. "JAMIE, YOU'RE A FUCKING STUPID FUCKFACE!" On campus, I took a seat in the surprisingly crowded softball stadium, where the Wounded Warriors Amputee Softball Team was taking on a squad of Fighting Irish coaches and celebrities.

I took one look at the field and – POOF! – any bit of self-pity I was feeling vanished. Every guy on the team was missing at least one limb, and several players were missing *two*.

Broken car window? Not an actual problem.

Thank you, Wounded Warrior Amputee Softball Team, for helping me put things in perspective.

And, oh, by the way? These guys can play ball as well as any of the All-Army guys I played with during my service in Japan. After a few innings, I even forgot that their bodies were not whole.

Do yourself and your families a favor and go see them, too. You can check out their schedule here:

http://www.woundedwarrioramputeesoftballteam.org

DAY TWENTY-SIX

Monday, September 30th. Herndon, Virginia.

Starting the day, I faced a frantic seven-hour drive from a hotel in eastern Ohio to a Washington, D.C. hotel for an appointment at 3:00. This jaunt was not on the original Sports Year schedule; I was supposed to be leisurely heading to Pittsburgh for a few days before hitting New Jersey on Wednesday for a Division-III field hockey match at Montclair State.

But I got an exceedingly rare invitation that I could not decline: taping an interview for a television documentary about the 90s that would air on National Geographic channel in 2014. The producers naturally wanted to do a segment on Viagra, the biggest pop culture pharmaceutical of all time. After reading my book, they asked me to sit down for an on-camera interview. Unfortunately, the New York and Los Angeles tapings didn't work for my schedule. The DC session wasn't on my route, but the inconvenience paled in comparison to the opportunity to be featured on the show and possibly sell some books.

I was even more pumped up about meeting the person on the interview schedule ahead of me: James Carville. The legendary political strategist just happened to be an avid sports fan, particularly rabid about his beloved LSU Tigers. I figured my recent visit to Death Valley would pique his interest and – who knows? – maybe he'd offer to give Sports Year some Twitter love. Mr. Carville was scheduled to tape at 3:00, so I needed to be at the hotel before that.

Two hours into the trip, I desperately needed caffeine. (The *Breaking Bad* series finale aired last night, ending at 11:00PM. Afterwards, I stayed up very late reading reviews online.) At a Pennsylvania Turnpike Starbucks, I grabbed a venti iced mocha latte. Congratulating myself for a record-fast pit stop, I gunned the Saab back onto the highway. As the car leaned left, the latte leaned right – and toppled out of the dashboard's drink holder. (Physics was never a strong suit of mine.) The plastic top did not stay sealed, letting liquid splash all over the passenger side of the car, soaking the carpet. Subsequently, I learned that rage could be as effective as espresso at reviving a sleepy person.

Thankfully, I thought back to the amputee softball players from yesterday and managed to remember that spilled latte was not actually a problem at all. I did not, however, stop to clean up the mess, which – in case you are unfamiliar with this less-than-macho coffee order – contained a lot of milk. You know, a liquid that turns sour.

At the Pennsylvania-West Virginia border, I hit standstill traffic, the result of one of those "Somebody definitely better have died!" accidents. Forty minutes later, I reached the crash site and instantly felt like a total tool, as the wreckage left little doubt somebody had indeed died there. When I finally got to the hotel at 3:15, I comforted myself with the assurance that James Carville was most definitely still taping. I raced to the large ballroom the producers had reserved for the shoot. Only, no taping was in progress; the crew members were just sitting around looking at their phones. James Carville was nowhere to be seen.

Turned out, he'd asked to come in early for his interview. He'd already departed an hour beforehand; even if I'd been on time I would've missed him. Dumbfounded and disappointed, I asked the producer, "Does that happen a lot, celebrities offering to come in early?" He shook his head in amazement. "First time."

I shook off the disappointment to give a one-hour interview. (Fifteen seconds were used in Part 3 of the documentary.) From the hotel, I headed to a house that was not my originally scheduled crash pad tonight. Two factors kept me from staying at my sister's: she lived in a sketchy neighborhood and didn't have a garage. Parking my car with the garbage bag-as-rear-window didn't seem like a smart option security-wise. (Maybe the D.C. criminals would have turned up their noses at my stuff, too, like their South Bend cronies?) Fortunately, an old friend and his family offered to host me at their home in Herndon, a northern Virginia suburb.

Terry and Patty serve as a cautionary tale for young couples in their neighborhood; trying for a fourth child, they were blessed with twins. Five kids under fifteen years old made for an active household. The energy proved irresistible, and I wished I could've stayed for days. Not sure Team Redican felt the same way.

Tonight, Terry and his two oldest daughters took me to watch their high school's girls' volleyball team. Emi and Anna eagerly shared their dream to play on that court someday. When a senior star smiled and said hi to them, they practically squealed with delight.

That reaction transported me back to my sophomore year in high school. I remembered passing Chris Campbell, a badass senior safety and team captain, in the hallway. He nodded at me. No words or smile, mind you; merely a nod.

But I am pretty sure I squealed, too.

DAY TWENTY-EIGHT

Wednesday, October 2nd, Cleveland, Ohio.

My long-awaited stop in Pittsburgh got ditched for a better offer: two free tickets to the Cleveland Indians' win-or-go-home playoff game tonight. A college roommate, who worked in the sports-management business, called me with the news last night. No way I could pass that up.

Unfortunately, I was forced to exceed the Pennsylvania and Ohio official speed limits *and* the Saab's unofficial speed limit for seven hours in order to make it to his office before 5:00 PM. (He was out of town and had stressed the fact that the receptionists would be departing promptly at closing time.)

From I-76 and I-80, I called both the Cleveland Veterans Affairs (VA) office and the VFW, trying to find a wounded veteran to join me. Neither organization could help me. In fact, a woman at the VA chided me for waiting until the last minute. "These men are wounded. They can't just make decisions and – BOOM! – get themselves to a ball game!" Ouch. I felt shorter than a batting tee after that, even though I'd had no control over when I received the offer of tickets. It had never occurred to me that these veterans might not be able to maneuver their schedules as easily as I could. Chastened, I thanked that woman for her insight.

My buddy had tempered my enthusiasm for the seats by cautioning me, "I have no idea how good they are." Uh, pretty good: 31 rows up from the Indians' dugout! The atmosphere at Progressive Field was electric, as the Tribe's fans madly waved white towels like Tom Hanks in *Castaway* trying to flag down a passing airplane.

Yep, Cleveland was pumped for its first playoff appearance in five seasons. Especially my new friend Sue:

Sue's been doing this since '95. That's her *third* headdress.

Despite that kind of support, though, the Indians lost. Of the four MLB games I'd attended so far, the home teams went 0-4. When I texted that fact to my ticket donor, he responded that he wished that statistical information had been in his possession much earlier.

After the game, I headed to the hotel bar for a nightcap. There, amongst the angry Indian fans, I met a pair of Tampa Bay Rays supporters, who'd flown in on a whim that very day from Florida. And they were still flying high post-game! A nightcap turned into several pops for me; I smiled all the way to my room, thrilled with the direction Sports Year was taking.

That's when I learned that a girl I watched play volleyball last week for Ursuline Academy in Cincinnati had died.

Her name was Jordan Hoak and she was sixteen years old. She died from injuries she suffered in a car accident the very next morning after her team won the league championship.

I'd be lying if I said I recalled her from the match. But, still, her death shook me.

Imagine Jordan waking up and realizing it's Friday. *FRIDAY*! Then she remembers that she and her teammates just pounded their biggest rivals last night. *A sweep?! In an away match?!* She gets behind the wheel – at sixteen she couldn't have had her license for very long – and drives herself to school, the place where everybody's going to be congratulating her all day on the victory. Maybe her favorite song comes on the radio and she can't believe it. *OMG!* She's feeling like life could not possibly get any better, and she never sees the other car…

I hope her last thoughts were joyous. It helps to think they were.

DAY THIRTY

Friday, October 4th. Ann Arbor, Michigan.

In a growing pattern, let me start out by saying I wasn't supposed to be here. I was supposed to be somewhere in the Mid-Atlantic States, en route to Annapolis, Maryland, for a regatta. In fact, I had no intention of even driving through Ann Arbor during Sports Year, let alone setting foot in this godforsaken city. But, once again, a donor changed my itinerary for his own selfish and evil purposes. I'll get to that in a bit.

On Day 27, I attended a men's soccer game at American University in Washington, D.C. Working the ticket table outside the field were two charming freshman athletes: Grace (field hockey) and Nicole (lacrosse). I told them what I was doing with Sports Year, and they both loved the idea.

Grace, who has a future in marketing, instantly said, "Then you need to come see our field hockey game on Saturday!" I appreciated her enthusiasm, but mostly I liked being told what to do by a pretty, young woman. Alas, I couldn't be make it, I explained, because I'd be 500 miles away at the University of Michigan football game.

"That's my hometown!" Grace responded. "Go see Pioneer High School's field hockey team. We won the state championship last year." Uh, okay. Will do.

DAY THIRTY-ONE

Saturday, October 5th. Ann Arbor, Michigan.

Regardless of the college you went to, you recall some entrepreneurial students selling funny T-shirts about a rival school. One of my favorites was "Muck Fichigan." (My favorite, unsurprisingly, was "Catholics Vs. Convicts," recently made famous by Patrick Creadon's outstanding *30 for 30* documentary on ESPN.)

As an undergrad at Notre Dame, I attended two football games at "The Big House," a.k.a. Michigan Stadium. In the chapter for Day Two, I related my talking smack with Dr. Sanjay Gupta regarding the "Rocket game" from 1989 and the "Desmond Howard game" from 1991. After the latter, I had no need to ever set foot in Michigan Stadium ever again.

But, as I wrote in yesterday's chapter, somebody decided otherwise. Bob, a Michigan native and UM grad, invoked his right as a $1000 donor to pick what game I'd see with him. He thought Homecoming Weekend would be perfect for me. *With friends like these...*

I girded myself for a thoroughly annoying day surrounded by Wolverines congratulating themselves on how wonderful it was to be a Wolverine. But I did not prepare myself for meeting a Wolverine coaching legend.

Since my host demanded I sport Michigan colors, we had to stop at the bookstore to get me some gear. (While an affront to my Notre Dame fandom, a yellow T-shirt would be a vast improvement over the Fighting Irish *leprechaun costume* Bob had been considering making me wear all day.) En route, I spotted a well-dressed older man walking by himself in our direction. At first, I seriously thought he was former United States Secretary of State John Kerry. I quickly rejected that identification, though, reasoning that the diplomat would be surrounded by security. Finally, I realized who it was.

As we neared him, I stopped and said, "Coach! Can I please get a picture with you?" He cringed, clearly unhappy at the intrusion. Knowing he'd been a high school English teacher in an early stage of his career, I thought he might appreciate the literal and metaphorical journey I was on. So, I hit him with a rapid-fire explanation of Sports Year, "I'm on Day 31 of a sports road trip where I'm attending a different event every day for 365 days." His face changed completely, tension replaced by delight.

"That's amazing!" he said. "I'd be happy to take a picture with you."

I quickly switched my iPhone to video and handed it to Bob, who happily assumed cameraman duties. As Coach and I posed with our arms around each other, he asked me where I was from. Sheepish, I admitted, "Actually, I'm a Notre Dame guy." He groaned and moved to pull away from me.

I assured him, with a gentle fist to the shoulder, "I have a great deal of respect for you and everything you stood for."

That seemed to appease him and he stayed put. With a clock ticking in my head, I motioned for Bob to begin shooting the video. He gave me the thumbs up, and I started to narrate. "Sports Year, here with Michigan's national championship winning football coach... Gary Moeller." As I said the words, they clanged in my ear – off key.

That's because they were.

Majorly offended, the former coach stepped away from me. "Nope. I'm not Moeller." I blinked in confusion as sweat slid down my back.

Finally, my lead-lined brain realized this was Lloyd Carr, the man who had *replaced* Gary Moeller, a guy who got run out of town after getting a DUI (and, more importantly, losing too many football games). Coach Carr *had* won the national title, proving that I had totally known what I was talking about. Except, you know, for his name.

As Coach Carr walked away, Bob just stood there gawking at my stupidity. I closed my eyes for a second before slowly extending my arm, fist up, and then opening my hand. "Gimme the phone." *I really, really don't want to see that video, but, goddamn it, I need to see that video.* Cringing, I pressed play. The action began with my starting to tell the Hall of Fame coach that I was actually a Notre Dame grad, but the video stopped after one second. Huh? I tried again. And again. Same result each time.

Turned out that Bob, a Samsung guy unfamiliar with the iPhone, had pressed "record" and then *pressed it again*, thus stopping the recording. But he stood there "filming" the entire time. Part of my spirit soared: there's no evidence of my ignorance! The rest of me knew, though, that a video of my stupidity would have had the potential to go viral. *Irish Idiot Insults Wolverine Legend! Domer Dunce Degrades Big Blue Coach!* Michigan fans, delighted at an ND fan's self-inflicted humiliation, definitely would've shared that link, possibly helping me catch the eye of a corporate sponsor.

Secret or public, my gaffe ruined my day. I prided myself on my sports knowledge. After all, I had known Coach Carr had been an English teacher early in his career, hadn't I?! Yet, I confused his name for that of the bozo he'd replaced. There'd be no mulligan for me. (Two days later, I sent Coach Carr an apology letter c/o the UM athletic department.)

Inside the stadium, everyone treated me very nicely, which shocked me until I realized they all assumed I was a Wolverine fan.

Bob had brought Marlin, his then girlfriend and now wife, and her 16-year old daughter, to Ann Arbor for the weekend, too. Tina had never been to a big-time school for a football game before, so, naturally, she was gaga over all things Wolverine.

Still bitter over my forced T-shirt, I exacted some small revenge on Bob, when I taught Tina the "real" words to the University of Michigan fight song:

"Hail! Hail! To Michigan the assholes of the world…"

119

DAY THIRTY-TWO

Sunday, October 6th. Lansing, Michigan.

Rough morning for me, as I nearly puked on the dashboard when I got behind the wheel. No, not due to a hangover.

Remember that iced mocha latte I spilled on Monday? Yeah, so, I never did get around to cleaning that up. *Ripe.* At the self-serve car wash, I was the only customer using that big soapy broom to clean *inside* his car.

But that didn't get my spirits down, since, for only the second time, I was heading to an event at the invitation of a stranger. Dawn, a mom of two in the small town of Holt, Facebook messaged me a few weeks ago: her daughter's 4th and 5th grade squad would be cheering for the Holt Rams today. Would I like to join? Of course!

Alas, to my thin "beach blood," the rain and cold merited my Gore-Tex ski jacket. But, I didn't think that was the most macho way to make a good first impression on Midwesterners. Of course, my alternative wasn't exactly the height of manliness, either:

Author doing the "Michigan-is-a-hand" thing to point out Holt's location.

The quality of play did not reach Big Ten levels, but these boys gave it their all under miserable conditions. Surprisingly, the most interesting action took place off the field. At one point, the head coach chewed out his son – the team's star running back – only to then get heckled by the boy's grandfather, leaning against the fence a few feet from me. The coach turned to *his* dad and told him to shut it. Grandpa was ready to rumble.

"Tell me to 'shut up?' I'll whip your ass!"

The head coach, now conveniently back to focusing on the game, said nothing else. I would've kept my mouth shut, too. In fact, I didn't even video the exchange, for fear of getting *my* ass whupped.

Besides, I wasn't there for the game. I was there for the cheerleaders. (That sounds a lot pervier than it should have.) They sported clear plastic ponchos over their uniforms.

Unfortunately, the cheerleading coach called off the halftime routine due to legitimate muddy turf-related injury concerns.

Dawn, thanks for the invitation! (And the homemade chocolate chip cookies.) Wet and cold was a small price for me to pay for experiencing the fun and warmth of a small town. Go Rams!

DAY THIRTY-FOUR

Tuesday, October 8th. Vernon Hills, Illinois.

Today marked yet another Sports Year first: attending the game of a child of classmates of mine. (There's gotta be a better way of phrasing that.) Tim and Margaret met during our junior year at Notre Dame. Their daughter Kate played volleyball for St. Joseph School in Chicago's northern suburbs.

I'd completely forgotten how small Catholic school gyms can be; this one only had room for bleachers on one baseline.

This was also the first time that I saw my new favorite sport played below the high school level. Tim, a major donor to Sports Year and a regular reader of the blog, made sure to temper my expectations regarding the quality of competition.

"The girls try hard."

I asked if it's more like Newcomb ball, that game from elementary school that's like volleyball only with just throwing and catching the ball. The proud papa hesitated a second before sheepishly shrugging, "Put it this way: Nobody's spiking."

He was not sandbagging. When one of "our" girls served overhand, our opponents – and their parents – gasped in surprise. Mostly, the players tried to get the ball over the net, no matter if it was the team's first or second touch. The only blocking occurred when one parent stood up in front of another to go to the concession stand, thus obscuring the view.

Despite the lack of volleyball skills, however, I thoroughly enjoyed myself. Is it trite or condescending to describe the scene as "innocent"? That's the word that leapt to mind. Innocent. Many of the players seemed happy just to simply be on the team.

One girl, more of a Mathlete than Class Jock or Miss Popularity, melted my heart when it came her turn to serve. She half-walked/half-ran to the service line, right in front of us. When a teammate bounced her the ball, she caught it stiffly. She smiled nervously. "Oh, jeez!" she gushed. Like, she actually said those words loud enough for everyone in the bleachers to hear. I wanted to hug her and tell her everything was going to be all right. But I didn't actually believe the latter.

Despite her mighty underhanded swing, the ball barely reached the net. Fault. I feared she might cry. I feared *I* might cry. But her teammates circled up and patted her on the back and the parents yelled out support. My favorite player smiled bravely and got ready for her team to receive serve.

I felt like I'd aged a year. Which begged the question: How the hell could I ever survive being a parent if I couldn't handle someone *else's* kid's low points?

DAY THIRTY-FIVE

Wednesday, October 9th. Normal, Illinois.

Tonight in St. Louis, the Cardinals hosted the Pittsburgh Pirates in Game 5, the finale of their National League Divisional playoff series. I'd seen close out games before (1998 ALCS, Yankees taking Game 6 from the Indians; 1998 World Series, Yankees winning Game 4 in San Diego to clinch the sweep of the Padres), but I'd never seen a do-or-die game (5 or 7). So, this was something I definitely wanted to do. But the Sports Year accounting firm didn't love the idea of scalping a ticket with prices above $100.

St. Louis was a five-hour drive from Chicago's northern suburbs. Last night, as I sat on Tim and Margaret's couch after the volleyball game, I checked my iPhone's map and saw that the strangely named town of Normal-Bloomington, in Illinois, sits at the approximate halfway point. After Googling "bowling alley," I found Circle Lanes. A brief phone call got me my event: a women's bowling league that started at 9:30 AM.

Which is how I found myself awake at 6:30 this morning, rolling south on I-55.

I walked into Circle Lanes with some trepidation.

For the first bowling event two weeks ago in Georgia, things were different: Club 55 was coed. So, I didn't stand out, aside from my age. But here in Illinois, I'd be the weird lurker being trailed by a guy with a video camera. (That reminds me: I forgot to mention that Carl, a longtime buddy, joined me yesterday. I picked him up at O'Hare. He'd be serving as my cameraman/drinking buddy/wingman for the next ten days.)

Fortunately, the ladies welcomed me, anyway. 54 women participated in the weekly league, "The Young and The Rest of Us."

I met an opera singer. As one typically does in a bowling alley.

Tracy Marie Koch teaches at the Midwest Institute of Opera. When I asked this first-year league member if she liked living in Normal-Bloomington, she seemed to take offense. "No, no, you gotta understand this, my man. Some people are from here" – she paused to play air guitar while making the sounds of the chords from the

"Dueling Banjos," a.k.a. the song from the movie *Deliverance* – "and some people are transplants." I did not need to ask which category she was in. Later, Tracy asked me, "So how do you make money driving around the country like this?" Uhhhhhh.

The nice ladies even let me bowl once! (It's worth watching the video to see me bite it thanks to my socks.)

Bowling alleys had become such dependable spots for me, I decided to start hitting them for a morning session once per week. Words I never thought I'd think.

Since I'd already seen an event this morning, we could enjoy a night on the town in St. Louis. After checking into the hotel, Carl and I hit The Oyster Bar, a cool spot directly across from Busch Stadium with live music, great Cajun food and a fun NOLA vibe.

We met a lively group of women and Carl quickly connected with the comeliest one. She and her pals invited us to join them at a sports bar to watch the last few innings of the game. Apparently, after showering earlier I'd doused myself with female repellent, since none of the women paid attention to me. But Carl played a long game of tonsil hockey with the hottie while I stood by myself watching playoff baseball on the TV. The Cardinals prevailed, sending the bar crowd into a frenzy like the ball had just dropped on December 31st. And even though I'd arrived not caring if the hometown team won, I found myself grinning like an idiot and high fiving like everybody else.

The good vibes ended for me when we got back to the hotel, where my electronic room key failed to unlock our door. At the front desk, I learned that when I had checked in that afternoon, the guy had not run my credit card right away. Later, my bank declined the transaction because I had exceeded my spending limit, so the hotel manager turned off my room key. I didn't even try to give the night clerk the old, "Huh? That's so weird. Must be a computer glitch!"

Thankfully (for me, anyway), Carl's new friend had declined his offer to sleep in her bed, so he was with me at the front desk to swap in his credit card. On the downside, that also meant he was an eyewitness to my embarrassment. "Someday we'll laugh about this," he assured me, like a good friend would.

But that comfort proved fleeting. Sleep eluded me, as the stress from the financial foolishness of this journey spread throughout my shoulders and upper back like insidious cement, hardening into knots.

I couldn't keep Tracy the opera singer's question from echoing in my head. "So how do you make money driving around the country like this?"

DAY THIRTY-EIGHT

Saturday, October 12th. Oxford, Mississippi.

Today. Was. Finally. Here. Finally.

Ole Miss. I'd been waiting decades for the opportunity to visit this hallowed ground. But gridiron glory had not granted the University of Mississippi instant membership in Sports Year's Top 10 list. No, suh, I was here for the girls and The Grove.

After all, Rebel football fans had only experienced one truly great football season in fifty years. But, to their everlasting credit, they never let on-field performance diminish their off-field production. As "Grovers" like to say, "We may not win every game, but we never lost a party!"

Joe, the sales guy at Fox Sports and Ole Miss grad, contacted his former fraternity brother on my behalf. This is part of the email he sent to introduce us:

> Jamie – David is my buddy that has been gracious enough to offer up two of his tickets and a free pass to the world famous Millard Society tailgate in the Grove.
>
> David – Jamie is making the trip of a lifetime and traveling to all 50 states and attending a sporting event everyday for a year! He unfortunately, is a Notre Dame fan, but don't hold that against him.

That email felt like validation to me; even though Joe and his sales reps at Fox hadn't been able to land Sports Year a sponsorship deal, he still felt strongly enough about it that he went out of his way to hook me up at his alma mater.

David's response pumped me up:

> Jamie, Looking forward to beginning the conversion process-- I can assure you by the time you leave Oxford, you will have a special place in your heart for our little slice of heaven. Looking forward to meeting you and you bringing some luck of the Irish to Oxford. Hotty Toddy!!!

Hotty Toddy? Dude. Isn't that a frou frou drink at ski resorts? Suddenly, I wasn't as excited for this experience as I had been. Within ten seconds of our setting foot on campus, however, Carl and I heard someone happily shout, "Hotty Toddy!" Immediately, several other happy people shouted back, "Hotty Toddy!" This apparently is a Mississippi fan's thing; it's simultaneously a rallying cry, a password to get into the club and an instruction to drink. Once again, Sports Year opened my eyes to my own cluelessness.

But there was more to "Hotty Toddy" than just being similar to a rallying cry like "Go Irish" or "Roll Tide" or "Fight On." I learned there's also an entire chant to it. Anybody can start it with a simple, "ARE YOU READY?" Then, any fans nearby boisterously respond,

Hell Yeah! Damn Right!

Hotty Toddy, Gosh Almighty,

Who The Hell Are We? Hey!

Flim Flam, Bim Bam

Ole Miss By Damn!

After cracking the code, Carl and I eagerly yelled "Hotty Toddy" the first time we approached a group of people in red shirts. When they responded in kind, we grinned like 4th graders on the school bus who made that pulling-down-fist motion at big rigs and got a trucker to blast the horn. We picked up our pace to David's tailgater.

Er, excuse me, *Bubba's* tailgater. Despite his having matured into a respected physician, husband and father, David's college buddies still called him Bubba. I loved that. He and his regular crew of fraternity brothers and their wives welcomed Carl and I better than the prodigal son. Their tailgater even had a name: The Millard Society, conveniently located directly behind Ventriss Hall, which is one of only two buildings actually inside the Grove. Catered with a well-stocked bar – first class, all the way. Bubba even refused to accept our cash for the tickets. "It's our pleasure to have you. Welcome to The Grove!"

For the sake of my mother and anyone else who hasn't heard, let me explain that The Grove plays host to the most legendary tailgating experience in college football. Actually, "legendary" might not even cover it.

By my count, eight unique attributes distinguish it from other schools' pre-games:

First, The Grove is located in the center of campus, giving it a true collegiate feel. Second, because oaks, elms and magnolias surround the ten-acre plot, it provides fans with a cozy feeling, natural beauty and, maybe most importantly in September, shade. Third, "The Pride of The South," a.k.a. the marching band, performs in front of The Grove stage, adding to the uniquely collegiate atmosphere. Fourth, since 1991 no cars or RVs have been allowed in the area. Fifth, each tailgating spot features a red, blue or white tent under which never ending streams of food and beverages are served, not necessarily in that order. Sixth, the "Walk of Champions" takes the

Rebel players down a sidewalk through the Grove to the stadium, splitting a sea of adoring fans. (Other schools do something similar, but that doesn't make this any less endearing.) Seventh, Dixie; the day was filled with southern drawls, southern traditions (a lot of people dress like they're attending an outdoor wedding) and southern charms.

Speaking of which, the hospitality Carl and I received was not limited to The Millard Society. While wandering aimlessly, we witnessed a woman give a girl in her early 20s a pair of cowboy boots. That would've been normal if they'd known each other. But they clearly did not. I totally had to get the scoop on that, so Carl and I crashed the donor's tailgate party, which just so happened to be the fanciest one we saw.

Jane was one of the hostesses at the famous Zebra Tent, so named because of the huge canopy's white and black pattern. She and her family had been rolling out the red carpet at every home game since 2001. She said that for her and the others, game day was "Bigger than Christmas because we do it so often." As much as I *really* wanted to debate that logic, I moved on to my reason for trespassing. "You didn't know that girl you gave the boots to, right?"

Jane modestly shook her head, not wanting me to build the gesture up into something more than it was in her mind. The attractive brunette spoke on camera in an accent sweeter than sweet tea. "Well, we had a downpour of rain and I saw this poor girl – her flip flop had broken, her sandal – and she was so cute, she was just walking through the mud. And I always bring a wardrobe change in case of rain. So I had my cowboy boots, my jeans and my baseball cap – everything – and I asked her what size shoe she wore, she wore my size, so I said, 'Come to my tent, get some boots and we'll catch up tomorrow.'"

At that point, complete disbelief at the fact that this kind woman gave a total stranger shoes without exchanging cell phone numbers or anything must have flashed across my face, because Jane rushed to explain, "I just hated to see that cute, little, precious girl just walking in the mud! We can't do that, we're southern belles!"

And that brings me to the eighth wonder of the world: The women at The Grove.

As an English major, I should have been on a mission to explore Oxford, this literary haven that spawned William Faulkner and other famous authors. But today, I fancied myself a social scientist conducting a research project. Once and for all, I would finally have an answer to the question: did the University of Mississippi boast the prettiest coeds in the country?

People half-jokingly say "Ole Miss redshirts Miss Americas," because *so many* attractive girls go there. This reputation started, appropriately enough, with an actual Miss America.

In 1959, sorority girl Mary Ann Mobley won the coveted crown. Apparently, seeing this smart beauty walk across their television screens convinced mothers throughout the South to send their daughters to college in Oxford, MS. From there, it was just a matter of genetics: attractive women mated with attractive or at least not butt ugly guys they met at Ole Miss, then they had attractive kids who attended their parents' alma mater and mated with other children of attractive parents... and pretty soon the whole campus had turned into a Ralph Lauren ad. But, still, there was no way reality could match the hype, right? And I knew the sights would never surpass Sevilla.

In the fall of my junior year of college, I spent the semester in London. Over October break, my roommate Bill and I visited Spain. After only half a day in Sevilla, he turned to me and said, "Dude, my neck hurts from looking at all the chicks." I nodded and proclaimed, "I will never see more pretty girls in one place again in my life."

23 years later, Ole Miss proved me wrong. *Hotty* Toddy, indeed! Seemingly every step we took brought us to another gorgeous gal in a sundress. Teeth whitening companies should really scout Rebel home games for "after" models. Carl, who had arrived intent on keeping the Camcorder rolling all day, actually put it away because he felt so pervy. Not everything, however, was all bourbon-flavored peaches and cream.

As if the depletion of both my hairline and memory were not sufficient evidence of my entering middle age, The Grove provided irrefutable proof: rather than checking out the comely coeds, I found myself marveling at their *moms*. Speaking of which, Carl and I sat next to one of the latter at the game. Unfortunately, Karen was there with her husband, David (who, from what I've seen on Facebook, appears to be a frequent hunter, so I will now stop talking about his delightful bride).

The game! I almost forgot.

Sold out Vaught-Hemingway Stadium crackled with a palpable buzz for this highly anticipated, primetime matchup between the better-than-usual home team and #9 Texas A&M. Quarterback and defending Heisman Trophy winner Johnny Manziel led the Aggies, and his daring style of play and cocky persona brought an extra level of excitement. (At this point in time, no one at The Grove had learned that Johnny Football liked to drink more than anyone at The Grove.) This would mark my seventh time seeing a player who had won or would later win college sports' most prestigious award. Unfortunately, I wasn't old enough to have seen a Notre Dame player who'd won it. Instead, in addition to the aforementioned Desmond Howard, I'd seen one Nebraska Cornhusker (Eric Crouch – 2001), three USC Trojans (Carson Palmer – 2002, Matt Leinart – 2004, and

Reggie Bush – 2005) and one Ohio State Buckeye (Troy Smith – 2006) punch their Heisman tickets with epic performances against ND. Not that I was still bitter, or anything.

At Ole Miss, our tickets turned out to be incredible: twenty rows up at the 45-yard line on the A&M side. Carl and I were caught off guard when, just before kickoff, all the fans instinctively turned toward the Jumbotron, eagerly awaiting *something*. Karen explained that, in a recent tradition, Ole Miss had a "mystery" celebrity tape the "ARE YOU READY?" and then the video gets played, firing up the crowd. Our secret celeb turned out to be comedian Steve Harvey. Sure enough, in response to the question 70,000 people screamed "HELL YEAAHHHH!" like it could get them into heaven.

Our primo seats gave me a unique insight into Manziel's interactions with his teammates, which did not occur. Seriously. The QB accepted high fives whenever he came off the field, but spoke to only one of his peers, All-American wide receiver Mike Evans. Instead, Johnny sat on the end of the bench by himself. Odd, I thought. He definitely wasn't one of the guys.

In an entertaining game, the Heisman winner struggled early before living up to his heroic reputation. He overcame a first half leg injury and two turnovers to lead the Aggies on a long game-tying touchdown with three minutes to go in the 4th quarter. But, that meant Ole Miss still had a chance to win! Carl and I noticed the home fans torn between praying for the offense to score and praying that they just wouldn't give the ball back to Johnny Football with any time left in regulation. Unfortunately, the Rebels offense could not deliver on either prayer. Manziel got the last chance and made it count, putting his squad into position for a game-winning field goal with three seconds left.

The fans around us knew it was over. They were right.

You know what else was over? The night. Bars in Oxford had last call at midnight. You read that correctly. 12:00 a.m., no more alcohol. The game kicked off at 7:30 and ended close to 11:00. By the time Carl and I would have walked downtown, entered a bar and ordered drinks, we would've been ordered by the bouncers to slam them. Instead, we hustled to our car and beat traffic. (See: earlier, proof-that-I'm-old statement.)

Still, the experience at The Grove lived up to the hype as college football's best tailgating experience. More importantly, my social science experiment confirmed that Ole Miss does boast the prettiest girls in America.

Bubba and the gang at the Millard Society tailgater invited me back. That merely spared us all the awkwardness of my inviting myself.

Hotty Toddy!

DAY THIRTY-NINE

Sunday, October 13th. Memphis, Tennessee.

Today gutted me. There may be no recovering from this.

No, I didn't lose my wallet, or miss my event (coed, adult soccer league), or get in a car accident. It was much, much worse.

After the Ole Miss game, Carl and I drove the eighty miles back to Memphis, where we stayed at the home of friends from the Army, Suzy and Chris, and their sons.

A few days overdue for a haircut, I got my clippers out of the Saab's trunk. Inside the guest bathroom, I inserted the #2 guard, just like I always did. But, as the blades hummed, I paused. Turning my head and looking at my reflection several times, I wondered, Should I take it down further? *Yikes! A #1 guard?! No way.*

Most bald guys struggle with being bald. Sure, Michael Jordan probably doesn't, because he so freaking *unfairly* has a perfectly shaped and ding-free dome. But the rest of us mortals are not so lucky, especially pale white guys like me. In addition to increasing one's risk for melanomas, ghostly skin accentuates bumps and blemishes. That fact didn't help my skull, which had more dents than my Saab.

So, dropping down to a #1 guard represented a terrifying new frontier for me. I simply was not ready for all that, and started cutting again with my standard #2. Then, in a surprising reversal, I stopped. *Screw it.* I'd take it down as far as I could without shaving it with a razor. (*That* was too much for me to even consider.) I inserted the #1 guard.

Post-shower, I kept running my hand over my scalp. In the mirror, my appearance looked noticeably different. I wondered how

Carl and our hosts would react. I braced myself for Uncle Fester jokes.

As I nervously navigated the stairs to the first floor, the aroma from a scrumptious breakfast greeted me, courtesy of Suzy's considerable culinary skills. When I entered the kitchen, she smiled broadly. *Whew. She likes the new haircut.* But, no, that apparently was not it. Suzy was simply happy to be in her element: cooking for a houseful of people. Hmmmm.

I entered the rec room to find Carl (cool, spiky hair) – "Hey, dude" – and Chris (closely cropped, but thick hair) – "Hey, man" – watching an NFL pre-game show. The two boys Camden and Colton, entranced by the video game they were playing, didn't even notice my arrival. *No big deal; guys don't always notice stuff like haircuts, anyway.* I reminded myself to simply remain patient.

That attitude lasted until breakfast was done. Then, sounding exactly like an irritated wife on a 70s sitcom, I asked, "So, does anybody notice anything *different*?"

Five pairs of eyes looked up at me. Five sets of eyebrows furrowed. A few heads tilted to their sides.

Nope. To them, bald was bald.

I didn't get drunk yesterday. But I got drunk today.

DAY FORTY

Monday, October 14th. Nashville, Tennessee.

For me, fate doesn't exist and things don't happen for a reason. I view those as crutches people lean on when results don't go their way. Occasionally, though, certain occurrences weaken the rhetorical cement in which I stand.

Today Carl and I were driving three and a half hours from Memphis to Nashville. And it was Columbus Day.

I'm not Italian or Native American so I never really cared about this holiday, aside from the fact that it provided a day off from school and, later, the Army. (As Owen Wilson objected in *You, Me & Dupree*, upon learning that the company with which he was interviewing did not take a day off in honor of Columbus's birthday, "He discovered *America!*" Am I the first person to ever quote that movie in a book? I'm thinking yes.)

But now that I was on Sports Year, I suddenly hated both Signore Columbus and the resulting annual celebration: no scholastic or youth league games were being played in Music City and none of the area's colleges had athletic contests, either.

Thankfully, though, as I sped east on I-40, my copilot Carl utilized his iPhone to find a coed softball league in action. The first game didn't start until 6:30 PM, which would still allow for plenty of time afterwards to catch a singer/songwriter or two at a bar on Broadway while downing too many locally brewed beers. I hadn't partied in "Nash-Vegas" for fifteen years, but people tell me I enjoyed myself thoroughly on that instance. Carl and I anticipated an epic night, despite it being a Monday.

Our rosy outlook got even better when we arrived in town earlier than expected, providing Carl time to address a work SNAFU and me time for a workout at the hotel prior to the game. But then things went sideways. *Stay off the internet, Jamie!* We didn't get out the door *until* 6:30, and we had not yet eaten dinner. At 7:20 we finally arrived at McGavock High School.

Driving on the school's street, I stared one hundred yards ahead at the two well-lit ball fields atop a plateau overlooking the parking lot. Softball games were being played on both diamonds. Having spotted a parking lot to the immediate right, I began my turn – all the while stupidly still checking out the action. "DUDE!" Carl howled. I slammed on the brakes, stopping just inches from the thick chain stretched across that entrance. *Whew*.

With my pulse at a Sports Year high, I managed to park the car without further incident. The schlep up the grassy hill transported me back to 1979-80; my mom hated a similar walk at an elementary school in Pomona, New York, where I played a lot of my Little League games. Apparently, lugging all the crap required for my brother and sister, both under two years old at the time, was not an enjoyable, twice-weekly experience. But I never minded the hike because it led to ball fields on which I'd had some great performances. (For example, in third grade I struck out three batters in a row on nine pitches. And, yes, it is sad that I still think about that feat.) Huffing up the slope in Nashville, that childhood memory made me smile; suddenly, I had an overwhelmingly positive feeling about whatever game we were about to see.

Carl and I turned toward the diamond on our right, but then a huge cheer arose from the other field, arresting our attention. Male and female players wearing red T-shirts emblazoned with "Torches" on the front rejoiced in the third base dugout like they'd just won the league championship. Their fans – wait, *fans*?! – were on their feet in the three-rows high bleachers, hooting and hollering. But their opponents' fielders – some confused, some annoyed – remained at their positions, meaning the game wasn't over. Maybe somebody hit an unlikely home run? I looked for a batter trotting slowly around the bags, but saw no runner.

I did spot a woman standing on first base. *That's* what had sparked such exultation: a batter had managed to not make an out. Such enthusiasm made my choice an easy one – I did a 180 and hustled toward them. Carl eagerly pulled out the video camera, predicting, "This is gonna be good."

But two minutes later, the red team lined up in the middle of the infield for the postgame handshake. Game over. Shit balls! Carl put away the video camera.

Knowing there'd be another game on that field, I plopped down in the red team's bleachers, berating myself for the Facebook folly that had caused me to miss watching this fun bunch play ball. That's when I noticed that the red team's spouses and significant others were still seated in the bleachers, rather than racing to the parking lot like normal people would've done, happy to be through with their obligatory spectating of crappy softball.

I asked one of the women why they were still hanging around. Krista, a jovial blonde who should be on the payroll of Nashville's board of tourism, wore a red T-shirt just like the players on the field. This blew me away. She told me that The Torches had just completed Game One of a doubleheader. *Hallelujah*! My cameraman/copilot would definitely get some good footage of me interacting with this happy group. "The next game is our last one of the season," she said. I quickly explained what I was doing with Sports Year. She and her husband Jesse loved the idea. Sincerely intrigued, they asked a lot of questions about where I'd been so far and what I'd seen. Their natural warmth and curiosity were endearing.

I asked for the team's backstory. Krista explained that the players and many of the fans worked for Gideon International. As she said those last two words, she cocked her head as if assessing my reaction. I probably wouldn't have thought twice about it, but her look caused me to reassess. *Gideon International.* I blinked a few times.

"You mean, like… the Bibles-in-the-hotel-nightstands? You're *that* company?!"

Krista nodded with a big smile. She told me that this was The Torches' inaugural season in any softball league ever, and they'd yet to win a game. Bingo; I now understood the celebration over the woman reaching first base. "But we got a lot better!" several other fans chimed in simultaneously. After getting clobbered 28-1 in their first game, the Torches only lost their last few by six runs or less. For 99% of the rec league teams I've encountered in my life, that statistic would neither have been seen as a positive nor shared with strangers. For Torch fans, though, it prompted proud grins all around. Carl and I exchanged a quick look. *What are these people on?*

On cue, Krista reached into her large purse and rummaged around. Finally, she pulled out two pocket-sized Bibles, one robin's egg blue and one tan. As Carl and I stared dumbfounded, she handed one to each of us. Somehow, this did not creep me out.

"We're the Torches… like from the Book of Judges," she said casually, as if two dudes from out of town would know that. We shrugged, like, Duh. (In case you're wondering: Judges 7:19-20, in which Gideon and his one-hundred men grasped torches in their left hands and trumpets in their right. Of course, when I learned that through Google later, I began singing, "Clowns to the left of me, jokers to the right…") Our impromptu Bible study was interrupted when, without warning, raucous cheering erupted at home plate. "We won! We finally won a game!"

Turned out that although The Torches' would-be extinguishers had more than nine players, they didn't have the league-mandated minimum of three females – a common problem in coed sports leagues. As the result, they had to forfeit the game. Hence, the glee; it was the Good Guys' first win of the year in their last chance to do so.

In an impressive show of sportsmanship, the fully stocked Torches offered to lend two of their gals to the other squad so that the teams could play a friendly scrimmage. Unfortunately, the Torch captain decided to loan Leslie. "One of our best players," Jesse grumbled, shaking his head like any second-guessing fan would. His wife felt secure about the decision, though, and reminded him, "Gideon won the battle with what he had." Others in the stands nodded in agreement. Not me, though.

"I dunno, does 'What Would Jesus Do?' transfer to the softball field?" That earned a surprisingly big laugh.

As the scrimmage got going, I tried to figure out what to do with my Bible. We hadn't brought a bag to the game. Carl was having the same issue. We cracked up; Bibles simply weren't something we'd planned for. Since they were pocket-sized, we each shoved one into our back pocket. This threw off our natural sitting balance. Carl pointed out, "It's like Costanza's wallet!"

Thankfully, the scrimmage gave me the chance to speak more with Krista, her fellow employees, and the spouses and significant others. These people oozed such happiness that I couldn't help assuming this was a cult. I mean, who the hell *wanted* to watch somebody else's softball game, especially when the quality of play was so poor?

The Gideons did. Get this: they genuinely liked their colleagues and wanted to spend time with them outside of work. Obviously, it helped that they all had dedicated their lives to spreading the word of the Lord. But, still. I felt bad that I had questioned their narcotic and cult statuses. (And that I typed "hell" in the previous paragraph.)

Two innings into the game, Carl dropped an F-bomb. I immediately cringed and elbowed him. Sheepish, he apologized. Krista just laughed. "Oh, like we haven't heard that word before!" Even so, we avoided cursing again for the remainder of the game, a feat I normally achieved only in the presence of my mom and the nuns at the family shelter where I volunteered back in LA.

During the game, Carl shot video as I interacted with the Gideon fans. Adria, a confident and assertive brunette, proved especially insightful. When I asked to meet the coach, she told me he wasn't there. When I queried why, she said, "He's actually in Peru on an international Bible scripture blitz." I laughed, "If I had a nickel for every time I've heard that excuse..."

After I requested suggestions for a terrific lunch spot for tomorrow that only locals knew about, Jesse insisted that we try "hot chicken." Unable to keep my ignorance a secret, I asked, "Isn't all chicken cooked?" He patiently explained that "hot chicken" is a regional version of fried chicken that's called "hot" due to the large amount of cayenne pepper used. He recommended we try Prince's. (Unfortunately, Carl's stupid work issues prevented this from happening. I have not forgiven him, despite the fact that The Torches would have.)

Back on the diamond, "we" lost 6-0, but still claimed the win in the record book due to the forfeit. Judging by the joyous reaction on the field and in the bleachers, a passerby would not have suspected a win by forfeit. The Torches captured the moment with a team victory photo behind their dugout. Carl suggested I jump in. I thought that was pushing our luck, but the team waved me over.

In fact, Rodney, the senior executive present, giddily rubbed my scalp between photos. I asked him, "Does that count for church?" No, their heads shakes told me, that did not. I mentioned being a "CEO" Catholic – Christmas, Easter, Occasion – and braced myself for the inevitable recruiting pitch for Christianity. But it didn't come. The Torches had more pressing matters at hand, like determining the location for the postgame par-tay. Krista even invited us to join them.

Carl and I could not nod our acceptances fast enough. My mind filled with wonder: at what famous Nashville joint do the *Gideons* celebrate their first ever softball victory??? That would be a little honky tonk called... Baskin-Robbins.

We followed behind a caravan of cars. At first, I was concerned that we hadn't gotten any of the Gideons' cell phone numbers; what if we got stuck at a red light and lost them? Fortunately, the Christian-themed bumper stickers made that impossible. The ice cream shop stood alone next to a strip mall and featured a patio out front with concrete tables and benches. Inside, I ordered a double scoop of chocolate chip in a sugar cone. As I pulled out my wallet, Jesse lightly put his hand on my forearm. "This is on us." I protested, but the others drowned me out with their own insistences. Well aware that I'd stumbled onto an amazing anecdote I'd be telling for decades to come, I knew I should have been paying for all of *their* ice creams. Yet, shamelessly, I accepted their generosity. They even treated Carl, too.

On the patio, the majority of the Gideons quizzed me about Sports Year, while Carl spoke off to the side with a few women. Suddenly, one of those gals burst into my circle with a stunned look on her face. She thrust her iPhone forward, the screen filled with an image of Jake Gyllenhaal. This stunned and delighted the rest of her colleagues. "You're famous!" one exclaimed. I disagreed, pointing out that if they hadn't heard of me before then I obviously wasn't famous. As movie questions began to fly at me, I glanced quickly at my copilot, well aware he'd bragged about me once again.

Ever since *Love and Other Drugs* premiered in November of 2010, Carl had been one of my biggest cheerleaders, always proudly talking up my success. This was not completely altruistic on his part, though. At bars, it had served him well as a conversation starter with women. "Do you like Jake Gyllenhaal?" *Yes.* He'd point at me. "See my buddy right there? Jake played him in a movie." *Nuh-uh!* This was never said in an, "OMG, that's so cool!" kind of way, but in a, "There's no chance *that* guy served as the basis for Jake Gyllenhaal" kind of way. That response always gave Carl plenty of opportunity to chat up the doubting young lady as she Googled me. He had reaped incredible rewards. But had I ever benefitted similarly? Not so much.

Standing outside the Baskin-Robbins in Nashville, I asked the ladies my standard question, "I look just like Jake, right?" They all laughed a little too hard for my liking – the universal reaction.

Later, Rodney, Jesse and I stood off to the side, talking about our respective colleges. The exec asked, "Four years at Notre Dame, yet you don't attend church, huh?" *Here we go.* I am a firm believer in the "no religion or politics talk" rule. Opinions don't get changed, but feelings do get hurt. Yet, in this instance, I decided to push it. "And don't forget the four years I spent in Catholic high school! I'm a huge disappointment to my parents and teachers." The two men chuckled, which was not the feedback I'd expected.

Rodney asked why I didn't attend weekly services. I told him the truth. "Sure, I've got a number of issues with the Catholic church, like the Pope's alleged infallibility and the lack of female priests, not to mention the sex abuse scandal. But that's a convenient excuse for me. Really, I just don't pay attention when I go. I think about what happened in my life last week and what's gonna happen next week… so, what's the point in going if I'm not praying and thinking about God?" Neither man commented for a moment.

Finally, Rodney said, "God doesn't care if you go to church." As he paused, you could've pushed me over with one of those paper wrappers the ice cream guy puts on a cone. "He just wants you to think about Him during a quiet time in your mind." I considered calling my parents right then and there. *Mom, I'm putting you on the phone with this wise man named Rodney. I am seriously considering converting to whatever Christian group he belongs to.*

I kept waiting for the Gideons' impassioned appeals urging me to accept the Lord Jesus Christ as my savior. Once again, they never came. In fact, at one point Rodney joked, "Jamie, you're probably wondering how you got caught up with these crazy Christians!" He was right. Only, to my complete surprise, they didn't seem that crazy.

Out of nowhere, I remembered that today marked Day Forty of my trip. Forty is obviously a number with great significance in the Bible. Initially, I decided to keep that information myself, so as to not prolong the religious discussion. For some reason, though, I shared it with the potentially Crazy Christians. Armed with an easy opening to a conversion conversation, they just nodded. Rodney gently said,

"Maybe the Lord is trying to tell you something." And he left it at that.

Once we had all finished our ice creams, Rodney asked permission from Carl and me to hold a prayer circle for us. I'm fairly certain women have prayed for me to leave their beds the morning after, but no one had ever prayed aloud for me in front of me. Honored and a little embarrassed, we consented.

The Gideons obviously did this often, moving with military synchronization to join hands and bow their heads. Rodney's prayer lasted about a minute, but this was the part that stuck with me: "Lord, please help Jamie and Carl as they look for a new story every day, and keep them safe on their journey." He'd done a better job of summing up my project than I ever had; I *was* on a journey looking for a new story every day. We said our goodbyes, handshakes and hugs all around. I'd made several new friends (with whom I stay in touch on Facebook).

In the car, at first neither Carl nor I could say much more than, "Holy shit!" (Pun unintended.) Eventually, he admitted regret for not stepping back from the prayer circle so he could video The Gideons praying around me. But in talking it through, we agreed that it was better to simply have the memory; not everything in this day and age had to be captured and posted on social media.

We began to recount the things that had to occur to enable our unlikely encounter with the happiest team in Tennessee. First, I had to spend too much time online in our hotel room. Second, before dinner I had to give in when Chris wanted to go in and sit down at Taco Bell rather than my preference of hitting the drive-thru and eating at the field. Third, we had to arrive at the school just moments before one of the female Torches miraculously managed to reach first base, prompting the wild cheering that caught our attention. Fourth, their opponents in the second game of the doubleheader had to be short two women, forcing the forfeit that gave The Torches their first win of the season and led to their celebrating over ice cream. Lastly, they had to invite us to join the party at Baskin-Robbins.

Had we hit an extra red light or if the Taco Bell staff had taken too long with our orders, we would have watched the softball game closest to our parking spot; never even knowing the Gideon Bible team was playing just three hundred feet away. "Maybe things do happen for a reason," I said, hardly believing those words had just fallen from my mouth.

As I gunned it back to the hotel, we continuously shook our heads with dopey grins on our faces. The Saab screeched into the parking lot, an audible expression of my eagerness to hit downtown where we'd down beers, enjoy live music and check out southern belles doing both of the same.

Inside our room, Carl needed to get online so he could check on something for work. "Just ten minutes," he assured me. With time to kill, I made the rookie mistake of plopping down on the couch. Once I got comfy, a wave of exhaustion hit me and soon I began yawning like a hippopotamus. Content, I leaned my head back against the wall.

Some time later, I sensed an angry presence in the room. I opened my eyes to find Carl towering over me. He wore a "going out" shirt with his spiky hair sufficiently gelled. Pointing at my lack of readiness, he barked, "Are you kidding me? Dude, let's go."

I turned the key in my body's ignition, but the battery clicked like I'd left the headlights on all night.

Clapping excitedly, Carl bounced on the balls of his feet. Channeling Vince Vaughn, he yelled "Nashville, baby! Nashville!"

I tried to rally, fully aware that, in addition to attending a different sporting event for forty consecutive days, I had failed to kiss a woman for the same amount of time, let alone had sex. Music City seemed to present an outstanding opportunity to break one or both of those ignominious streaks. But I just couldn't summon the energy. I got halfway to my feet before slumping back into the couch like Apollo Creed at the end of *Rocky II.*

A sinner arrived in Nashville intent on raising hell, spent two hours with The Gideons and then went to bed at 10:30. Sober.

Coincidence?

DAY FORTY-ONE

Tuesday, October 15th. Knoxville, Tennessee.

Today I attended an 8th grade football game at the invitation of Trip Tierney, a college buddy and "Score-Checker-at-A-Funeral" donor ($500) to Sports Year. Watching his son Grant star at running back made me feel more ancient than anything else on this trip so far.

As I observed how skilled some of the players were, I wanted to call my father and complain *yet again* about his refusal to let me play weight football prior to high school. (Back then, we called it "midget football," which, I am told, is no longer acceptable terminology.) Dad based his stance on the dubious claim that he read an article in which Joe Paterno, then in the middle of his infallible period at Penn State, declared, "No boys should play tackle until age 14." Naturally, my old man could not produce a copy of this interview or even remember the name of the publication in which it appeared. Short of writing to Coach Paterno for confirmation, then, it was impossible for me to refute the no-tackle-before-14 rule. And, I realized, even if I *had* sent a letter to Penn State's football office, JoePa likely would have backed my father in a show of paternal unity.

Long story endless, my first attempt to catch a pass while wearing a helmet as a receiver occurred on my first day of freshman football tryouts. The ball hit me right in the facemask and bounced away. The humiliation stayed with me.

Trip's son did not have such problems. Despite being a 7th grader on an 8th grade team, Grant looked like the clichéd man among boys. In fact, his natural athletic abilities provided me the coveted opportunity to ask my friend, "Do you know who his father is?"

In this, the season finale, our team won in a shutout. Afterwards, I got the privilege of eavesdropping on the head coach's final post-game talk. As the boys circled around him and took a knee,

I realized that some things don't change regardless of geography. I'd heard a variation of the impending speech numerous times, yet I still got pumped up. The coach thanked them for their hard work and dedication, expressing his eternal pride in the squad. He gave the three assistants the opportunity to say a few words, and each coach emphasized his pride and appreciation for the team's effort. The head coach took center stage again, reminding the players who'd be moving on to high school next season that they could always come back to see him, that he'd always be there to help. Finally, he brought the team in to "break it down one last time." I had to fight the urge to join the boys as they squeezed close together, hands raised and touching in the center, and executed their team clap/cheer with gusto.

On the ride home, I sat in back with Grant, who still wore his sweaty T-shirt and football pants. I'd forgotten how "ripe" football pads get during a game. *Barf.* I made a mental note to apologize to Loretta Reidy for all the stenches she endured in her career as a sports mom.

Grant's parents and I seemed way more excited about the game's outcome than he was. The man of the hour did, however, flash some enthusiasm when we stopped at the drive-thru of Cook Out, a regional chain near the University of Tennessee's campus, for burgers and cheese fries.

Several hours later, the look on Trip's face still said, "I'm so happy he's my son!" I felt lucky to have witnessed excellence, let alone have it be my friend's kid. I looked forward to following Grant's exploits over the next four seasons.

DAY FORTY-FIVE

Saturday, October 19th. Notre Dame, Indiana.

In every odd numbered year, USC plays at ND in the middle of October. Heated rivalry + Indian Summer = great time. Adding to the fun today, a wounded veteran was going to join me for the action.

After last month's Wounded Warrior Amputee Softball Team's game, I mingled on the field with some of the players and fans. There I met Brett, a former soldier from Cincinnati, who lost both his legs in Iraq. He had driven four hours to see complete strangers play softball, simply because they shared a bond with him. He had been seeking both inspiration and commiseration. I asked Brett if he had attended the previous day's debacle against Oklahoma. Nope, he'd only come up on Sunday, specifically for the Wounded Warriors. He'd never seen Notre Dame play football in person.

That was all I needed to hear. I invited him to the USC game and offered him a place to stay here in town. Brett happily accepted, leaving me both psyched – to bring a wounded veteran I'd already met and liked – and relieved – to have already identified someone a month out from the game. Finding suitable guests had become my biggest challenge of Sports Year.

My friends Mary and Wes, already $500 donors to the cause, had generously bought me a pair of tickets, too. I knew they'd be proud to host a man who had sacrificed so much for our country. Brett repeatedly told me, "This is so great! This is so great!!" We shook hands before I gave him my card and told him to follow up with me.

Why didn't I take *his* number? I have no idea. But my failure to do so still gnaws at me. What, was I some big shot producer who said, "Have your people call my people" or something? After three weeks passed with no word from Brett, I started to get anxious, so I tried to find him. My Googling and searching social media turned up nothing.

I caught a break when a friend got me in touch with the amputee softball team's coach; I held out hope that one of his players had struck up a friendship with Brett after the game and exchanged contact info. Unfortunately, nobody on the team knew him.

Right up until kickoff, I thought Brett might call at the last minute. He did not. I hoped he was okay.

The Trojans versus the Fighting Irish is the best non-conference rivalry in America. In a reflection of that lofty status, this would be only the third night game in Notre Dame Stadium history. The crowd pulsed with anticipation. Well, most did.

There may have been people inside Notre Dame Stadium who wanted to be there less than Mary did, but they likely numbered fewer than USC's Heisman Trophy winners. No, Mary was not an Al-Qaeda plant. Rather, she hadn't gone to ND, she knew nothing about football and, despite having lived in South Bend since the Gerry Faust Era, she didn't care about the Irish. This actually marked her first time attending a game! Mary had, however, enjoyed dozens of tailgate parties over the years.

Alas, the weather did not meet Indian Summer traditions. For the past six weeks, every time I popped the trunk my ski jacket mocked me. *Why the hell did I bring you?* For days like this; hello, 40-degrees. Yes, Snow Miser was not far off. With the wind making it seem much colder, fans needed some excitement on the field to stay warm. Unfortunately, the football players did not deliver. The schools combined for zero – 0! – second half points, but the Irish held on for the 14-10 win.

Mary, despite bringing us good luck, assured me she wouldn't be back to a game.

Jamie Reidy

DAY FIFTY-TWO

Saturday, October 26th. Montvale, New Jersey.

This was a momentous day for Sports Year: my – gasp! – 25th high school reunion. More than 5000 people were expected to be in attendance.

But, not all of them for my reunion.

The St. Joe's Regional Green Knights, ranked #3 in the nation, were hosting the Paramus Catholic Paladins, the team that *had been ranked* #3 in the nation one week ago. Nobody predicted that before the season started. (How times have changed; when I was a freshman, the two varsity squads were 0-8, facing off on Thanksgiving Day for the right to not finish the season winless.) This P.C. High squad featured the top recruit in the country: Jabrill Peppers, who would turn into a 2016 Heisman Trophy finalist at Michigan.

Today's game was being broadcast on MSG Network, but another network was there to cover me! My friend John Klekamp, then a news anchor at NJ-12, had heard about my journey from his partner Mike Huckman. (In 2005, as the CNBC producer who covered the pharmaceutical industry, Mike had actually orchestrated my live television debut after my book came out. We stayed friends despite his being a USC grad.) John put me in touch with the NJ-12 sports anchor Nick Meidanis, who arrived at my high school with a cameraman in tow. My high school buddies choked on their tailgate beers in disbelief that I merited a news story, making the whole thing that much sweeter.

Nick needed a quieter place to conduct the interview than the crowded parking lot where my friends were telling the same lies they'd been telling for nearly thirty years and the opposing team's band was tuning up its instruments. I suggested the gymnasium, the place where all the school records in track and field are memorialized.

154

Once inside, in a new personal low of shamelessness, I pointed to a placard featuring my name as part of the three-man 400-meter intermediate hurdle relay team that won the 1988 Bergen County championship, obliterating the previous school record by three seconds. (In my – weak – defense, I *did* emphasize that I had been the caboose of the team, far slower than Craig Collins and Alex Callahan.) The cameraman man videoed me staring at my own name on the wall, and that scene made it into the NJ-12 sports "Friday Night Feature" the following week. Big thanks to Nick Meidanis for the support! (The next day, my father busted my balls big time about the school record thing.)

Today was perfect for football: bright sunshine, autumn leaves, a crisp feel to the air. A huge sign greeted enemy fans, letting them know they had entered the presence of champions. In my senior year, my teammates and I captured the first state title in school history. We had no idea we had started a dynasty.

As my teammates and I watched the boys on the field today, we determined that only three, *maybe* four of our starters could be first-string for this squad. I was not even considered in the conversation, FYI. Nowadays, I'd be running cross-country if I wanted to participate in a fall sport. That's a team that doesn't have cuts.

How was it possible that I had grown old enough to see my defensive end bring *his* kids, one of whom wore his father's jersey from our *freshman* year?

Rob Healy and his son Owen.

And how had I lived so long that a nickname of shame had morphed into one of endearment? In the fall of 1985, my sophomore team hosted Don Bosco Prep, one of our two big rivals. I was an undersized cornerback who had yet to grow into his size 11 feet. My starting role in the secondary had more to do with the previous first-stringer's truancy from practice than it did my "skill set."

Late in the second quarter, the Ironmen had the ball facing third down and thirty yards to go from their own six-yard line. 3rd and 30. As we waited in the huddle for the defensive call, I was thinking, *OK, coach, just drop eight guys back in a zone, force the QB to throw it short and let's get out of here with a punt and good field position.*

Our defensive coordinator called for an all-out blitz, which left me on an island in man-to-man coverage on an unusually muscular wide receiver. Behind center, the quarterback saw this matchup and promptly audibled. *That's weird*, I thought. After the snap, he threw a quick slant to my man, who I'd soon learn was named Derek Horner. I was right on his hip when he caught the ball, but as I reached to tackle him – Meep! Meep! I can still see the cloud of dust Horner kicked up on our barren field as he blazed ninety yards to pay dirt. I can also still hear my secondary coach's furious, "REE-DEE!" I was not allowed to play football in the second half. (Two years later, Derek Horner would win the 100-meter dash at the New Jersey state championships.)

At our first practice following the home loss, our first team Offense and first team Defense lined up to scrimmage. I didn't know if I was supposed to be out there; did I get benched just for the second half or did I get *benched* benched? The kid who had replaced me didn't know, either. It took the coaching staff a minute to figure out there were only ten players on defense. Finally, Barry Clark, the coach who had howled my name in anguish, noticed. He asked, loud enough for everybody to hear, "Who's starting at the other corner?" He paused for devastating effect. "Toast?"

In 1985, the New York Giants had a cornerback named Elvis Patterson, who, during practices, had an unfortunate habit of getting beat deep for touchdowns by wide receivers. Bill Parcells, in his first head coaching role en route to the Pro Football Hall of Fame, sarcastically dubbed Patterson "Toast," because he got burned all the time. Seemingly everybody in northern New Jersey knew the story.

So, when Coach Clark tossed "Toast" out there, every muscle in my body tensed. *Maybe the other guys didn't hear?* As. Freaking. If.

My teammates erupted, falling all over each other in hysterics. Even the coaches cracked up. Intuitively, I sensed Toast wouldn't be one of those nicknames that fell to the wayside. Nope, it would stick.

For the remaining 2 and ¾ years of high school, guys used it whenever discussing our secondary's biggest liability: me. I don't know if the cheerleaders totally grasped the term's meaning, but they understood they didn't want to be dating a guy called Toast.

After today's blowout victory – Go, Green Knights! – my 25th reunion teammates and I walked onto the field. (The sparse grass and dirt we once scuffled on had been replaced by a state-of-the-art Field Turf.) Incredibly, several of our former coaches were still coaching, including Barry Clark. I approached him, ready to introduce myself, since I hadn't seen him since thirty pounds and a head of hair ago.

"Toast!" *Oh, c'mon!* I felt my face flush. "Toast!"

He was beaming at me, like I'd caught the game-winning pass in our state championship game. I extended my hand, but he pulled me in for a bear hug. "Jamie, it's so great to see you! Mr. *Author!*" I could not believe that he even knew about the book.

Coach Clark turned around and actively looked for my former head coach. "Tony! Get over here! Did you see Toast?!"

Suddenly, 28 years of embarrassment washed off me. What had started out as a dis had melted into a term of endearment. *Toast? That's me!* Damn right.

I wouldn't have predicted that at graduation.

Coach Barry Clark and the author.

DAY FIFTY-THREE

Sunday, October 27th. Westwood, New Jersey.

Much fun was had last night at my reunion. And a directly proportional hangover was in effect today. I wasn't suicidal, but I would've gladly swapped bodies with a dead person.

I had purposely not scheduled a sporting event for this morning, as I knew I might not be feeling so chipper. There was an all day equestrian competition in Bergen County, New Jersey, which would've been a first for me. But Rob Downes, a former wrestling teammate, had mentioned at reunion that his daughter had a soccer game at 2:30; a perfect start time for a guy who slept until 1:00.

I still showed up late, with the score 2-0 good girls, a.k.a. the Dragons.

Initially, I felt bad that I skipped the horse show. That would have been really cool to see. But, I got another Sports Year first: witnessing Rob's dog pee on Rob's mother-in-law's purse. How many sons-in-law would like to train their dog to do that?!

This soccer game was played on the field furthest from the parking lot. Teetering on the edge of dry heaving, I needed the hundred-yard walk like I needed a hole in my ball sac. After Rob introduced me to the other soccer dads, he handed me a red Solo cup. Happy for the hydration, I took a big gulp. And nearly puked the Bud Light back up.

Trying to keep it together, I gasped, "You guys *drink* at your kids' games?!" Six fathers raised their cups in response. Rob just snickered at me.

After climbing into my car, the wave of nausea hit. Luckily, I got the door open in time. *Ralph!* Sigh. Another Sports Year first.

Jamie Reidy

DAY FIFTY-FOUR

Monday, October 30th. Chestnut Ridge, New York.

Aside from occasional self-loathing sessions during my two Motel 6 stays, I hadn't spend much time thinking about how majorly I'd f'ed up my Kickstarter campaign. Today, however, that thought was on constant repeat on my internal iPod.

Since Kickstarter makes no money when a campaign fails to reach its crowdfunding goal, they go to great lengths to ensure each project's success. Based on real life lessons learned from other campaigns, the website offers incredibly specific instructions and helpful hints. Basically, it's like the professor who stands at the front of the class and stomps her foot on the ground a few times, saying, "You might see this on the test."

They even go so far as to coach you on the "rewards" you promise people for donating at various levels. Those rewards don't get triggered until *after* goal completion, so it shouldn't concern the Kickstarter folks; yet, they still want to make sure you maximize the funds you raised. (Even though I ended up using Indiegogo, I kept the same rewards.) To this end, they make it abundantly clear that you should check – and double check – the costs you'll bear when rewarding donors. "You don't want to find out the hard way that you're spending too much…" Naturally, I completely ignored that advice. Today, I literally paid the price.

Everyone who donated $10 or more got a Sports Year beer koozie, to be shipped no later than October 31st. I remembered that fact on October 24th, while captivated by NBC's dream Sunday Night Football matchup of Peyton Manning versus Andrew Luck. The jilted veteran faced off against his replacement in his return to the very arena he had made possible. Suddenly, during the third quarter, the image of a beer koozie flashed into my brain, which was strange since

160

I wasn't drinking. Regardless, I broke into a sweat and began feverishly searching online for companies that make koozies.

Before I'd set out on Sports Year, I thought it'd be cool to create a visual that explained the project quickly and simply. I envisioned a map of the United States with my circuitous route highlighted, featuring all of my planned stops. Budget constraints prevented me from hiring an illustrator or graphic designer to produce it. So, although I had never demonstrated any artistic ability whatsoever, I decided to try and draw it free hand. I went to Office Depot and bought a white board, brought it home and set it atop my coffee table. I figured I'd give it one shot, laugh at my spastic effort and then give the used white board to my friend Matt, a Sports Year's donor, the father of my goddaughter Tegan and a guy who happened to have told me the day before that he needed a whiteboard for his office. Staring at the enlarged map of the US on my Mac Book screen, I began drawing. On my first try, this is what I produced (minus the route, obviously):

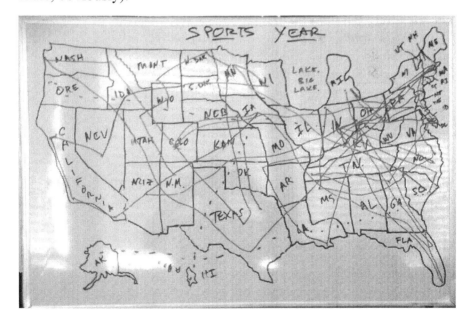

Sitting in my hotel room in western PA and watching the Colts upset the Broncos, I decided to place that image on the white, foam beer koozie every donor would be getting. I ordered 100, figuring I'd give the extras to people I met along the way. Maybe, if they became a hit, I'd even be able to sell them online and make a little scratch?

I paid $210 for the koozies plus $30 for express delivery to my parents' house. (With a little forethought, I could've saved by using normal delivery.) Since I had not followed the Kickstarter instructions re: budgeting in advance for rewards, this $2.30 per koozie didn't faze me. I figured, even with just a $10 donation, I'd be clearing nearly eight bucks. The clerk at the post office? She fazed me.

"It's too fat." *Excuse me?* "Your envelope, it's too fat. You're going to have to pay a handling fee because it won't fit through the normal mail feeder." My internal record player scratched.

When I had successfully squeezed the koozies into regular letter-sized envelopes, I was psyched. Since the koozies were so light, I figured each one would only require one stamp. But this close-to-retirement woman, straight out of central casting with her New Yawk accent and static-y hair poking every which way, explained that postage for a bulky item would cost $2.40. So, adding together the koozie cost and the postage, each $10 donation came out to only $5.30. A two-hundred dollar difference may not seem like much, but it was to me.

Standing in the post office line, feeling and hearing the frustrations of the customers stuck behind the idiot with the thick envelopes, I suddenly remembered the Kickstarter suggestions. And then I remembered how my friends had told me I was a moron for even attempting this journey. And, you know what?

I was starting to agree with them.

DAY FIFTY-FIVE

Tuesday, October 29ᵗʰ. Atlanta, Georgia.

One of Sports Year's main themes was helping others, so I was excited to add my brother to the list of beneficiaries. Thanks to this crazy project, Pat discovered a skill he did not know he possessed: searching online to find athletic events for his older sibling to attend. This was a tedious chore, but he exceled at it. (Not sure where he will list that talent on a resume, though.)

Given his track record so far, I was surprised when Pat called with bad news midway through my drive from North Carolina to his house in Decatur, Georgia. Despite his best efforts to find me a female event in the ATL, he'd failed to lock down a "guaranteed" one. The best he could do was an Emory University club volleyball league match that was listed on one team's site, yet not listed on the opponent's site. *Is it 'game on' or what?* Hmmmm. I couldn't risk getting to the campus and learning I'd been shut out. Today I really needed an event involving women because my male/female ratio had dropped well below my goal of 45%.

Feeling anxious about my chances, I reached into my past for a long shot. From 2000-2008, I played in a coed flag football league in Redondo Beach. Of the many rules, the most important one stipulated that every third play had to be thrown by or thrown to a woman. Every good team had at least one former D-1 male athlete who basically cancelled each other out. So, victory often came down to whether your girls were better than their girls. The games were fiercely competitive, but pretty much everybody headed to a dive bar afterwards for drinks and greasy food. I enjoyed the league so much that I scheduled my work trips to ensure I'd be home on Wednesday nights. (My mom once commented, "No wonder you're single; who wants to date a guy who sets up his life around flag football?") The organization that ran the flag football league also sponsored other coed sports leagues. Light bulb!

While filling up at a gas station, I Googled the national Sport and Social Club, which boasted membership in forty cities, including, thank goodness, Atlanta. Feeling like a total weirdo, I called up and dumped all this on the stranger who answered: "Hi, my name is Jamie. I'm an author who's writing a book about this crazy yearlong sports road trip I'm taking. Currently, I'm on Day 55. Any chance you have a coed sport I can see tonight?"

Surprisingly, a friendly guy named Kevin Cregan, the president and founder of the ASASC, didn't hang up on me. His club boasts 21 different leagues. He quickly mentioned flag football, but, then, sensing an opportunity, blurted out, "What about inner tube water polo?"

What ABOUT inner tube water polo???

Gloriously, inner tube water polo was exactly what the name implied. Five-on-five, coed teams who share the same color tubes. The rules were pretty simple: as long as you stayed in your tube, you could shoot the ball at the goal. The player with the ball could be flipped over by defenders. If you had the ball, you could also flip over other players. *What could be more fun than flipping people over?*

Imagine my surprise when these crazies invited me to play! Initially, I had to decline, since I had no swimsuit. Luckily, though, I recalled my backup suitcase in the Saab's trunk. (Like you don't have a backup suitcase.) Five minutes later, after changing in the locker room, I was splashing around in the pool.

While height is a desired quality in normal water polo, it's not necessary for the inner tube variety. Basically, this sport was just a lot of reverse paddling. And flipping people over. Talk about a fun workout; my back and shoulders were sore for days.

Apparently, inner tube water polo was catching on around the country. That came as no surprise to me. Did I mention that it was coed? And it took place *in a pool*? #SignMeUp

Er, not so fast. After the match, I made the mistake of merely changing clothes in the gym's locker room without first showering off. In the car, I suddenly felt a fierce itching on my hamstrings. Then it spread to my lower back and arm pits. As I raced to my brother's house, I imagined getting pulled over and having a cop ask me what the problem was. "Inner tube water polo, Officer."

Would he have just skipped the Breathalyzer and run me in right then and there? By the time I got to Pat's, I was ready to scratch my skin off with the house key. Thankfully, after a *Silkwood* scrubbing, I was back to normal.

On my note pad I scribbled, "Buy Benadryl," just in case I got asked at a future event to participate in a sport that wasn't really a sport.

Big shout out to Kevin Cregan who showed up to meet me in person and gave me an Atlanta Sport and Social Club T-shirt. My second sponsor!

DAY FIFTY-NINE

Saturday, November 2ⁿᵈ. Jacksonville, Florida.

The World's Largest Outdoor Cocktail Party – the name, alone, got this event into the original Sports Year Top 20 list.

Bitter rivals Florida and Georgia play annually on the first Saturday of November at a "neutral site" in Jacksonville. In normal seasons, this game kicked off in late afternoon or prime time due to CBS's desire to showcase this pair of SEC powerhouses. In 2013, though, matching mediocre 4-3 records relegated this clash to a 12:30 start. For the 84,000 attendees, though, that simply meant they needed to begin drinking earlier.

The fun started before we even got to the tailgating lot at EverBank Field, home of the NFL's Jaguars. Kevin, my former college roommate and current Jax resident, drove us to a cheap parking spot across the Saint Johns River from the stadium. On the way there, we passed a dual cab F-150 sporting Bulldog flags on the driver's side and Gator flags on the passenger side. #TruckDivided After parking, we waited in an hour-long line for a ferry to take us across the river. Nothing like watching a guy shotgun a beer, puke and rally at 9:00 a.m.

Once aboard the boat, we sat next to an entertaining couple in their mid-late 40s. Barney was wearing a brand new blue pullover, but he admitted he'd only been a UF fan for a few hours. I asked him why the sudden enthusiasm. He nodded toward his girlfriend and said, "She threatened to cut me off if I didn't cheer for the Gators." Kevin and I laughed. Holly simply smiled; she really would've denied her man sex for rooting for the hated Dawgs.

Despite the existence of GPS in smart phones, it took us nearly an hour to find our tailgater. This happened because Kevin is a pilot and the guys hosting the tailgate are pilots, and flyboys refuse to "cheat" by utilizing modern technology. Instead, they insist on using terrain markers and the like to guide them. Annoyingly, the light poles in EverBank Field's parking lots did not sport helpful letters and numbers, i.e. no A-6, to tell a person where he is. We laughed at the number of drunk football fans who must wander the expansive lot looking for their cars after Jaguar games. (But then we remembered that nobody actually goes to Jags' games.) One upside of our unexpected walk: sampling the hospitality of several tailgates. Again, Southerners did not disappoint. A friendly group of Gators brought a keg from Gainesville: "Swamp Head" beer.

This event will always have a warm spot in my heart because it is where I first learned about the game "Drop Shot."

It's Beer Pong meets Corn Hole: you toss a beanbag at the target which has a hole in the middle. One drastic twist: players do shots of booze instead of shots of beer when their opponents sink the bean bag.

After Drop Shot, UF's Miss America contestant gave me her card! (I should probably mention that Ms. Hart gave everybody her card. Everybody, that is, except for my friends Mark and Rick!)

Rachel Hart with the author.

UGA and UF are given equal numbers of tickets, so the stands end up split down the middle with an amazingly cool red and black/blue and orange line of demarcation from end zone to end zone.

But don't let anyone tell you that The World's Largest Outdoor Cocktail Party is the best party in college football. Basically, it's the same as every Sunday pre-game in an NFL stadium parking lot. No grass or trees, just acres of blacktop. Good time? Sure. But nowhere near the spirited atmosphere of other big games played on campuses.

That said, this marked the first time I ever met identical *cousins*. Tailgating post-game, I met Wesley and Jason, a pair of Georgia fans, who, based on the fact that their faces were identical, I took to be twin brothers. They gave me matching, "We get that all the time" looks, before explaining that their moms are sisters who gave birth on the same day. I demanded to see photo IDs. One guy pulled out his driver's license and the other showed his... concealed carry permit. Did I mention that they were from Georgia?

Although I did a video interview with Jason and Wesley, my lack of sobriety kept my iPhone's flash off. In the dark. As the result, I have no proof of their uncanny resemblance.

The World's Largest Outdoor Cocktail Party, indeed.

DAY SIXTY-TWO

Tuesday, November 5ᵗʰ. Louisville, Kentucky.

Today began with the long-awaited car problem.

Last night I stayed with my Army buddy Joe, his wife Nahoko and son YJ. Joe was the genius who suggested I save the nascent Sports Year streak by finding a bowling alley back on September 21ˢᵗ. Pulling out of his driveway with a hangover this morning, I was less than excited to see an unfamiliar yellow light appear on my dashboard. A quick check of the owner's manual induced panic in its owner: "Engine Malfunction. Contact Saab dealer."

Psst! There *were no* Saab dealers, anymore. At that moment my decision to take a cross-country journey in a ten-year old car made by a defunct Swedish automaker seemed particularly unwise. Joe suggested that it was probably nothing – "probably just you screwed the gas cap back on wrong." But I just couldn't trust the car.

I used the Google and found a repair shop – Sovereign Automotive – that worked on Swedish cars. *Douche bag, party of one?* It was an hour away in Roswell, GA. Dread quickly turned to relief when the owners Bob and Cathy made me feel right at home. (Small world story: Cathy once lived in Hermosa Beach, CA, one town south from my town, Manhattan Beach!) The mechanic's diagnosis: an improperly screwed in gas cap prompted my car's computer to register the "malfunction" alert. I freaking hate when my friends are right. And I hate it more when I'm stupid.

Due to the potential travel day lost to repairs, I hadn't planned an event, as I wasn't sure if I'd have to stay with Joe another night. Back on the road in thirty minutes without being charged – thanks, Bob and Cathy! – I figured I'd just drive to Nashville, three hours away, and search for a game there. But then I recalled that my friends Tim and John had company basketball games every Tuesday. In

Louisville; three and half hours north of Music City. Boom! I turned right on I-65, rolling to Derby City without first calling the guys to see if they would, in fact, be playing basketball this evening.

Of course, they were not; work and family, blah, blah, blah. Even worse, I didn't get to town in time to just show up and watch any of their league's other games. And every high school and college was event-less, also. Fittingly, considering that I crashed at Joe's house last night, I resorted to Sports Year's tried and true fallback.

Rose Bowl Lane's "Striking Concepts" league featured a lively crew worthy of its clever name. I saw a baby with a bottle of milk and his grandpa with a bottle of Bud. I didn't identify any Buddhists.

How Hettie, a disarming woman with a warm smile, began her pitch for religious conversion, I do not know. One minute we were talking about bowling leagues and how helpful they had been to keeping my streak alive and, the next thing I knew, I was seated at a side table and being told all about the wonders of Buddhism. Hettie whipped out what I thought was a business card, but it was actually a chant: Nam, Myoho, Renge, Kyo!

Hettie: Buddhist and bowler

She promised that daily repetition of the phrase would "Transform your life, gain full potential, world peace, individual happiness." Sensing a conspiracy, I asked if my mom had called her. Hettie cracked up and said, with absolute sincerity, "I don't know your Mom!"

Feeling fortunate to have kept the streak alive, let alone met such welcoming folks, I felt like having a beer. But I worried it was not kosher to drink in front of Buddhists. Hettie's man Tony pointed to his own beer to assure me I'd be okay. I bought him a round.

In addition to receiving life-changing spiritual guidance, I picked up a car tip. Greg, a bourbon drinker who had just won his team the nightly raffle by bowling a clutch strike after his raffle number was picked at random, told me what to do the next time the Saab's check engine light came on. "It might be just a computer glitch. So, the way you find out is you disconnect the positive and negative cables to your battery and keep it like that for fifteen minutes. When you reconnect it, if the light is gone, you're good to go. If it's still there, you need to go to the mechanic." So, readers, keep that trick in mind!

Hettie and I hugged goodbye, and later she friend requested me on Facebook. Hopefully, through my pics and posts she has noticed an increase in my personal potential maximization!

DAY SIXTY-SIX

Saturday, November 9th. Madison, Wisconsin.

Generally, I don't trust people who were born in Los Angeles. Nothing against them, personally – except for, you know, the lack of trust. But introduce me to somebody from Iowa, Minnesota or Wisconsin? I'd be fine giving them my SSN and mother's maiden name.

Understandably, then, I was happy to visit the Cheese State's capital. Even better, I was getting a personal tour from a former local. David LeFevre, the chef whose sister played viola in the chamber music concert in Houston, grew up in Madison. During the Sports Year planning stages, I texted him that I was gonna do the Wisconsin Football Weekend: Badgers on Saturday and the Packers on Sunday. He texted back, "Not without me you're not!" Adding to the fun, his brother in law, David Spath, the guy who gave me the cooler, wanted in, too.

For as much praise as Ole Miss has received as a college football paradise, Madison gets a lot of first places votes, too. In fact, *Sports Illustrated* ranked it the #1 college sports town in America. *Bleacher Report* picked Madison as its Best College Football Town. Additionally, *SI* did a "Greatest College Football Traditions" bracket on its website and the Wisconsin student body's 4th quarter ritual of jumping like lunatics to the House of Pain song "Jump Around" claimed the top spot. Needless to say, I woke up excited to get today started. Just outside of town, we stopped at a convenient store to grab a case of beer.

Seemingly every person in Madison wore red, white and/or black. With my red, black and white ski jacket, I fit right in. Being a white guy helped that feeling; Madison was the most Caucasian place I'd been outside of Utah. That comparison turned out to be appropriate, since the home team's opponent was Brigham Young University.

We ate brats inside the student center, which is located smack in the middle of downtown. Afterwards, I popped into the Peet's Coffee and returned with three empty coffee cups. Both of the Davids raised an eyebrow. Bro-in-law asked me what I was doing. I smiled broadly, happy to share my genius. Stealthily cracking a beer can and pouring the contents into a cup, I explained, "Now, the cops will be none the wiser as we walk to the stadium." The guys erupted in completely mocking laughter. Chef dramatically backed up with his arm extended, as if he was ushering me into enlightenment. Finally, I looked around at the throngs of people in the streets – *every* person had a beer in their hand. Holy shit did I feel like a dunce. "Thanks, Jamie!" the guys pounded me on the shoulders, still laughing.

Being a short walk from home to the game is nice perk; plus, it allows tailgating at home. Housegating?

To get to Camp Randall Stadium we first walked through the Camp Randall Arch, a gray, granite structure reminiscent of West

Point. That observation made sense, since the Arch is a monument dedicated to the soldiers who trained at the Army post before fighting for the Union in the Civil War. I didn't expect to get a brief history lesson today, so that was a neat surprise.

Just outside our stadium entrance we passed a statue for Barry Alvarez, the former Badger head football coach and current athletic director. I had not realized that Mr. Alvarez's sensational career – he singlehandedly turned Wisconsin into a powerhouse – had been immortalized in bronze. This discovery nearly ruined my day.

I was more than familiar with Barry Alvarez, who served as defensive coordinator during Notre Dame's stellar 22-1 run in 1988-89. He left South Bend to take the Wisconsin head coaching position. Seven years later, Lou Holtz retired/got forced out and many fans, myself included, pushed for the university to bring back Barry Alvarez, who had achieved some impressive successes in Madison. Notre Dame brass, however, chose to hire Bob Davie, a man lacking both head-coaching experience and intelligence. The Irish have mostly been mired in mediocrity ever since, whereas Coach Alvarez got a larger-than-fucking-life statue.

Thankfully, the Badgers' rowdy and engaged fan base roused me from my funk. Everything people hyped about the UW football experience - the students, the band, the running game – proved worthy of the praise. During "Jump Around," I hopped up and down like a fool, finding myself deliriously happy. And I also thoroughly enjoyed the "5th Quarter," a twenty minute segment after the game during which the marching band plays fun songs like "The Chicken Dance" and "Tequila."

I'd come back in a something-faster-than-a-heartbeat.

DAY SIXTY-SEVEN

Sunday, November 10th. Green Bay, Wisconsin.

For me, life is all about tempering expectations – others' and my own.

As the Gin Blossoms sing (sang?) in "Hey, Jealousy," their biggest hit, "If you don't expect too much from me, you *might* not be let down." (In case you've never heard of the Gin Blossoms, their first album was one of the my favorite debuts of the 90s. Sadly, they couldn't keep the momentum going.) The weight of expectations threatened to crush today; I didn't want my first trip to Lambeau Field to be a let down.

When I made my Top 10 venues list, Lambeau was a no-brainer occupant of the #1 spot. (Augusta National finished runner up.) Even my *mom* knows that the frozen tundra in Green Bay is hallowed ground. Rolling into town with that level of expectation, then, set me on edge. How could the experience possibly measure up?

On top of all that, I was finally bringing another wounded veteran to a game. It had been six weeks since Aaron accompanied me to LSU's Death Valley. Six weeks?! That was unacceptable. But thank goodness for Iraq and Afghanistan Veterans of America (IAVA.org)! They did what I'd wanted Wounded Warriors Project to do two months beforehand: posted my link to the group's homepage. Within an hour, I got this email from a former Army sergeant:

Jamie,
I was wounded in Iraq in 2006 from an IED. My life long dream is to see the Packers play in Green Bay. I saw what you are doing on Facebook and figured I'd give it a shot.
Thanks for offering the opportunity
Justin

First of all, I couldn't believe somebody contacted me so quickly. Even better, he wanted to attend a game – Green Bay Packers – to which I was already committed. I emailed Justin back, thanked him for being first to respond, and told him he was going to Lambeau.

His response made my chest hurt:

Jamie,
Please tell me that this is not a joke. I have the worst luck in the world and knowing how that is I don't want this to be a scam. Me saying this is not in anyway meant to sound insulting to you I just can't believe that it's legit.
Justin

You can imagine how good it felt to reassure Justin that his luck was changing. In further email correspondence, he asked if he could bring his grandfather. Internally, I balked at that due to my own financial concerns. But then I read Justin's explanation that the older man had to drive him because, due to Justin's PTSD, his family didn't let him operate a motor vehicle. Also, they preferred that he didn't go anywhere by himself. *Uh, yes, your grandfather is more than welcome to join us!* Neither of the Packer fans had ever been to Lambeau. I was thrilled to be able to facilitate their first visit to Mecca.

Sunshine greeted us in the morning, but shortly afterwards the day wobbled like a shanked punt. The Davids had bought the tickets for Justin and his grandpa (J&G) on StubHub, but they hadn't looked at them since the purchase. So, during our hour-long drive to the game, I opened the email file on my iPhone. Surprisingly, I did not see a PDF version of the tickets. Instead, I saw a *photo* of them. Like, the seller had taken a picture of the two actual tickets and simply uploaded that. Uh oh. My stomach dropped.

Typically, I was a wuss when it came to filing complaints or demanding better service; not as bad as Henry Winkler's character

Chuck in *Night Shift*, but not assertive, like Michael Keaton's Billy Blazejowski, either. Yet, dialing the number for StubHub's help desk, I found myself ready to unload on whatever poor sap answered the phone.

Twenty minutes later, I hung up completely disarmed and thoroughly impressed. The rep immediately apologized for the blunder that had escaped StubHub's quality assurance process and then offered to replace the false tickets we purchased with two "better" seats. And by better, he meant, "On the 50-yard line." I quickly accepted that fix! But, in texting with Justin this morning, I kept that new and exciting information to myself.

After a quick trip to Kinko's to print out the PDFs of the tickets, The Davids and I parked in a family's front yard not far from the stadium. As we strolled through the crisp and sunny morning, I could hear John Facenda's legendary voice from *NFL Films* in my head.

We arrived before Justin and Grandpa at the rendezvous point: Kroll's West, a bar across the street from Lambeau Field that provided a vast outdoor drinking area. We had just enough time to pound a Bloody Mary and buy a second round, including beverages for our guests, of course. Justin had texted me a description of what they were wearing, so it was easy to spot two men with beards of similar length, one red and one white. Justin sported a #92 Reggie White home jersey with green Packers gloves. Grandpa rocked a Packers hat, scarf and coat. Seeing them decked out like that, I became even happier about what was about to happen.

(Justin and Derald, both utilizing the limited edition Sports Year beer koozie!)

Turned out that Justin had "inherited" his Packer fandom from Derald – "it's like 'Gerald' but with a 'D'!" Derald explained that he grew up in Iowa, "We didn't have – I'm older than dirt – we didn't have television, but we listened to the Packers on the radio every

Sunday." Justin had never heard that story before, which made me feel pretty good that he gained some insight into his grandpa thanks to Sports Year. As if on cue, Derald launched into his best radio announcer impression, "Live from City Field, it's the Green Bay Packers!" Both Justin and I paused. "Wait. *City* Field? You mean Lambeau Field?" The older gentleman simply gave us a look that suggested we should not doubt him. (Later, I just had to Google it; sure enough, Lambeau Field wasn't built until 1957.)

After another beer, I figured it was time for the big surprise. As Chef filmed with my iPhone, I handed our guests their 50-yard line tickets. "Are you shitting me?!" Justin asked, incredulous.

"Twenty rows up on the Fifty!" Chef chimed in.

"Ho-lee shit!" Justin said. Derald simply kept looking around in disbelief. Both men hugged me, their sincere appreciation for us as obvious as their devotion to the Pack. Then they hugged The Davids. We all could have floated to our seats.

Just like in Madison, on game day in Green Bay it's legal to walk out of a bar with an open beer. My friend Mark explained it with, "It's fucking *Wisconsin*. Of course you can!"

Justin and Derald needed to walk back to their cars to get some stuff, so The Davids and I waited outside our gate for them. As the minutes ticked away, I grew anxious that the Iowans would miss kickoff. Seemingly thousands of fans had squeezed in one last beer at their tailgaters before heading over, so we found ourselves mired in an interminable line.

Finally, our guests arrived with grins nearly as wide as the bulky seat cushions each man carried. Those tripped alarms in my brain. At the Ravens-Broncos game two months earlier, I'd heard numerous complaints from female fans who were denied entrance due to the NFL's new policy limiting the size of bags. (Why this took twelve years after 9/11 to implement, I dunno.) If women couldn't bring a large purse into the stadium, I doubted Justin and Derald's seat cushions would make the cut.

After I gave the guys the bad news, Justin shook his head, certain they'd be fine. I offered a solution, "Seriously, let me go with your grandpa back to your car. We'll still have time to get back before kickoff." Negative. Justin remained convinced.

What were these guys gonna do when the guards made them leave their cushions outside? Unfortunately, we found out soon enough. After the security guy informed J&G that they could not bring in the seat cushions, rage flashed across Justin's face, hotter than phosphorous. I moved to step between him and the guard. And then – whoosh! – it was gone. Justin's shoulders relaxed and he nodded in resignation. Sadly, the men left their new purchases against the outside wall of Lambeau. "A small price to pay for today," Derald said with encouragement.

Inside Lambeau, I was immediately struck by the similarities with Fenway Park; both shrines are tiny compared to their modern day counterparts and the stands are right on top of the fields. Like Red Sox fans, Packer backers were rabid. I expected the mood to be a bit somber, since star quarterback and NFL icon Aaron Rodgers had suffered an injury the week before, and wouldn't be playing today. In his place, backup quarterback Seneca Wallace made his first start for the team. The fans cheered his introduction like he was the MVP. Beers and brats in hand, sunshine on my back, I cheered like a local. I hoped Justin and his grandpa would get to see a victory from their seats on the 50-yard line.

Sadly, the Packers fell to the Eagles in a lackluster game. The rest of us won big time, though. "Thank you" falls woefully short in expressing my eternal gratitude to IAVA for providing the means by which Justin found me, to StubHub for turning disaster into a dream come true for Justin and Derald, and to The Davids, for treating us all to the game.

Lying in bed tonight, I came to an important place mentally. If the accounting office's prediction proved true and Sports Year did run out of funds before the end of November, I'd proudly look back on Sunday November 10th as the pinnacle of what I tried to accomplish: friends and strangers united to help me help wounded veterans cross off items on their sports Bucket Lists. Today made it all worthwhile.

That's the thing about expectations: sometimes you can't set them high enough.

DAY SIXTY-EIGHT

Monday, November 11th. Chicago, Illinois.

Obviously, on Veteran's Day I felt especially compelled to bring a wounded service member to a game. But considering how difficult it had been to find someone, I didn't like my odds of achieving my goal two days in a row.

Thankfully for me – and an Army staff sergeant named Lamar – my friend Marianne didn't get bogged down in paradigms. She found an *active* duty serviceman who'd been injured in Iraq. He proudly rocked his Army sweats to the United Center for the Bulls' home game against the Cavaliers. (In case you're wondering, no LeBron – he didn't rejoin Cleveland until the next season.)

It had never occurred to me to seek out men and women who had remained on active duty following their wartime wounds. I guess I assumed everybody would take the disability payment and exit the service as quickly as possible; I mean, that's what I would've done. Lamar suffered a life-threatening spinal injury during a dangerous convoy run; the truck in which he was riding shotgun crashed into the one in front of it. He broke three of his upper cervical discs and remained paralyzed for seven months. Yet, despite the fact that he could have retired on a 100% medical disability, he *still reenlisted and continued his Army service*. I could not begin to fathom that level of commitment. He simply loved taking care of his soldiers and refused to give that up.

During the game, dozens of red t-shirts dropped from the ceiling. Fittingly, Lamar caught one.

In his current role, Lamar serves as the senior enlisted soldier for an Army Reserve unit in Chicago. His younger troops most certainly benefited from the example he set everyday. Talk about a true patriot.

What a pleasure to catch a game with a current soldier. I would have been honored to meet Lamar on any day, but Veteran's Day provided an even better perspective. Hooah!

DAY SIXTY-NINE

Tuesday, November 12th. Edina, Minnesota.

When I was in high school many Stanley Cups ago, I would have scoffed at the idea of members of the fairer sex playing hockey. *It's too rough. They'll get cold. What if they break a nail?* Thank goodness these girls proved me stupid today.

If not for the ponytails, I would have assumed I was watching boys compete. These young ladies played fast and aggressive hockey. Consider me hooked. (Hockey pun unintended.) I couldn't wait to catch the University of Minnesota's Lady Gophers play in the spring, and I made a mental note to grab a good seat on the couch when the USA women took the ice in Sochi.

But it was *off* the ice that I learned my biggest lesson of the day. My hosts, Sarah and Lindsay, college classmates of mine, cooked me a wonderful meal. After we had finished and their three kids (15, 13, 11) had completed their assigned chores, Sarah announced, "Game time!"

I assumed this meant, time for the kids to entertain themselves on their various electronic devices. Uh, no.

As the box containing Ticket to Ride, a board game I'd never heard of that involves trains, suddenly appeared, I realized that "Game time" meant, The Knapp family will now play a board game at the kitchen table. Like, with each other.

I didn't realize families did that any more. Shot, SCORE!

DAY SEVENTY-ONE

Thursday, November 14th. Sioux Falls, South Dakota.

Ah, my first Sports Year crush: female indoor volleyball.

Once again, like in Cincy, we had high school D-R-A-M-A! Bishop O'Gorman, the top-ranked team in the state, had been upset in its previous match, thus jeopardizing its entry into the state playoffs. In order to stamp their passports to the postseason, the Knights needed to beat the hungry underdog Lincoln High Patriots.

Today marked my first South Dakota sojourn. Better yet, in another Sports Year first, I'm staying with a friend's *parents*. (Actually, wait, you kinda already know the guy: Kevin, my Day One host in Denver.) I arrived at his childhood home hoping the post-match dinner with Dr. and Mrs. McGreevy would lead to many embarrassing revelations about their son. I planned on promising them I would not share said scandals, but then promptly emailing all our college chums with the dirt.

Little did I know that my hosts are royalty in Sioux Falls, especially at Bishop O'Gorman High. Conservatively speaking, every single person wearing light blue said, at a minimum, hello to them, and most stopped to chat. Thanks to my simply having arrived with The McGreevys, the people working the snack stand gave me extra popcorn. Psyched for the match, I began chomping those kernels like my own kids were playing.

The volleyball tension dissipated quickly, as B.O. – which, I'm fairly certain, they don't like being called – dominated. The Knights swept the first three games, led by Taryn Kloth, their 6' 3" star outside hitter. I'd happily pay to watch this young lady play college volleyball in *two* more years. (Update: Taryn signed with Creighton in 2015.)

Despite departing the gym high on victory, The McGreevys did not divulge any embarrassing information about their youngest son. This forced me to question my faith in my coercive abilities. Kevin's parents undoubtedly questioned my social abilities.

During a delightful dinner, I couldn't stop yawning. Walking to their car, my hosts suggested we stop for a nightcap. Having stayed up late the night before with an old roommate in Minneapolis, all I could think about was nighty night. A nightcap? I would've voted no, if I'd been given a vote.

We hit the hot spot in town, in the lobby of a hotel, and met a friend of theirs: a man of the cloth. I felt like I was living the set up for a joke: Two septuagenarians, a priest and a 43-year old walk into a bar; only the youngest guy didn't drink.

No joke. I imbibed ice waters while they knocked back vodka and white wine. WTF has happened to me?

DAY SEVENTY-THREE

Saturday, November 16th. Lincoln, Nebraska.

When I originally planned my itinerary, I intended to only make repeat visits to Atlanta, home of The Greatest Person to Ever Live, a.k.a, my nephew Danny. Certainly, a return to Nebraska was not a consideration. Yet, here I was. And, no, it wasn't the Indian food that did it. I came back for a job.

Scott, my chaperone on Day 2, had told me he wanted me to be his SoCal rep in the new medical device company for which he served as national sales director. Two and a half months ago, hearing that was good for my ego; I didn't seriously consider the offer. But now, staring down the barrel of $75K in credit card debt, a sales gig simply was good for *me*.

In the opening chapter, I shared how I'd applied to work at Starbucks and didn't even get an interview. But that wasn't the only job ring into which I'd thrown my hat.

In the summer of 2012, I read a blog written by an incredibly smart entrepreneur, a guy with a bold vision for changing the way corporate marketing teams use content. He and his cofounder started a company based around proprietary software they'd created. This company was hiring sales people. I looked up the blogger on LinkedIn and found one common connection, my longtime friend "Tyrell." This buddy did not make introductions lightly. Rather, I had to fill out a specific and lengthy form explaining why I wanted to meet the co-founder. Despite my lack of experience in media sales or marketing, Tyrell agreed to make the introduction.

A few days later, I got a call from the other cofounder. We spoke on the phone for more than an hour, and he invited me to NYC for an interview. Once there, I instantly responded to the energy in the open office space, which could have served as the setting of a romantic comedy in an advertising agency. Young, happy people zipped around, buzzed on their jobs and the free gourmet coffee. (Or maybe it was the endorphins from the free gym memberships given to employees.) All of the sudden, I grew tired of working by myself in my dumpy beach apartment. I wanted to join a team. I wanted to live in New York City for the first time in my life. I wanted to move close to my parents.

After that in person meeting, I felt great about my chances. The cofounder asked if I could return after the weekend to make a presentation to the startup's sales team; if the four members gave me the thumb's up, then I got the gig. My positivity soared when the cofounder sent me the Power Point slides in advance, positioning me for peak performance. After staying at my parents' house on Sunday night, I caught a ride with Dad to the train station.

"Knock 'em dead, Stinks!" He'd given me that nickname in my infancy and used it throughout my childhood, but only when my friends were not around. Except, of course, for that time at an 8th grade C.Y.O basketball game when, frustrated with my refusal to shoot from the outside, he yelled, "Shoot, Stinks!" I don't think I've yet recovered from the subsequent humiliation. That said, his using that nickname now, ahead of this hugely important interview, filled me with warm feelings and positivity.

I arrived in SoHo with enough time for a leisurely iced mocha and banana. Then I showed up at the company early, just like I'd learned in the Army and at Pfizer. The salespeople, two men and two women with a combined age of less than 100, greeted me enthusiastically. For the presentation they sat at a table while I stood. In my two and half years as a sales trainer at Eli Lilly, I always grooved on having a captive audience and being the center of attention. Giddy up.

First, I gave them a rundown on my work history. The two women couldn't believe I knew Jake Gyllenhaal. After learning that one of the guys had graduated from USC, I shared how difficult it had been to live in Manhattan Beach as an ND fan during the Pete Carroll glory years. He ate that up. In the presentation, I'd be selling those four Twentysomethings their own product, but in reality I was actually selling them my favorite product – me. Having already rehearsed the slide deck a dozen times at home and on the train, I pulled up Slide One, feeling invincible.

And then I suffered a mental meltdown of Mickelson-on-the-18th-at-Winged-Foot proportions. Suddenly, I forgot how to work Power Point. Seriously. Presenting in front of strangers for the first time in seven and a half years, I forgot that pressing Enter advanced from Slide One to Slide Two. I also forgot that I could accomplish the same basic task by using the down arrow key. Instead, I tried to use the MacBook's mouse – my nervous energy skipped me three slides ahead, and then, once I had recognized my blunder, I zipped all the way back to the beginning. I cracked a self-effacing joke, but then promptly spazzed with the slides again. Sweat slid down my back. Rather than looking like a confident, modern salesman wielding a commonly used tool of the trade, I resembled my father trying to get voice mails from his iPhone. Finally, the axons fired, and I finished strong. Well, at least without further urination down my leg.

I was not surprised when the cofounder emailed me four days later to say *he* wanted to hire me but had been surprised to learn the sales team did not support that decision. He didn't mention the Power Point disaster, but he didn't have to. He gave me some specific feedback, writing, "They didn't think you fully appreciated our value prop." Actually, that analysis was spot on, since until that email I'd never heard of the term "value proposition." Re-reading that message, I felt like Austin fucking Powers; all I needed was a Tab.

Over a year later, in November 2013, I still believed in my natural ability to sell. But, in football kicker terms, I'd iced myself. Now, I doubted whether I'd pass muster if asked to present to a group. *What new freaking Power Point are they using out there now?!* For all I knew, Scott could have been joking in September when he offered me a job. Today, I planned on locking one down.

Two weeks ago, I emailed Scott and David, my producer acquaintance who'd connected me with Scott in the first place, and told them that my plan to hit a University of Texas football game in Austin had fallen through. That was only partly true; I had originally intended to attend the Longhorns game against the Cowboys of Oklahoma State, but once I'd seen how freaking far it was from South Dakota to Austin, I nixed it. (Common flaw of Sports Year: unreasonable distances between events. #planning) Plus, I needed a job. So, I explained to the guys that I'd love to take in my first Cornhusker game as my fallback. "Anybody got a couch and/or a ticket with my name on it?" David responded that he had a guestroom for me. Scott said he had a ride, a tailgate party and a ticket for me. Boom!

If David's wife Ginny harbored any misgivings about hosting a stranger, she did an amazing job of hiding them. They cooked me dinner on Friday night and made me feel like an old friend. David lent me a legit Nebraska sweatshirt for the game, and they even dialed up a crisp and sunny autumn day.

Scott, resuming his tour guide role, picked me up with plenty of time for tailgating. Similar to the scene in Madison, red dominated the streets of Lincoln. We started pre-gaming at a bar, where a guy who I'd only met twenty minutes earlier insisted I do an Irish Car Bomb with him. That was a lifetime first; although I had Car Bombed many times, I'd never done so while the sun was still in the sky. Scott told two Husker hotties in their twenties that Jake Gyllenhaal played me in a movie. Sizing me up, they understandably did not believe this information. So, they Googled me. (I have video of this.) When proven wrong, they laughed with delight. Then they laughed harder, "You're *forty three*!" I did not realize that that information was on the internet.

En route to the stadium, Scott and I invited ourselves to a tailgater held in back of a former ambulance. In front of the "ER" on the back, the owner had painted "Husk." I pictured the self-satisfied nod that guy must've given himself on the six or seven Saturdays a year when he pulled that baby into his usual parking spot.

On game day, Memorial Stadium's 90,000 capacity counts as the third-largest city in the Cornhusker State. Nebraska fans were the best I'd ever seen. They filled the stands early, universally decked out in the same shade of red. Talk about *intimidating*. (Pet peeve alert: Notre Dame fans will never get it together and settle on either navy blue or Kelly green and then wear *only* that color. Yellow, white, pink... So annoying.) Scott got us down to field level for pre-game warm-ups, which gave me an excellent perspective on the fandom.

Five minutes before kickoff, a vaguely familiar guitar riff blared from the speakers, igniting a fireball of fanaticism in the crowd. "What the hell?!" I had to scream the words to Scott. He just smiled, drunk from devotion (and the tailgating). Everyone in attendance turned to the giant Jumbotron. I spun in a slow circle, gawking at the people gawking at the live video feed of the Husker players walking from their locker room through the tunnel and, finally, onto the field. (Later, I Googled this tradition and learned that it's called "The Tunnel Walk." Less predictable was the name of the rock band and its song that sparked the delirium: the Alan Parson's Project's "Sirius.") After the first home team touchdown, hundreds of red balloons were released into the sky. While beautiful to see, I shuddered at the environmental impact of that weekly stunt. Certainly, that wouldn't be allowed in, say, Los Angeles, San Francisco or Seattle.

At different times, athletic department employees wielding cannons fired hot dogs into the crowd. I learned this when one frank, wrapped in a plastic bag and secured with a rubber band, ricocheted off the right side of Scott's head and into my left temple. Startled, I stooped down and picked it up, beyond confused. "How often do people sue?" I asked him. He, and several people around us, cocked an eyebrow at the question. "You know, from losing an eye?" The other people just scoffed. Scott put a patient hand on my shoulder. "Nobody sues. This is *Nebraska*." Pretty good hot dog, by the way.

Cornhusker fans impressed me big time with their enthusiasm and dedication. Down three scores midway late in the 4th quarter? I'd have been in the parking lot drowning my sorrows in a 12-ounce can. Not these folks; seemingly all of them stayed until the final whistle. I looked forward to a return trip to Memorial Stadium.

When Scott pulled up to my host's curb, I reached into my ski jacket pocket, pulled out my folded resume and offered it to him.

 He shook his head. "Jamie, that guy we did the Car Bomb with?" I nodded, not sure where he was going with this. "He's a doc that I called on forever. He said he felt like he'd known you for twenty years. If I had any doubts about you, which I didn't, that clinched it for me. I told you: the job is yours."

That came as a relief, but also a death knell.

Need One

DAY SEVENTY-EIGHT

Thursday, November 21ˢᵗ. San Francisco, California.

Originally, I'd been excited to meet a college buddy for sushi. But that was before I lost my appetite from dread over the phone call I had to make: to instruct my father, a Certified Financial Planner, to cash out my 401k. For him, this was anathema. Rich Reidy would go vegan before he'd let any client, let alone his own son, raid a retirement fund. He'd gladly trade O'Reilly for Maddow every night than allow somebody to give up the reward of compounded interest.

"Hold on," Dad said, putting down the phone. I assumed he was trudging to the liquor cabinet to pour himself a stiff one as he contemplated where he'd gone wrong in raising me. But, strangely, I didn't hear any ice cubes dancing in a glass. After a moment, he returned to the call.

"You're not cashing out your 401k." Before I could object, he continued, "You can thank your mother for this…" They were wiring $8.5K of their own money into my bank account first thing the next morning.

I could've refused the offer. I *should have* refused it. But I didn't. Forty-three years old and I was still borrowing money from Mommy and Daddy. What. A. Fucking. Loser. I said as much to him. Thankfully, my folks didn't see it that way. "You just keep going," Dad said. "This is all gonna work out."

I arrived late to dinner, explaining to my buddy I'd somehow gotten lost even though I'd chosen the sushi joint. In truth, I'd needed time to stop crying. Were they tears of humiliation or relief?

Yes.

193

<u>DAY EIGHTY</u>

Saturday, November 23rd. Palo Alto, California.

My friend Joey is kinda famous in San Francisco, as the result of having appeared in Season One of a local reality show in 1996. My liver thinks he's infamous, though, thanks to his love of Fernet, a poisonous liqueur that should probably be illegal.

When Joey heard about Sports Year, he offered me a place to crash. Two weeks before The Big Game, a.k.a. Stanford versus Cal, he called with a hookup for me, which was confusing. "But you didn't go to either school," I pointed out. His sneer could be felt through the speakerphone.

A work colleague of his hosted a killer tailgater and, after hearing about my journey, had extended me an invite. Joey instructed me, "Just don't wear anything red." No problem. I happily rocked a Cal hat and t-shirt to express my sincere appreciation for the free food and booze. Jason's crew welcomed me like a long lost classmate.

My friends Dan and Carol Winters, parents of Kristi, my old neighbor in Manhattan Beach, graciously took me to the game. Before kickoff, we hit a Stanford tailgater.

Much like the Cal gathering, I couldn't shake the feeling that I was the only attendee under 50 who had yet to make millions with a tech startup. Lots of "market disruption" talk. Wasn't disruption a bad thing?

Constant thought in my brain: I am so unemployable.

DAY EIGHTY-ONE

Sunday, November 24th. Oakland, California.

After Lambeau Field, Oakland Coliseum ranked second on my list of NFL stadiums. I wanted to see the former for its history, the latter for its hilarity. At a Packer game, pretty much everybody looked the same: like a person from Wisconsin. At the Raider game, many fans didn't look like people.

Raider Nation is famous for its extreme devotion, especially The Black Hole. I wished Raider games were like cricket matches, so I could spend an entire weekend in sections 104-107. If you are a "people watcher," get to Oakland Coliseum STAT.

(Duh. It's "*Raider*juice.")

This marked the first time I'd ever attended a football game that felt like something else, something bigger. I experienced a similar feeling at my first Grateful Dead concert. I guess that made sense, considering that The Dead were born just across the Bay.

My favorite thing about a Raiders game? The women. Fellas, if you prefer dark haired, dark eyed beauties who drink draft beer, then be sure to schedule a game for next season. And if you like the aforementioned *plus* tattoos? Move to Oakland and buy season tickets to the Silver & Black. Please invite me to your wedding or, in seventeen years, your daughter's quinceañera.

Post-game, on my walk to the BART station, I passed a panhandler who urged people, "Don't hate, *donate*."

Yeah, brother, even though I'd been asking people for money, myself, that pitch earned him some dough.

DAY EIGHTY-FOUR

Wednesday, November 26ʰ. Inglewood, California.

This morning, after I did my usual online research into the local high school sports schedule, I paused and rechecked my info. Commence the following internal dialogue: *Uh, do I really need to see girls' hoops today? Uh, yeah, dude. It's been four straight days of guy sports. Remember the male-to-female ratio goal of 45%?*

And that's how I ended up here:

This marked my second solo venture to Inglewood in my thirteen years of living in the LA area. This city was only a fifteen-minute drive from my apartment, so it wasn't distance that had kept me away. Nope, it was fear. I'd been guilty of assuming that Crips or Bloods would put a cap in my ass had I dared venture onto their streets. *W'sup, guy who's seen* Boyz in The Hood *too many times.*

My first trip there also occurred as part of a poorly thought out book project. In summer 2011, I was working on "Going Groupon: Thirty Days of Daily Deals of The Day," a nonfiction account of my obsession with Living Social and the like. (Unfortunately, I was six months too late with the premise; the idiot CEO of Groupon refused the $1B and then the stock plummeted and all the secrets came out re: the crappy results for small businesses. Nobody wanted to publish a book about a cheapskate bachelor buying a Groupon every day.) I set up rules I had to follow, which led to my purchasing an amazing meal deal at a soul food restaurant in Inglewood. This provoked great trepidation in the author, and much self-flagellation over the contrived rules. But, a deal – ahem – is a deal.

What an enjoyable lunch I had! Contrary to my pre-meal racist fears, I emerged with my ass cap-free. I promised the delightful waitress, whose family owned the restaurant, I'd be back with friends, including a Michelin star-winning chef. She smiled brightly, but I wonder if she knew I wouldn't return. I certainly didn't know that; I strode out the door buoyed by my newfound open mindedness. But then a thing, and then another thing... and two years slipped by without my making the short drive northeast for the delicious cornbread made from her grandmother's recipe.

So, today I drove at night – gasp! – to a girls' holiday tournament in Inglewood. Where I watched teams from Manhattan Beach and Beverly Hills – two of LA's whitest towns – play basketball. My big takeaway from a whopping two games of spectating: the girls missed a *lot* of layups. Like, way more than their male counterparts did in games I'd seen. From my uneducated perch in the bleachers, I couldn't help but wonder: why are the rims at the same height for boys and girls?

In volleyball, for instance, the net rests six inches lower for the women than the men. This allows for more hitting (only squares say "spike"), which leads to an increase in scoring, which is a big crowd pleaser.

Basketball fans would certainly applaud more scoring rather than less scoring. So, why don't we lower the rims for girls' basketball?

DAY EIGHTY-SEVEN

Saturday, November 30th. Torrance, California.

I took more notes at today's event than I had at any other during Sports Year. Aside from the Wounded Warriors Amputee Softball Team's game, this was my favorite event so far. (Technicality: tailgating at Ole Miss's The Grove did not count as a sporting event.)

You see, I was finally home; at a high school wrestling tournament.

I walked on the wrestling team at Notre Dame, where I wrestled neither well nor often. Teammates cranky from cutting weight occasionally got into fights over who got me as their partner at the end of practice, since everybody was tired and wanted an easy match.

But before I could be lousy in college, I had to be *really* bad in high school. And as a freshman new to the sport in 1985, I lowered the bar.

I had no intention of ever wrestling. I was a basketball player – point guard. Toward the end of football season, my P.E. teacher Coach Jeff Levy asked me what sport I was going to play in the winter. "Basketball," I chirped, my prepubescent voice nearly cracking glass.

He shook his head. "No, you're not. When you get cut, come out for wrestling." Now it was time for me to shake my head. "I've never been cut from anything, Coach!" This man, who had watched the 5' 3" 102 pound Jamie Reidy play hoops in his gym class for three months, didn't bother arguing. He simply said, "Wrestling tryouts are the Monday after Thanksgiving."

Ten minutes into basketball tryouts, I knew I would not be making the squad. Forget my lack of height; a point guard needed to be able to dribble with both hands. I couldn't brush my teeth with my left hand, let alone beat a guy off the dribble. Plus, the argument could have been made that I could barely go right. *Y'know, come to think of it, our CYO team did suck...* Just as Coach Levy had predicted, the Monday after Thanksgiving found me at wrestling tryouts. Looking around the cramped room with a low ceiling and padded floor and walls, I gaped at the seemingly neck-less boys, all of them wearing layers of sweats. One guy rocked a dockworker hat like a thug version of The Edge. Their collective intensity unnerved me. *What are they so angry about?* If I'd known the pain that awaited me, I'd have sprinted to the Winter Track team's practice.

Twenty-eight years later, as I sat in wooden bleachers on a Saturday morning, memories flooded back. My first match took place on a day just like this, albeit a helluva lot colder in New Jersey than Southern California. After two weeks of practice, I stepped onto the mat positioned in the center of the basketball court; our opponent's gym suddenly seemed cavernous and chilly.

The ref blew the whistle and I felt naked. I'd played sports all my life, but I'd never done it as an individual. T-shirts popular among wrestlers boast, "No timeouts. Nowhere to hide. No one to blame." Adrift without the benefit of having a power forward or shortstop or linebacker to rely on, I circled my opponent alone. And terrified.

Locked in a clench, I became overwhelmed by utter confusion, similar to accounts I've read describing being trapped in a burning house. Panicked, I gasped for air and searched for an escape route. Even when I did something good, I'd end up in another room afire. This is a sport I chose *voluntarily*? The referee penalized me twice for using an illegal move, a Full Nelson. I had no idea what he meant. Kneeling beside the mat, Coach Levy demonstrated on an assistant coach both what I had done wrong and what I needed to do – a *Half* Nelson. Again, I had no clue.

Somehow, I was winning the match late in the third period when I erred badly, ending up on my back. The other boy instantly pinned me. As I left the mat, tears streamed down my face. This was nothing new; growing up, I cried every time my baseball team lost a game. But these tears weren't grounded in the knowledge that I should have done better. No, these tears sprung from humiliation. I had no idea what I was doing, and I knew the whole world recognized that.

On the drive home, my father seemed to be attempting to crush the steering wheel in his hands. "This crying bullshit stops *now*." It did. In public, at least.

In the bleachers today, I sat one row in front of two mothers new to the sport of wrestling. That fact proved easily discernible from their conversation. Listening to them made me wish I could go back and hear tapes of my mom in 1985. Instead of watching me wrestle, my friends in the stands used to watch *her* watch me wrestle. Apparently, she'd contort her body into the positions she thought I should be utilizing to escape the clutches of whatever much more heavily muscled boy was crushing her baby. My weight class was 112. I weighed 110, making me the only kid on the team who didn't have to cut at least a little weight.

Today my 43-year old brain short-circuited when I realized one of the wrestlers I'd been watching was not a boy. I'd read about girl wrestlers, but I'd never seen one. Wow. As I told myself to "get with the times," the moms behind me declared they were fully against it. Another female grappler walked by. I couldn't help but notice that she had boobs. *What are the guys in the locker room saying beforehand and after? Does she have a boyfriend?* These are the questions I asked myself, embarrassed to be such a dinosaur.

Many girls wore a swim cap-type thing beneath their headgear. On mat #2, the wrestler's swim cap came off, revealing two pig tails, but the ref didn't give her the opportunity to rig it. The scoreboard operator stepped in, alerting the official to the problem. He then paused the match and gave the wrestler ample time to fix the swim cap. Obviously, the referees were adjusting to the times, too.

She lost, but managed to not get pinned. Coming off the mat, gasping and frustrated, she asked the coach, "What *is* a 'mule kick?!'" This melted my heart, because it echoed my own Full Nelson-Half Nelson confusion. It was so pure. New wrestlers don't know anything! After, what, two weeks of practice? Coaches scream out years' worth of advice to athletes with hours of knowledge. During my pharmaceutical sales career, we were constantly reminded that doctors must hear a message *seven* times before it sank into their brains. So, it wasn't surprising that a 14-year old girl didn't retain "mule kick." (Parents, keep that "seven times" rule in mind when your kids don't adhere to new rules. So says the guy with no kids.)

I found myself rooting for all the skinny and weak kids who staggered off the mat in defeat, wobbling like newborn foals. I wanted to throw my arm around their shoulders and say, "You can change this. If you work hard, you can be 1st team All League someday, too." *And after that you can have guys fight over who gets to wrestle you at the end of college practices because you're one of the worst on the team.*

At a wrestling tournament, it's easy to spot the veteran athletes. I don't mean the guys who are already shaving. I'm talking about the competitors who look like they have "been there before." They are focused, but easily navigate the paths around the mats. They spend their downtime between matches wisely, conserving their energy as they sit comfortably. They eat healthy snacks.

The green wrestlers, on the other hand, stumble around like the new guy in a war movie. Between matches, they sprawl across the bleachers, putting kinks in their backs. They chow down on Doritos and guzzle soda.

Even as a senior in high school, I still felt like a newbie. I simply hadn't wrestled often enough to understand what I was doing, to recognize the patterns and adjust accordingly. On the team in college, I carefully observed the starters as they went about their match day routines. *Man, I wish I knew all this four years ago.*

Sitting here at this tournament, I realize that's a good metaphor for my love life. Until my late thirties, I hadn't spent enough time in committed relationships to know what the hell I was doing. I did some dumb things and said a lot of dumber things. I didn't appreciate the impact my self-centeredness had on my partners (possibly the result of being so damn self-centered). Rather than communicate my desires or complaints, I assumed women could read my mind. Sometimes they could, but not nearly often enough to compensate for my silence.

Every time I lost a wrestling match, I learned something useful for a future contest, whether in preparation or execution of a move. Today, coming off a pair of failed relationships, I'm looking forward to putting my newfound experiences to good use.

<u>DAY NINETY-THREE</u>

Friday, December 6th. Redondo Beach, California.

Priorities. *Sigh.* I like to say that "Life is all about delivery," meaning that the way you deliver a message or the way you deliver on promises is key to your happiness and that of others. And I still believe that to be true. But, man, priorities are huge, too.

Like tonight, for example. I was scheduled to attend the NCAA women's indoor volleyball regional at USC (25 minutes northeast), which started at 7:00 PM. No, that's not completely accurate: I was *psyched* to be there. After all, discovering the thrill of women's indoor volleyball had been the biggest surprise of Sports Year. So, then, I was jacked to see me some tall girls pounding the daylights out of some Wilsons.

And then I got the email: Gus is in town and we're going to dinner at MB Post at 6:30. *Hello, dilemma.*

A legendarily fun character in our group of friends, Gus moved to Seattle a few years ago. Now, thanks to the combination of his family duties and his general laziness, we hadn't seen him at the past few of our annual Ryder Cup-esque golf trips to Santa Barbara. But, getting beyond that bitterness, I couldn't deny that I wanted to hang out with him. Gus = Good time. But so did the collegiate volleyball players vying for a shot at the national title!

Did they serve bourbon at USC's Galen Center? No, the nice lady on the phone told me, they did not.

But they did serve very good bourbon – and incredible food – at Chef David LeFevre's flagship restaurant, M.B. Post. And I hadn't eaten there since I'd returned to the area, which was sacrilege since I had been the first customer through the door on opening night three years ago.

Sorry, volleyball girls. And, thank you, high school basketball girls who play at the convenient time of 3:30!

Dinner proved predictably hilarious and delicious, but I ditched the dudes halfway through after my pal Laura sent me a life-altering text: "Having some people over. Amy's here."

I'd met Amy at a beach party on July 4, 2009. Whether or not she was interested in me, I dunno, but I was just off a break up and not in the market for, uh, smart, independent women. Fast forward to July of 2013; we were both at Laura's 40th birthday party, and the hostess asked if we knew each other. Amy shook her head, but I said, "Yes we do." And I explained that we'd met on 16th Street in Hermosa Beach. *Nothing.* At a party on the volleyball courts. *Nada.* The sun was going down and there was a DJ and people were dancing. Laura was giving me a look. *Good god, man, have some pride!* "Amy, you were wearing a blue sweatshirt..." Just as Laura prepared to alert hotel security, Amy's face lit up in recognition. "Oh, yeah!" (Later, it became obvious she was merely recalling being at that party, not necessarily remembering meeting me.)

But after that 40th fest in July, I failed to follow up properly. She lived in San Francisco, so it wasn't like I could see her easily. And then I left on Sports Year. But I remained smitten.

Catch ya next time, Gus!

DAY NINETY-NINE

Thursday, December 12th. Suffern, New York.

Tonight, my father dropped me off at a high school to watch a basketball game.

Afterwards, I called him to come pick me up, and then waited in the lobby with dozens of teenagers who were also waiting for their parents to come get them. I spoke to none of the girls. Was it 2013 or 1985? Seemingly, I had not progressed in life at all.

Well, to be fair, *this time* I used my iPhone to call home. My family lived in New York state, but I attended high school in New Jersey. Out-of-state calls were much pricier than a local call. Thus, The Reidys utilized an "elaborate" pay phone scam in which I'd dial 0 for the operator and tell the person I wanted to make a "collect call," which meant the receiving party would pay for it. After asking my name, the lady would connect me to my parents' house and say, "I have a collect call from Jamie. Do you accept the charges?" This was a signal, you see. Whoever answered the phone at my house only had to say, "No," and the operator would apologize to me and then disconnect. Fifteen minutes later, one of my parents would pull into the school parking lot. Team Reidy batted a thousand with this ruse, saving a lot of money in long distance NJ-NY.

But it was never that simple with Rich Reidy. No, my old man couldn't *just* refuse the collect call. Instead, he felt it necessary to disguise his voice in a comically bad impersonation of an elderly nanny. In response to the operator's question, Dad would say, "Uh, I'm sorry, but I'm just the baby sitter. I'm not authorized to accept collect calls!" On more than one occasion, I swear to God, the operator laughed at him.

Tonight, I looked for a payphone to use, just for old time's sake. But I didn't find one. Wouldn't have mattered, anyway, as I didn't have any coins and it had been so long since I used a calling card that I didn't know how to make a call anymore.

Standing by myself in a lobby crowded with teens made me feel creepier than ever, so I walked outside and waited for my Dad. In the snow.

DAY ONE HUNDRED AND ONE

Saturday, December 14th. Philadelphia, Pennsylvania.

The Army-Navy game was an original Top-Ten event on the Sports Year agenda. As a football fan, it was a no brainer. As a former Army officer, the game meant a little more, especially now that I'd met four wounded veterans during my journey and had seen firsthand the sacrifices these men made in defending our country.

The fact that today just happened to be Day 101 seemed fitting, too, like the 101st Airborne Division's Screaming Eagles. In the shower, I found myself singing a cadence from basic training: "One-oh-one! Patch on my shoul-der! Pick up your weapon and follow me! I am the In-fan-try!" (In the Army, I was the opposite of infantry: Personnel, a.k.a. Human Resources. Our training school motto: We don't retreat, we backspace.)

Frustratingly, my trend of struggling to find a wounded veteran to bring to an event continued for the Army-Navy game. My early plan fell through, leaving me panicked. C'mon, this is Army-Navy; I *had* to bring a wounded veteran! Fortunately, Team RWB (Red, White, and Blue) saved the day for me.

The organization's goal is "Enriching the lives of America's veterans." I found them through my cousin Brian, who played lacrosse at West Point prior to his becoming an Infantry officer and a Ranger. I've had the pleasure of partying with him and several of his classmates many times. I sent an email to them asking for help in finding a veteran's organization that could hook me up with a guest for Army-Navy. (One of the guys responded with a screed against Wounded Warriors, revealing that the organization had turned off many people with its budget that only focused 60% of resources on veterans. Nearly three years later, that imbalance blew up in a scandal.)

Two days after my email to Brian and his buddies, a volunteer at RWB cyber-introduced me to Tom Lee, a former sailor *and* a former soldier. Three questions came to mind: who could possibly be better to bring to Army-Navy than that guy? How many "two service guys" are there? Mathematically, what were the odds that I'd get set up with one? Thank you Team RWB!

Tom Lee texted that he'd arrive at Lincoln Field an hour after me, so I did some tailgate reconnaissance. Holy flags! In no other stadium parking lot had I ever seen so many people flying the Stars and Stripes. The patriotism felt palpable, right down to the presence of West Point cadets and Naval Academy midshipmen. (I was surprised to learn that even the female students are called "midshipmen.") The students looked so out of place in their grey and black, respectively, dress uniforms, but they yucked it up like normal college kids. Their uniforms, however, served as stark reminders that these young men and women would soon be putting themselves in harm's way so that the rest of us could maintain our God-given right to simultaneously down Fireball shots from a four-person Shot-ski.

The author, far left, displaying piss poor posture.

One Army tailgater I invited myself to boasted camouflage beach chairs. The host's 18-year old son was attending his 18th Army-Navy game. Wow. Go Army!

Tom and I met up at the Team RWB tent, which was thankfully heated. Food and drink abounded. A spirited game of Flip Cup broke out, not a surprising development among a group of competitive men and women. My team lost, dammit!

Tom has a contagious positivity, the kind of person around whom you can't help smiling. He lost a leg as the result of an IED in Afghanistan. Now, he competes in triathlons. Think about that the next time you come up with an excuse to skip the gym.

Phil Hoffman, the Ravens team photographer I had a few beers with the night before the Broncos game, also served as the Naval Academy's team photographer. Back in Denver, he told me to contact him a few weeks before Army-Navy because he had something special for my guest and me. I followed orders and I'm so glad I did; Phil came through big time, with a pair of pre-game field passes.

But, in typical Sports Year fashion, I failed to lock down the exact pickup location. This resulted in Tom and my traipsing outside *and* inside Lincoln Field for thirty minutes. At one point he smiled and shook his head, admonishing himself. "If I'd have known how much walking I was gonna do today, I would've brought my 'running' leg." *Ooof.* My stomach turned into a cauldron of self-loathing. Apparently, it showed on my face, so Tom warmly slapped me on the shoulder and smiled, "It's all good!"

Tom Lee on the sideline while rocking a Team RWB scarf.

An the game, we'd be sitting with a different Phil, this one a college roommate of mine. His brother Mike had generously donated our seats, which were in section 234, row 26. After Phil, Tom and I began hiking up the increasingly slippery stairs, I quickly realized we were heading to the literal top of the stadium. My old roomie and I exchanged a worried look; Tom, with his prosthetic leg, could certainly have difficulties with the climb. Turned out, Phil and I could certainly have difficulties sizing up our guest. Tom made it to the top without a problem or a word of complaint. He also wasn't gasping, like Phil and I were, our breath visible in the 26-degree air.

This was the first Sports Year event blessed by snow. Our section at "The Linc," as Lincoln Field is called by Philly locals, was apparently designed by an architect planning to give his ex mother-in-law season tickets: the wind blew continuously in our faces, as did the snow, then sleet, then rain. Sitting three rows from the top, my fear of heights kicked into overdrive. The guy sitting behind us cracked that a Blue Angel almost hit him during the pre-game flyover. How did Tom, a native of Hawaii, react to our chilly perch? With a joke, of course. "Thanks for the great seats, guys!"

I am a fair-weather fan in the sense that I prefer fair weather. At the opening kickoff, I began calculating how long we'd have to stay before gracefully sneaking off to a warm bar. Phil must have sensed this. Midway through the second quarter, he leaned over to me and, with his teeth chattering, whispered, "We are *not* leaving before a guy with one leg." Obviously, we would never have considered ditching Tom. My old friend was merely commenting on how much mas macho Tom was than we were or ever had been. Unfortunately, the veteran did not appear to have any desire to leave early. Fortunately, we took a break from the relentless weather by hiding in the concourse during halftime.

(At halftime, the grounds crewmembers used snow blowers to clear off the yardage lines.)

There, we met up with my cousin Brian and his buddies, who offered us some of their "rations." (Years ago, these guys devised a method for sneaking booze into stadiums: fill double-seal Ziploc bags with bourbon and hide them under a shirt or coat. Even if security were to pat down the mule, the bag would feel like a love handle! Once you were safely inside, all you needed was a concession stand soda in which to pour the booze. #genius). Tom declined the drink, so I did the same for solidarity. But I was thankful to avoid the ice cold Coke that would have further lowered my core body temperature. As we prepared ourselves to once again brave the elements, Tom turned to Phil and I with a sheepish look. "Guys, I've had a great time. Great! But I've got an hour's drive in this weather. I should probably get on the road." *What?! Huh?! No way! Aw, that's too bad... you know what? We might as well walk you out.*

Tom and I are now Facebook friends. Six days a week the triathlete posts his workout results. Normally, I get annoyed with people who share their fitness stats with the world – *cough! CrossFit cult members, cough!* – but I enjoy seeing Tom's updates everyday. This is a man who was given an understandable reason to wallow in his plight, to wave the white flag at the world. But he didn't.

He just figures out which leg he needs for the day's mission – walking or running – and rucks up.

DAY ONE HUNDRED AND TWO

Sunday, December 15ᵗʰ. Delran, New Jersey.

Today marked the first time I watched a family member play a sport. Well, it was my brother's nephew by marriage. Regardless, I felt nervous enough pre-game that Jack might as well be my nephew, too. 5th grade CYO basketball can do that to you.

Gotta love a church that doubles as a gym:

"Three-point Jesus"?

Unfortunately, Jack's team couldn't pull out the W, losing by three. But the defeat didn't seem to matter after one of his teammates hit a meaningless three-pointer at the buzzer (to cut the lead from six to three).

The players and their parents erupted in cheers, and they all bounced out of the gym as if they'd won.

And you know what? With that attitude, maybe they did.

<u>DAY ONE HUNDRED AND FOUR</u>

Tuesday, December 17ᵗʰ. Montvale, New Jersey.

The weatherman predicted snow in the morning, but assured his viewers the white stuff would stop quickly. Apparently, Mother Nature didn't watch local TV. I shoveled my parents' driveway twice, but you never would have known it from the smooth white blanket. (At least I got in two workouts, though. I pretended I was Rocky Balboa training in Siberia for his match with Ivan Drago.)

Strangely, it took me a while to realize that the unexpected snowfall could jeopardize the Sports Year streak. Sure enough, I checked school websites only to find big red alerts: gymnastics cancelled, wrestling cancelled, basketball cancelled. ("Neidermeyer? DEAD! Stratten? DEAD!") By now, you know the play call: bowling.

Not so fast. A call to the local alley informed me that Benjamin Moore Paint Company, a huge local employer, had cancelled its league for the night. "Two other leagues haven't called in to cancel yet," the manager told me. "But it doesn't look good." Regardless, I announced to my folks that I'd be heading to Montvale Lanes, four miles away in the New Jersey town where I attended high school at St. Joe's.

Unexpectedly, my father told my mother, "I'm gonna drive Jamie." I figured he was worried about his beach bum of a son handling the unfamiliar wintry conditions. Turned out, he wanted to see just what the hell I was doing in Sports Year.

The bowling alley's parking lot had fewer cars than a church on Monday. Inside, I approached the main counter and Jerry Seinfeld's voice filled my brain. *Why do bowling alleys have elevated counters? What, do they think they're pharmacists or something?*

After introducing myself to the guy in charge, I described my project. He gave me the familiar look: tilted head, arched brow, half-grin. He was clearly considering calling the cops, but grudgingly shared that his name was Rich. "Same as my father's!" I turned to point over my shoulder at my old man, only to discover he was standing *right* behind me. Suddenly, I felt like a pharmaceutical rep again, with a trainer lurking close by and monitoring every word of my sales pitch. Good thing Dad was there, though, because his presence reminded me that I grew up in the area.

"I graduated from Joe's," I explained, using the local nickname for my high school. "My dad even drove me over here tonight!" The guys behind the counter chuckled at that. "But this snow screwed up my schedule and the streak will be over at Day 104 if I don't watch some people bowl in a league tonight." Now, the manager got it: I was crazy, but harmless.

Hoping to curry favor, I explained to Rich the manager that two of my buddies from high school used to work at this bowling alley decades ago. He brought Jason, an employee in his early 30s, into the conversation. The new addition heard my friends' names and said with a mixture of bitterness and fondness, "They used to kick the shit out of me every Sunday." Yep, that would be my skinny pals, Semp and Waldo, thrilled to have somebody smaller to pick on.

Since there were both a Ladies' League and a Men's League in action, I chose the former so I could get another female sport on the scorecard. But I also counted on the ladies being more open and chatty, making it a win-win. The employees pointed out a pair of women who'd be particularly good for me to talk with.

Members of "The Bowling Grandmas," Joan and Edna both had sons who'd graduated from my high school a few years before me. That certainly helped put them at ease with the random, middle-aged bald guy whose father hovered ten feet away. (At this point I realized

I might be mistaken for a mentally challenged adult getting some supervised time out in public.) The ladies offered me food from their impressive potluck holiday buffet – shrimp! – that took up two long tables. Sadly, I learned that one of the sons had died recently.

The grandmas graciously let me video them as they somehow managed to simultaneously bowl a league game and exchange Christmas presents. I expected controversy to erupt after Joan answered her cell phone just as she was reaching for her bowling ball on the rack. WTF?! But, nobody else seemed to care. When I asked if any gambling took place during the games, Edna looked around suspiciously before admitting, "We used to." After half an hour of visiting, I thanked them for their time and food, and was rewarded with two big Merry Christmas hugs.

On my way out, I asked one more question. "Two other leagues cancelled tonight, but you ladies still showed up. How come?"

Edna answered, "We're *grandmas*! We do anything."

Joan and Edna. (Sorry for the poor photo quality, ladies!)

Snow fell as my father and I walked to the car. He asked, "Can I buy you a beer?" Yes, sir.

Belly up at his local Irish drinking club, he beamed as we clinked pint glasses. Seeing Sports Year in action had obviously helped him understand what the hell I was trying to do in this project.

With a proud nod, Dad said, "That was really cool."

DAY ONE HUNDRED AND EIGHT

Bronxville, New York. Saturday, December 21ˢᵗ.

Today marked the first time I attended consecutive events with the same family. The names of those fortunate people might surprise you.

Jenn and Mark Redman were the evildoers who forced me to wear a Joe Flacco jersey to the Ravens-Broncos game in Denver. But, despite their finding humor in the risk to my physical wellbeing, I just couldn't quit them.

Last night they and their two boys took me to Madison Square Garden for the ultimate local rivalry game: Islanders-Rangers. Under normal circumstances, I could care less about who won a hockey game, but tonight there was no question which team I was rooting for; Jenn, you see, grew up with Ranger PJs. Her father, George, (RIP, Mr. Romano!) had been a season-ticket holder for years, so she attended dozens of games. In fact, Jenn was present at the most infamous hockey game in Madison Square Garden history: the night in 1979 when the Boston Bruins went over the glass and into the stands to fight Ranger fans!

Unfortunately, the home team lost to their hated rivals. Fortunately, Mark has a terrific collection of Scotch at their house. After a late night and a sleepover in their older son's room (Thanks for moving out, Luke!), I got to hang out with them on Saturday, too. The Redman's younger son Will had an eight-year old hoops game in a local CYO league, even though his team is Episcopalian. (Don't ask.)

What fun to watch my friends' son lead his team in scoring en route to victory. But a bummer to recall that I never led my CYO team in scoring. Or to victory.

Thankfully, I'm all about Will, not me! Right?

DAY ONE HUNDRED AND NINE

Long Island, New York. Sunday, December 22nd.

In keeping with my theme of KOF (Kids of Friends), I awoke at 5:15 to attend my best pal from high school's 10-year old son's hockey game.

Scarce were the circumstances under which I would ever even consider doing such an insane thing as rising before dawn to drive an hour away. But today was super special: the boys were playing at Nassau Coliseum, the home of, coincidentally enough, the New York Islanders!

The trip started on a humorous note when Denis pulled into our *neighbor's* driveway at 5:45 AM. I stood silently in my driveway watching him, thinking, NOOOOOOOO! Then I ran up the hill, waving my arms like mad. He didn't see me. I couldn't yell to him, because I didn't want to wake the neighborhood, so I quickly texted him. No use. He actually got out of the car and started walking to knock on the kitchen door! Finally, I ran closer while doing the whisper-yell, "*DENIS! DENIS!*" Fortunately, he heard me before he'd made it to their door.

Inside the hallowed hockey arena, the boys seemed nonchalant about the venue. The parents, however, were far more excited about a game in The Coliseum. By the way, somebody needs to do a reality TV show called, *Hockey Moms*. Seriously. These ladies screamed at the officials like those men had called their babies ugly.

Our team got down 5-2, but roared back to tie the game with a minute to go. My friend's son Jameson had two assists in the rally. Seeing that, alone, would have been worth the lack of sleep.

But witnessing Denis's devotion as a father made the day particularly impactful. As a rule, hockey parents are crazy. Similar to swimming, hockey team practices are held early in the morning or late at night, due to the limited facilities. Beyond the scheduling inconveniences, though, hockey is far and away the most expensive sport, since the equipment costs big bucks and needs frequent replacing due to growth spurts. Toss in all the lengthy road trips to other states and Canada, and, yeah, hockey parents are crazy.

Denis, however, takes his commitment to a level I'd never seen. In the winter after his three kids fell in love with hockey, he bought a bunch of two-by-fours and framed a big rectangle in the backyard. Then he laid down tarps, turned on the hose and, voila, his kids had a rink they could skate on whenever they wanted. Once spring arrived, Denis turned a sales bonus into "Glice," an artificial ice flooring he installed in the basement; *now* his kids could skate year round. Finally, he joined a weekly men's hockey league. Important note: Denis did not know how to skate! But he wanted to learn, so he could spend more time with his children on the ice.

Talk about embracing fatherhood. Wow. Today, as I saw the joy on his face as he watched his son play, I finally began to understand.

Jamie Reidy

DAY ONE HUNDRED AND ELEVEN

Tuesday, December 24th. Montvale, New Jersey.

Is it weird to say I'd been dreading Christmas Eve? Ever since I started planning the Sports Year agenda, today made me uneasy. So it was probably fitting that I woke up hungover.

For the past eighteen years, Maureen, my closest friend at home, has organized a party celebrating the overlooked holiday of Christmas Eve *Eve*. (She also leads a bar crawl on Good Friday called WWJD: Where Would Jesus Drink?) Normally, the Yuletide fest takes place in a private room of a bar in New York City. This year, the location moved across the Hudson River to Hoboken, New Jersey. For fifty dollars per person we got all we could eat and drink. I got my money's worth, and I went to bed at 4:00 a.m. full of good tidings for all.

Four hours later, I awoke homicidal. Workmen at Maureen's condo complex chose eight o'clock on Christmas Eve morning to drill who-knows-what into the brick walls of her building. Every zizzz, zizzz felt like I was being lobotomized sans anesthesia. Since sleep was no longer an option, I skipped out faster than Santa, unshowered and wearing my clothes from last night. The sunny morning provided a stark contrast to my foggy brain.

Five minutes into the drive home to my parents' house, I remembered that I was on Day 111 of a little project called Sports Year. *Oh, that.* Then I remembered that it was December 24th; my months-old concern over today's sporting event sparked a wave of sweat and nausea.

Christmas Eve had no professional sports scheduled. Zilch. The NFL doesn't play on Tuesdays, obviously. The NBA had five games on Christmas Day, but none on the 24th. The NHL had none on either

222

day. The only college football bowl game on Christmas Eve was the Sheraton Hawaii Bowl.

Originally, I planned on being in Aloha Stadium for that contest and then taking a redeye flight to catch a Christmas Day NBA game in either Los Angeles (Lakers hosting the Heat) or San Francisco (Warriors hosting the Clippers). My decision rested entirely on game ticket availability. Unfortunately, the Sports Year accounting department nixed a quick trip to Honolulu. That didn't disappoint me too much, however, since I desperately wanted to see my 19-month old nephew Danny on what would be his first real Christmas. And two NYC teams, Knicks and Nets, were hosting games on the 25th.

Finding a sporting event in the Tri-State Area (New York, New Jersey and Connecticut) on Christmas Eve, however, became a major problem. Obviously, no high schools or youth leagues scheduled games on that day. My father had ingeniously called the Rockland County Jewish organization to see if they knew of any Jewish leagues playing that day. No luck. I took to Twitter and Facebook, pleading for help in finding a Jewish game in *any* sport on December 24th. I got no responses.

Driving home from Maureen's, I had no choice but to return to Montvale Lanes in the hope of catching a bowling league in action. I felt like a moron walking into a bowling alley in broad daylight dressed like I was heading out for a night on the town. Rich, the general manager with whom I'd spoken during my visit the week before, instantly sized up my situation. "Late night?" He and his coworker laughed as I recounted my wall-drilling wakeup.

"Any leagues going today?" I asked, fingers and toes crossed. They both shook their heads glumly. "We close at 1:00, too. Nobody bowls today, man." *Of course they don't.* I explained that that left me out of options.

"What about the racetrack?" the GM said, sounding hopeful. "They run those horses all the damn time for those degenerate gamblers!" Buoyed, I whipped out my iPhone and checked the webpage for Meadowlands Racetrack, just outside Met Life Stadium where the New York Giants and New York Jets play football in New Jersey. Alas, my 50-1 hopes pulled up lame: no racing scheduled.

I thanked the guys for their help and trudged outside. Sitting in the car, I put the key in the ignition, but I didn't turn on the engine. Instead, I opted to punish myself by freezing. I just sat there, shivering and self-loathing and questioning my decision to not break the bank to fly to Hawaii for the bowl game.

A dark blue, older model conversion van caught my peripheral vision as it pulled into the parking lot and came to a stop in front of the bowling alley's lobby. I watched in my rearview mirror as a man in his forties got out and walked around to the passenger side where he opened the sliding door and stepped inside. He then extended a ramp down to the sidewalk before walking over to open the lobby's two glass doors, propping them open. Curiosity piqued, I twisted in my seat to get a better look. A teenaged boy rolled down the ramp in a wheelchair. A few seconds after, a similar kid did the same. Both boys were slumped over to one side of their chairs, but they wheeled themselves inside. The man, who I assumed to be their father, then grabbed from the van a large, black, nylon bag that looked to be four feet by two feet.

I wanted to race inside and get the scoop, but I decided to wait, so they'd have time to get set up. Finally I turned on the engine, cranked up the heat and held my hands in front of the vents, trying to thaw them out so my introductory handshakes wouldn't freeze the recipients. The father reemerged to park the van before hustling back inside. I tossed some Altoids in my mouth and exited the car. My dress shoes clacked on the cold blacktop, a loud reminder of just how out of place I was.

The employees were more than a little surprised by my return. Sheepish, I said, "I saw the boys roll down the ramp and I just *had to* see what was going on." The GM motioned toward the wall near the doorway. "You can read about them!" Sure enough, an article about "the bowling Leo brothers" – framed and matted – hung proudly for everyone to see.

I learned that Nick and Matt Leo, a high school sophomore and freshman, respectively, suffered from Ataxia-Telangiectasia (A-T), a rare degenerative disease that causes a progressive lack of muscle control, while also impacting their speech. It wasn't tough to find the boys in the empty alley; I just followed the sound of bowling pins. Within sight distance, I paused, unsure if their father would welcome a pale stranger who smelled like last night and wanted to talk to his sons. I turned back to Rich at the counter. "Think it'd be okay for me to introduce myself?" He nodded with a smile. "Totally. Those kids love the attention."

Still not completely convinced, I walked over slowly. The brothers were only using one lane. As one boy looked on, the other got set to bowl: his wheelchair was positioned behind an alloy ramp atop of which sat a bowling ball. With a slight push, the teen sent the ball down toward the pins. Clearly, the bag I saw the man carry inside had contained these ramps.

Mr. Leo saw me as he picked up a bowling ball from the automatic ball return and placed it on the other son's ramp. I smiled and thumbed over my shoulder toward the employees. "Those guys said I *have* to talk to your sons!" He smiled briefly, waiting for me to get to the point. I quickly explained that I was on Day 111 of a yearlong cross-country sports road trip, and that I'd be writing a book about my experience. "Would it be all right if I shot some video of your boys bowling and maybe interviewed them on camera? This will definitely be its own chapter." The man's face lit up.

"Whaddaya think, guys?" he asked in a Brooklyn accent. "Do you wanna be in a *book*?" His sons both smiled and nodded their heads. I felt like hugging them. Their father extended a hand and gave me a hearty shake. "Stephen Leo. Merry Christmas!" Turned out that they were just killing time prior to driving to his brother's house in Brooklyn for the Italian tradition of a fish dinner on Christmas Eve.

Matt, the younger brother wearing a red hoodie, gave his father precise instructions on positioning the ramp. Dad then put Matt's pink and purple ball on top. The teen paused before pushing the ball. He left two pins on his roll and then picked up the spare. My jaw nearly hit my feet.

Nick, bespectacled and clad in a grey camouflage sweatshirt, pushed his wheelchair into place. Mr. Leo removed Matt's ramp and replaced it with Nick's. I furrowed my brow at this. "Why don't they just share the one ramp?" I asked, thinking merely of the cost savings. Their old man looked at me like I had a bowling ball for a brain.

"Would *you* share *your brother's* baseball glove?"

I realized that I'd just asked the dumbest question of my life, which was really saying something. "I'm an idiot!" I howled with embarrassed laughter. "No! Under absolutely no circumstances would I ever have shared a mitt with my brother." Suddenly, I stopped thinking of Nick and Matt as handicapped kids who bowled. Now, I just viewed them as kids who bowled.

After I asked Nick to explain how it works, he said, in halting cadence, "We mostly just adjust the ramps accordingly and then move the ball depending on the alley." His father added, "Tell Jamie about the center of gravity." Nick, focused on his next attempt, didn't say anything, so Mr. Leo continued. "The employees at the lane taught us this: the center of gravity is different because there are no holes in the ball." Since the boys can't hold it with three fingers like most bowlers, there is no need for holes. "So, they can move the ball on top of the ramp to where they want the center of gravity, and that affects which way it turns." To me, that sounded a lot harder than normal bowling.

On camera, Nick rolled a ball the color of nighttime sky. Boom! A strike. He waved his left hand, as if to say, "There you go." His father laughed gleefully. "How funny is that? Good shot!" Still videoing, I told Nick, "Come on, man, you gotta give me a thumbs up or something!" The boy got his right arm high in the air, but his left – the weaker of the two – barely lifted off his wheelchair's armrest. But both hands gave me the thumbs up I'd requested. He flashed a big, proud smile.

Dad gave me some backstory. Several years beforehand when the boys expressed their desire to bowl, Mr. Leo sought expert advice on how to approach it. Only, nobody really knew how. "We could find very little stuff on the internet about this." Now, the kids bowl for the Demarest High School team. "Nick is mad at me, " his father told me in an aside, "Because he can't try out for the baseball team." Suddenly, my eyes filled with tears.

On Nick's next frame, he knocked down nine pins before picking up the spare like a pro. "You're on fire," his proud papa cheered. The boys smiled when I said, "You guys are hustlers! I see what's going on, here. You're trying to take my money. I will *not* play you." I thanked the Leos for letting me spend some time with them and, after one handshake and two fist bumps, headed for the door.

At the car, I realized that my Sports Year streak of attending an event with a ref, ump or judge had just ended. The Leo brothers had only been practicing, the bowling equivalent of a pickup basketball game. The streak had ended at 110 days.

I thought I'd be furious or embarrassed or inconsolable. I *was* in pain, but it stemmed from my face hurting from all the smiling. What was an arbitrary streak compared to what I had just witnessed?

Nick and Matt, my surprise Secret Santas, gave me the gift of recognition: we are solely responsible for any limitations placed on us. I didn't expect to cry in public – or anywhere else – on Christmas Eve. But I'm happy to have had the chance to do so. Those construction guys at Maureen's condo complex did me a favor by drilling at eight o'clock in the morning.

The day I had dreaded most in Sports Year turned out to be my favorite – Merry Christmas, indeed.

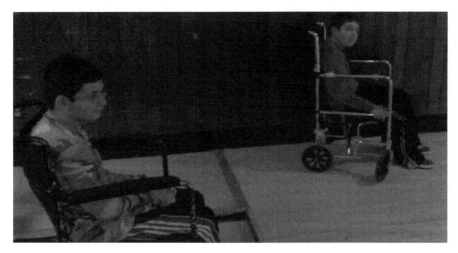

Matt and Nick Leo

DAY ONE HUNDRED AND TWELVE

Wednesday, December 25th. Brooklyn, New York.

As I explained yesterday, I had two NBA games in NYC to choose from today: Knicks and Nets. Once my schedule solidified, I crossed my fingers I'd get to see my favorite team play host in Madison Square Garden. Alas, they didn't tipoff until 2:00, which precluded me from making it to Christmas dinner at my aunt and uncle's in Fairfield, Connecticut. The Nets, the team that used to call New Jersey home but now played in Brooklyn, tipped off against the Bulls at noon.

My father dropped me at the train station for my journey to Brooklyn. Nothing makes me feel more like a Country Mouse than using mass transit. I don't know what my problem is, but I have a long history of missed stops and connections. At the Secaucus Junction station this morning, true to form, I missed my connecting train. It wasn't that I had spent too much time getting coffee or using the bathroom or staring at Twitter. No, I was standing *right there on the tracks* when the train pulled into the station. Only, I was at the wrong end of the train. Instead of, I dunno, looking around and seeing that all the other commuters were boarding fifty yards ahead, I stupidly stood in front of doors that never opened. (Insert: train whistle sound). The train left me behind.

Fortunately, I wasn't the only person who could've used some gingko biloba with his coffee. The Cohens, a family of five from Springfield, New Jersey, had also been futilely pounding on the wrong train doors, yelling in frustration. After successfully boarding the next train, we discovered that we were all heading to see the Nets. Well, since Team Cohen boasted more fans of Chicago than Brooklyn, they were heading to the "Bulls game." We had an enjoyable conversation along the way, and I explained what I'd been doing with Sports Year.

Amy Cohen made my day when she told her three children, "Look at this, kids. You should chase your dreams, just like Jamie." I liked the sound of that. (She and I are Facebook friends.)

We parted ways when they entered the Barclays Center as normal ticket-holding fans do. I still had to scalp a ticket. I nabbed a lower-level ticket with a face value of $77 for only $35. The gentleman had originally asked for one hundred. "Merry Christmas," he said, insincerely, upon completion of our illegal transaction.

Have you ever been to a professional sporting event by yourself? Under normal circumstances, it's an order of magnitude worse than going to a movie solo, but that sense of loser-ness was magnified on Christmas. My holiday spirit continued to fade when I paid $5 for a bottle of water. Bah humbug, Jay-Z! I did, however, perk up when I found my seat next to a guy wearing a yarmulke and drinking a beer. I hadn't realized those two things were allowed to occur at the same time. Chalk up another Sports Year first.

At halftime, I bolted Barclays and boarded a subway to Grand Central Station, where I caught an earlier Metro North train to Connecticut. Walking into the party at Uncle Gerald and Aunt Rosemary's house, I felt like a returning war hero, greeted with enthusiastic shouts and warm hugs.

Later, my mother and I were talking, off to the side of the party. I shared Amy Cohen's comments to her children on the train. Self-deprecatingly, I added, in a faux-maternal voice, "And, kids, if you chase your dreams, then maybe in your mid-40s you'll have to borrow money from your parents, too!"

Mom instantly snuck an arm around my hip, pulled me close and looked up at me. "We are happy to support you chasing your dreams." *Awwww, jeez, Ma.*

Crying two days in a row? Yep.

DAY ONE HUNDRED AND FIFTEEN

Saturday, December 28th. Bronx, New York.

As an alumnus, I truly wished Notre Dame's football team had enjoyed more success this season, which would have translated into playing in a "real" bowl game in Miami or New Orleans or Phoenix. But as a cash-strapped vagabond on an extended stay at his parents' house in New York, I was kinda happy that the Irish's sucking let us fall into the Pinstripe Bowl at Yankee Stadium.

Plus, this way I got to attend the game with my Uncle Gerald, who hosted us on Christmas Day, and two of my cousins, Brian and Mike Reidy. My father, Gerry's brother, chose not join us, claiming in an email that he didn't want to see the lousy matchup. "ND-Rutgers? No thanks!" Just copying and pasting that comment gets me annoyed all over again. But I think Dad's bowing out had more to do with what happened the last time we all attended a Fighting Irish game here.

In November 2010, Notre Dame and Army played in the first college football game hosted by the new Yankee Stadium. My father and I would be tailgating with classmates of mine, as well as my cousin Brian and his booze-smuggling buddies from West Point. As Dad and I drove from my folks' house into NYC for the game, I instructed him to pull into a liquor store so I could pick up some peppermint Schnapps. *Say what?*

I explained the double-seal Ziploc bag trick to him, adding that because of the bitter cold we'd be drinking a lot of hot chocolate inside the stadium. Rich Reidy was normally whip-smart, especially when it came to cocktails, but on this occasion he still didn't follow. "Dad, the Schnapps is *for* the hot chocolate." Ah ha! He found this entire caper to be hilarious. Outside Yankee Stadium, I asked him to serve as the booze mule.

He protested. "Why, because I have more *padding*?" Uh, Roger that. After a brief back and forth, he relented. Inside, we discovered that the location of our seats along the left field line prevented wind from hitting us. So, we actually found ourselves overheated; with no need for hot chocolate to warm us up, we forgot all about the Schnapps.

But, then, sometime during the third quarter, the air around us filled with a delightful peppermint aroma. Fans looked everywhere, trying to locate the source. My father and I didn't put it all together until we got back to our hotel room: he had managed to sit *on* the pocket of his parka that contained the double Ziploc of Schnapps. POP!

Apparently, it's hard to explain to your wife the next day both why a) your clothes reeked of peppermint and b) you needed a new cell phone.

So, yeah, I grudgingly came to see why Dad took a Pasadena on attending today's Notre Dame victory with one of his sons, one of his brothers and two of his nephews.

DAY ONE HUNDRED AND TWENTY

Simsbury, Connecticut. Thursday, January 2nd.

School officials in areas near Hartford, Connecticut, cancelled all scholastic activities today in advance of a blizzard... that never came.

I tried to find an event, I swear. My hosts Chris and Joanie Nelson are still chuckling at me for dragging them to the local hockey rink in the attempt to catch a "drop in" hockey game.

Alas, three players did not a game make. (Note: one dude not pictured.)

Now, I've just gotta double up on some other days in preparation for more cancellations. 365 in 365 is still doable!

<u>DAY ONE HUNDRED AND TWENTY TWO</u>

Saturday, January 4th. Fenway Park.

As I've said before, I'm not a hockey guy. I don't dislike it as much I do – I mean, *did*! – soccer, but I just don't follow it. Since Canada's favorite sport is clearly meant to be seen live, not televised, my exposure to it has been limited.

That said, I could not pass up the opportunity to see a college hockey game played outdoors at a baseball shrine. Talk about an aptly named event.

Even with my bias as a Yankee fan, I think the Red Sox have the big leagues' best ballpark. Since 2009, I've tried to make a pilgrimage each summer. On this trip to Fenway, though, the weather was a little different than usual.

I dressed accordingly. Down below, I wore two pairs of ski socks, a pair of compression shorts, two pairs of ski tights, and jeans. Up top, I sported a turtleneck, three long sleeved compression shirts, a fleece, a sweater, my Gore-Tex ski jacket, a Balaclava, and a ski hat. I also wore two pairs of gloves, just like Lloyd Christmas on the mini-bike.

Yet, I was still shivering thanks to the 10-degree temperature at the 4:00 face off between Merrimack College and Providence College. How chilly was it? The beer taps froze, forcing the concession stands to sell cans. God forbid fans didn't get their beer fix! (I scrapped my original plan to attend the Notre Dame - Boston College game; scholastic pride wasn't gonna keep warm at the 7:30 start.)

For diehard Sawx fans, here's a shot of Pesky's Pole in winter:

My takeaway from today? Outdoor hockey games are worse than televised ones, because it's impossible to follow the puck from your seat. That said, I got the feeling people weren't really attending for the actual hockey game.

Like me, they just wanted to be able to say they'd been there.

DAY ONE HUNDRED AND TWENTY THREE

Sunday, January 5ᵗʰ. Boston, Massachusetts.

One of my oft-stated purposes of Sports Year was to expand my horizons by attending sporting events that I would never normally attend. Today marked the most dramatic departure yet:

Opening day of the US Figure Skating Championships featured the "novice" division, skaters ranging in age from 11 to 15.

Full disclosure: I hate the saying, "If you had told me a year ago that I would be doing _____ I'd have said you were crazy." That said, if you had told me a year ago that I'd be attending opening day – or *any* day – of a figure skating event, I'd have said your cravat was tied too tight and cutting off blood flow to your brain.

Yet, there I was at 9:30 a.m., sitting in the stands with a lot of women, a few husbands (you could tell by the "I better be storing up major credits for this" faces), and what looked to be a number of gay men. But the latter judgment may well have been my presumptions talking.

By the time I arrived, the competitors were all sharing the ice for warm-ups. The loudspeaker played Smash Mouth's signature hit "All Star," which may not have been how the guys in the band pictured the song being used back when they released it in 1997.

Today, I, too, was in for a surprise. I had a freaking blast!

Like hockey, figure skating was much more impressive in person than on TV. Being up close allowed me to hear how physically demanding the sport is; the sound of blades against ice was intimidating. Also, the lack of Scott Hamilton's talking over every move allowed this rookie spectator to simply observe and appreciate what I was seeing for what it was: an incredible combination of athleticism and artistry.

Fortunately, I attended the session featuring "pairs" skating, so I got to see these youngsters work together as a team. Considering the fact that *I* was nervous for them, I can't even imagine what their parents were experiencing. There must be so much pressure on the competitors. The boys, skinnier than the coin toss kids in that Rockwell football painting, performed Herculean feats of strength. Seeing middle school girls with makeup caked on reminded me of photos of Jon Benet Ramsey, which, obviously, wasn't the best mental picture. And the outfits both sexes wore? Chris Hansen and the *To Catch A Predator* crew should set up shop at these events.

Here's a serious question that came to mind: What effect did staring into somebody's eyes for hours on end have on young kids? From 6th through 11th grade I could barely make eye contact with a girl. When skating pairs, these boys and girls hardly ever *broke* eye contact during their entire routines. I wondered if this would benefit them later in life, either dating-wise or in the business world. *Phil is so confident, the way he makes strong eye contact...* Or would it hinder them? *Phil is so creepy the way he's always staring right through you...*

In the stands, nobody spoke. The gallery surrounding the 18th green on Sunday at Augusta is louder than a figure skating crowd. Even during the breaks when the judges are judging, spectators only whisper. I wanted to yell *something*, but my lack of lingo kept me quiet.

When the skaters got close to the boards, it was quite a thrill: would they crash? But I felt guilty for even having thought that. I found myself rooting for all the teams to simply do their best. What a concept.

In Lincoln back in early September, my clueless questions may have ruined the spectating experience for a nice lady at the University of Nebraska's women's volleyball match. Today, a nice lady named Lisa had the misfortune of choosing an empty seat one away from mine. Hey, it was pretty much her own fault; she didn't have to sit near me.

Seconds after she'd settled in, I mentioned in a loud whisper that it looked like the contestants all did the same moves. "That's because they do," she responded. Ah ha! No wonder there were only two categories: Argentine Tango and Viennese Waltz.

Lisa's son was both a skater *and* an ice dancer. I did not realize that those were not the same thing. Her son was not competing today, though. The two of them were there to gauge how much he needed to improve, as well as to hopefully find some new partners. The latter task, she explained, was extremely tough to do. One pair competing today was actually brother and sister. That obviously made coordinating practice time a lot easier than it was for the parents of the team members from northern California, one of whom lived in San Jose and the other in San Francisco. Moms and/or Dads of skaters "are either driving to cold stands or sitting in cold stands," Lisa said.

And that was the exact moment at which figure skating got added to my list of sports the children I did not have would not be allowed to play someday. That was even before Lisa mentioned how crazy expensive skating was: you had to pay for a skating club membership fee, ice time and coaches. Even for a lousy coach, you'd be lucky to pay just $1 per minute. *Puck that noise.* (I realize that joke makes no sense, but I left it in because it still made me laugh.)

This morning I hadn't arrived wanting a drink, and it didn't even occur to me that I might be able to buy one at a juvenile event. After watching the "Bud Light" Zamboni clean the ice, though, I found myself thirsty. But the venue sold no alcohol. Bait and switch! Judging from the tense faces and clenched fists, most of the parents needed to take the edge off. But, the booze ban was probably smart given the fact that these kids certainly didn't need any *Great Santini* moments. (Although it would be pretty funny to see a drunk father bite it on the ice.)

Wowed by the competitors' precision, grace and strength, I would most definitely return to an ice skating event. With a date. And, maybe, a flask.

<u>DAY ONE HUNDRED AND TWENTY NINE</u>

Saturday, January 11th. Manhattan Beach, California.

Exactly one week ago at Fenway Park, all of my clothing layers made my arms stick out like the little brother's in *A Christmas Story*.

Today was a bit different.

Given a choice... I'm picking board shorts and flip-flops.

DAY ONE HUNDRED AND THIRTY THREE

Wednesday, January 15th. Redondo Beach, California.

"You're so full of shit," I said. "On both accounts."

Over drinks last night, my buddy Jim tried to tell me that not only were Luke Walton (two-time NBA champion with the Lakers) and Matt Leinart (Heisman Trophy-winning quarterback at USC) members of his basketball rec league, but those two men played on the *same* team. Jim raised his right hand. "I swear to God. They've got a playoff game tomorrow night."

This blew my mind. I had heard of former pro athletes playing in amateur leagues, when they were, like, old. Retired. Just looking to break a sweat. But Luke freaking Walton and Matt freaking Leinart?! They were 33 and 30, respectively. This, I had to see.

Luke Walton (9) and Matt Leinart

Apparently, I was pretty much the only person who felt that way, since merely one opponent's girlfriend and father joined me in the bleachers. Luke and Matt's team boasted an amusing name for a squad made up of all white guys: Wonder Bread.

Their opponents did not seem nearly as rattled as I had expected them to be. If that had been me out there on the court? Let's just say it would've been tough to D-up with my autograph book in hand. And that is coming from a guy who, as a Notre Dame grad, f'ing hates Matt Leinart. It was all I could do not to stand up and scream obscenities at him about the "Bush Push." Of course, considering the fact USC won that game, I doubt my barbs would've gotten into the head of Mr. Heisman 2004.

Leinart subbed out several times, while Walton never left the floor. That said, the former Laker didn't try to dominate until late, when they trailed by 18. Oh, I'm sorry, did I fail to mention that Wonderbread had been losing since the second minute of the game?

Their opponents, sponsored by Makai, a marketing and events company coincidentally owned by a friend of mine, rained threes like the trailer from *Noah*, with the majority of them dropping. One guy in particular, Pablo, had a game-long "heat check" going, which seemed fitting given that the other two fans were there to root him on. Meanwhile, neither Luke nor Matt could buy a shot from behind the arc. Moreover, the latter got a layup blocked from behind by a dude possessing average athletic ability, prompting me to nearly throw out my back from a joyous air punch. (Leinart is listed as 6' 5". He is the shortest tall guy I've ever seen.)

Once upon a time, I played in this gym, albeit as part of a six-feet-two-inches-and-under league, meaning nobody taller than 6' 2" could play. Eventually I had to quit, though, because my teams – which, as Captain, I had assembled – always sucked. Even worse, nobody went out drinking afterwards. Maybe full court action was too tiring or produced too much body odor, or maybe it was the league's lack of women, I dunno, but nobody ever went to a bar afterwards like we always did in the extremely fun coed flag-football league.

Anyways. Tonight, watching these two famous athletes miss threes in the same gym where I used to miss threes made me feel really good, the equivalent of watching a PGA guy duff a chip at my local muni. *But why the hell would a PGA guy play golf at my local muni?!*

The answer to that question eventually led a part of me to root for Wonder Bread, a turnabout that shook me right down to my flat feet. Whenever I'm not invested in a game, emotionally or financially, I root for the underdog; *obviously*, then, I should have been cheering for the stacked team to suck it. And I did just that for the first 34 minutes.

But then Luke and Matt locked in, two competitors who refused to lose despite their seemingly insurmountable deficit. That's not to say they hadn't been trying to win earlier in the game; such behavior would have been disrespectful to the game, and both men played with total class. This wasn't a case of when you were growing up and the older guys in the neighborhood finally declared, "No more messing around!" before pounding the crap out of you and your little pals after you mistakenly thought you might actually win a game when you were up big.

Walton and Leinart had been trying all along, but something clicked in their brains late in the contest, something tangible. Luke dove for loose balls. Matt, the only defender back on a fast break, fouled the guy hard, ensuring no layup. And, dammit, somehow I started rooting for the pair of former pros to pull off the miracle comeback. Walton hit two threes and Leinart added one; the lead was down to nine with 3:30 to go.

What was more stunning, that Luke Walton and Matt Leinart played on the same rec league team, or that said team *lost*?

Tonight was a victory for competition and camaraderie. Luke Walton played in the NBA alongside Kobe and had two championship rings at home. Matt Leinart starred in front of 94,000 fans at the L.A. Coliseum and had America's most famous sports trophy on his mantel. Each banked millions of dollars in his pro career. Yet, those two guys still came out on a Wednesday night to run with their buddies in a rec league game.

Sports!

Here's the link to the video from the game.

My YouTube video breakdown of the action racked up 17K viewings thanks to BustedCoverage.com posting the video, which was seen by somebody at Bleacher Report, who then reposted it. (Update: now 26K views.)

That was as close to going viral as Sports Year ever got.

DAY ONE HUNDRED AND THIRTY SIX

Saturday, January 18th. Manhattan Beach, California.

Today I caught a 12-year old rec league soccer game. Watching a regular team play, as opposed to a travel team, was an unusual experience. Most of the girls weren't aggressive, and many didn't seem to care who won or lost. The parents still yelled from the sideline, but their voices didn't reflect the stress and tension involved at the travel team level.

But that was actually okay with me, since I was dealing with a ton of internal stress and tension; I had a big job interview ahead of me.

Remember Scott, my chaperone in Nebraska who offered me a sales gig? His boss, the psychiatrist and entrepreneur who started the medical device company for which Scott served as national sales director, invited me to interview with him in San Diego later this afternoon. After the soccer game, I got on the 405 South toward America's Finest City. (I did not make up the nickname; that's what the city calls itself.) In fact, due to time constraints, I attended the youth soccer game in my blue suit, dress shirt, and tie, marking not just a Sports Year first, but a lifetime first. It made me think of black-and-white photos of World Series crowds, when all the fans dressed like that.

"Wally," the CEO, was in SD for a medical conference at the Hotel del Coronado. He invited me down for a grilling, since his initial reaction after Googling "Jamie Reidy" did not fill him with an overwhelming desire to hire me. (Apparently, if your previous employer fired you and then disparaged your morals to the media, it gives future bosses pause.) But Scott had assured him I was the right guy for the job, so Wally grudgingly agreed to judge for himself.

He may have expected me to be nervous; considering I hadn't had a real job in nine years, that was probably a safe assumption. Ever the shrink, he tried to mess with my head by postponing our meeting two hours at the last minute. *He's icing me!* But, little did the good doctor know that I had achieved a Rumeal Robinson-in early-April-of-1989 level of un-ice-ability.

For starters, while "The Del" required a road trip, this wouldn't be an away game for me. Pfizer had hosted two sales meetings there at which I'd, uh, enjoyed myself thoroughly. As the result, the hotel's iconic red roof looked to me like runway lights would look to a pilot in a blizzard. More importantly, in the 17-months since I screwed the PowerPoint pooch at the NYC marketing company, I had been work-shopping how I'd handle my next job interview.

Wally and I sat down to dinner, and I ordered the humble pie. "You know, my mother and father didn't raise me to lie to my bosses and game the system," I began. "They were embarrassed by some of the stuff in my book."

Wally could not hide his surprise. "I'm glad you said that, because I was going to ask about your parents." *Of course you were, Dr. Psychiatrist.*

From there, I explained that I had zero emotional investment during my time at Pfizer. Helping patients with their ear infections, allergies and hard-ons didn't motivate me. Despite being an extremely competitive person, I took no personal pride in my performance and I didn't mind just getting by. For me, it was a job, not a career. Yet, I still finished the year 2000 ranked #1 in the nation.

At Eli Lilly Oncology, however, my attitude changed after I saw the cancer patients who might receive my chemotherapy. Suddenly, I had a mission that motivated me. I worked harder than I ever had, and the results reflected it: my sales partner and I finished my first year ranked #1 in the country. I got promoted to sales trainer, coaching reps who lacked experience or success, or both. I was excelling in that role in March of 2005 when *Hard Sell* came out. Humiliated that one of their cadre wrote the book that pulled back the curtain on the pharma industry, Eli Lilly fired me.

Strangely, getting axed did not hurt my self-esteem. If anything, it fired up my ego to unprecedented heights. Nine years later, self-destructive pride had brought me to the brink of financial disaster. "Wally, I've learned that having a good job is not the worst thing in the world," I said with a self-mocking laugh. Fortunately, he laughed, too. Seizing the opening, I closed him. "Is there anything keeping you from giving Scott the okay to hire me?" Nope.

I drove the two hours back to Manhattan Beach, meeting friends at a bar just before last call. I ordered two bourbons and slammed them, signaling for two more.

Sports Year's closing time was fast approaching, and I wanted to blur that reality.

Jamie Reidy

DAY ONE HUNDRED AND THIRTY SEVEN

Sunday, January 19ᵗʰ. Redondo Beach, California.

Today marked the beginning of a lengthy eastbound road trip, the highlights of which would be the annual Ice Fishing Tournament in Brainerd, Minnesota on January 25ᵗʰ and the Super Bowl in New Jersey on February 3ʳᵈ. First stretch: six hungover hours to Scottsdale. There would definitely be a rest-stop nap in my future somewhere off I-10.

But I needed to catch a quick game before I departed. Didn't care what it was, but I gained a new favorite version of an old sport: six-year old girls' basketball.

My goddaughter Tegan's older sister Ahnika (sucking up alert!) had a game, so I killed two birds with one stone: finally saw her play and checked off my Sports Year event. But I was not prepared for the amount of comedy and adorability. At one point, our coach had to burn a timeout because a player – his daughter – refused to inbound the basketball. After a brief talking to, she relented.

Parents cheered baskets made by both teams. Talk about a love fest!

One big question, though: why have an official referee? Very few fouls were called and, despite the players' frequent failures to even attempt to dribble, no traveling violations were called. Most amazingly, *not one parent* hassled the ref, either. Get paid to watch hilarious and adorable little girls "play" basketball? Now that's a job I could do.

Four hours later I was still grinning like an idiot when I pulled over for my nap.

DAY ONE HUNDRED AND THIRTY EIGHT

Monday, January 20th. Scottsdale, Arizona.

Over the course of my 17,000+ miles on the road, I made plenty of questionable food choices. While I may not have found gas station sushi, like John Krasinski of *The Office* fame narrates in the Esurance TV ad, I *did* choke down gas station sandwiches with illegible "Sell By:___" dates and gas station beef jerky that could've been used to pry the hubcap off a tire rim. Some of those encounters led to, ahem, earlier than scheduled pit stops. On no occasion, however, did one of my cavalier culinary choices leave me within seconds of crapping my pants. Until, that is, I ate breakfast at my best friend's house.

One of my rules for successful freeloading is a paraphrasing of the most famous line from *When Harry Met Sally*, "Have what she's having." If your host announces, "We're having anchovy pizza," unless you are allergic *and* left your Epi-Pen at home, you need to mangia.

Accordingly, after Jenny Rooney, Mike's better half, offered to make me a bowl of her famous organic oatmeal this morning, I smiled and thanked her. But then I rolled my eyes at my buddy. What *happened* to you? Unlike me, the lady of the house took her health – and that of her husband – very seriously; after boiling the organic oatmeal in filtered water, she added organic blueberries, organic bananas, organic light brown sugar, and some soymilk.

Growing up, I loved oatmeal, the instant kind from Quaker Oats, specifically maple brown sugar. One of my mother's cabinets still contains the small, dented pot in which I'd boil the milk like a big boy. When she wasn't looking, I'd add a little syrup to my oatmeal, because I was a rebel like that. As you can imagine, then, the seemingly I.C.U.-approved Rooney version did not appeal to me. But, I ate enough to not be rude.

Hours later, Mike and I hit the Phoenix Coyotes game. (That's an NHL team, btw.) We grabbed beers on our way to the seats that he'd gotten gratis from a friend of his. *Shot, SCORE!* We enjoyed the action from twenty rows up. Well, I should say, Mike enjoyed the action. I listened to the entire second period from my seat in the men's room.

About halfway into beer #2, my belly rumbled ominously. Like a farmer gauging the arrival of rain by the gaps between thunderclaps, I guesstimated I still had an easy twenty minutes before I'd need to do a bathroom-and-beer run. *As if.* Seconds later, I leapt from my seat and did that clenched-ass-cheeks speed walk to the concourse, where I frantically searched for the restroom signs. Thankfully, one stall was unoccupied when I stormed in, forehead sweating like a junkie in need of a fix. Just how perilous was my predicament? I couldn't even spare the time to wipe down the toilet seat first. Ick.

Approximately thirty minutes later, I got a text from Mike inquiring as to my whereabouts and condition. I nearly had to text him back to ask him to come to the men's room and search other stalls to find me more toilet paper.

Please do not, however, think I am blaming my gastrointestinal disaster on my hostess or the meal she kindly served me. Perhaps, after five months of fast food, bad food and countless Diet Cokes, my digestive track had become a den of iniquity that simply collapsed under the virginal purity of Jenny's organic oatmeal.

Maybe next time, though, we can go out for breakfast – my treat.

DAY ONE HUNDRED AND THIRTY NINE

Tuesday, January 21st. Grants, New Mexico.

Today things got silly in a way only Hollywood could have orchestrated.

The schedule called for me to drive 460-miles from Scottsdale to Albuquerque, where I'd stop to see a girls' high school hoops game before crashing in a motel. Then tomorrow I'd drive six hours northeast to Denver, followed on Thursday by a long haul to South Dakota; all of this en route to one my most anticipated events.

After I'd set the original Sports Year schedule with all of the predictable big games and must sees, I did a lot of online searching for goofy sporting contests. My favorite one: the world's largest ice fishing contest in Brainerd, Minnesota. Oh, the questions I wanted answered! How suicidal-ly boring would an ice fishing contest be? Did women compete? How cold was -20 degrees, *really*? Would contestants invite me into their little cabins to warm up? Would that be as creepy as it sounded? I couldn't wait to find out.

Before leaving Scottsdale, I got a forwarded email from my buddy Allan, the guy who tried to get me sponsored at Fox Sports. A friend of his worked as an associate producer on the daytime talk show, *The Doctors*. She had emailed everybody she knew with an invitation for bachelors to apply to appear on an upcoming dating episode. One of the female hosts was single and, despite being an attractive physician, had difficulty meeting suitable guys. So, a dating expert would help her choose between three suitors.

The segment would be taped on Friday, three days from today, in Los Angeles. *This*, I thought, was the kind of pointless thing I would normally drop everything to do. But, seeing as how I was on

Sports Year *and* had no guarantee I'd be chosen for the show, I needed to forget the distraction of TV dating and stick to my plan.

But, still, there was, like, no way I wasn't at least applying, just to see where I stacked up. So, I sent the producer an email with the subject line, "Jake Gyllenhaal played me in a movie." Then I got into the Saab and headed north on I-17, as scheduled.

An hour later, I stopped to gas up in the little town of Black Canyon City. In the men's room, I read a funny note written on the urinal wall. In a goofy mood, and since I was in Arizona, I decided to tweet a picture of the wall at Meghan McCain, who I followed on Twitter. (That was the first and last time I've ever tweeted somebody after reading a bathroom wall.)

Amazingly, the Senator's daughter, who is now a successful TV personality on Fox News, responded quickly.

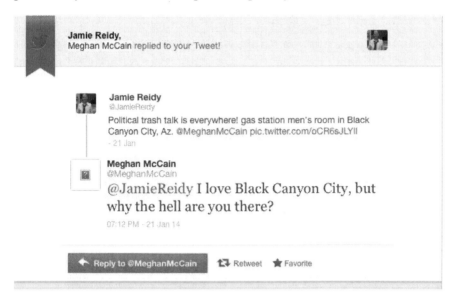

Jamie Reidy,
Meghan McCain replied to your Tweet!

Jamie Reidy
@JamieReidy
Political trash talk is everywhere! gas station men's room in Black Canyon City, Az. @MeghanMcCain pic.twitter.com/oCR6sJLYll
- 21 Jan

Meghan McCain
@MeghanMcCain
@JamieReidy I love Black Canyon City, but why the hell are you there?
07:12 PM - 21 Jan 14

↰ Reply to @MeghanMcCain   ⇄ Retweet   ★ Favorite

Getting a Twitter response from a minor celebrity seemed like a good omen for the TV show. Turned out, it was: the producer from *The Doctors* called me shortly thereafter to tell me I'd been picked.

That news merited a celebratory lunch next door at Chihuahua's, an RV serving up killer burritos with the slogan "Chillin + Grillin." While eating, I got an email from the NBC Sports Network.

Some backstory: on Halloween, Jay Busbee, a cool and funny columnist for Yahoo Sports, interviewed me in Atlanta. (Unrelated: in spring 2016, he published his first book, *Earnhardt Nation: The Full-Throttle Saga of NASCAR's First Family*. #Bestseller.) We met at a crowded Starbucks and hit it off to the point that we both wished we'd scheduled beers rather than coffee. He wondered aloud why I hadn't appeared on NBC Sports Network yet. I told him I wondered the same thing. Jay offered to introduce me to the producers of "SportsDash," a show he'd been on several times. Now, those same producers were asking me to do a TV interview on Thursday. In *Los Angeles*.

This seemed too good to be true. Suddenly, I had a huge decision to make: stick to my plan and attend ice fishing or scrap that whole Midwestern swing (and the subsequent drive to New York; I'd have to fly to the Super Bowl) in order to return to LA for NBC Sports and *The Doctors* dating show.

Who was I kidding? There was no decision to make at all. A successful appearance on NBC Sports Network – "Next up, a writer who's living a sports fan's dream adventure…" – could have led to a fulltime or part-time contributor gig, maybe even a corporate sponsorship. In any of those cases, the money would have enabled me to decline the medical device sales job offer and continue on Sports Year. And the dating episode of *The Doctors*? Well, at the very least it would be a good story.

Although the decision seemed easy, it was not without one major risk: the pump fake. After *Hard Sell* came out, my agent encouraged a friend of hers to write a profile on me for the *Los Angeles Times*. (Afterwards, I sent my agent flowers as a token of appreciation for her manipulating the media on my behalf. I figured that was a no-brainer move. Apparently, not. She thanked me profusely, saying, "No client has ever sent me flowers!" That stunned me, but illustrated two good life lessons: most people in Hollywood suck and sending flowers to a woman is always a good idea.)

The newspaper writer came up with a unique setting for the interview: the Hustler store in Hollywood. She thought it'd be fun to talk with "the Viagra guy" in a porn shop. It ended up being the longest profile any newspaper did on me. (Naturally, my friends busted my balls no end. In fact, Charles Randolph, the screenwriter who adapted my book into the film *Love and Other Drugs* sent me an email, "Look at the media darling!" Five years later when the movie came out, Charles didn't win any awards for his work, unfortunately. But, in 2016, he took home a little statue named Oscar for co-writing *The Big Short.* Amazing what he could do with a quality piece of source material, huh?!)

The day after the piece ran in the paper – June 24, 2005, in case you were wondering, not that I have it memorized, or anything – I got a call from a deliriously happy woman at my publishing house. She had just spoken to the person in charge of booking guests for *The Tonight Show with Jay Leno.* Jay's booker loved the article and wanted to speak with me in order to gauge whether I'd be a good guest on the show. Yes, please! We chatted on the phone for thirty minutes and she laughed a number of times in the right places – always a good sign. I explained that I lived locally and would be ready to hop in the car to shoot up to Burbank any day that summer. She said she'd definitely be in touch. Yeah, no. I never did get invited to sit on Jay Leno's couch.

Now, I worried, would I get let down by NBC again?

Having decided to abort my drive toward the east coast, I got off at the next exit on I-10 in New Mexico and did some Googling for a sporting event that night. I found a girls' basketball game, Grants High hosting Miyamura High. Unbeknownst to me, Grants was a town in Native American reservation country. I'd never even gambled at an Indian casino, let alone spent any time in one of these areas. Walking into the school, I instantly recognized that I was a minority.

I recognized the warm up song, though: "Basketball" by Kurtis Blow. Uh, scratch that; apparently, Bow Wow remade it. Now, I felt whiter *and* older than everyone else in attendance. That tune was followed up by Kid Rock's "All Summer Long," which seemed an odd choice for a sanctioned school event, given the song's celebration of underage drinking, pot smoking, and lovemaking.

The quality of play was sloppy, turnovers and missed layups aplenty. But what the gymnasium lacked in hoops talent it made up for in vocal fans; the family and friends in the stands provided louder and more frequent commentary than I'd experienced at any high school basketball game. Between the first and second quarters, the P.A. system cranked up "The Chicken Dance" song, prompting enthusiastic participation among the fans, myself included. It was strange to see so many ponytails in the stands – on men.

My favorite part of the game involved the gymnasium itself. The baseline wall featured large, framed photos of the girls' and boys' varsity squads; that had to be a cool feeling for an athlete to see his or her picture on the wall every day.

Pinching pennies led me to buy dinner at the concession stand (tastiest hot dogs I'd had so far) and to sleep at a Motel 6. This was just my second Sports Year stay at that chain, far below any pre-trip Over/Under predictions. As I tried to get warm underneath one of those thin, used-to-be-light-brown blankets, I wondered, Why didn't I reach out to Motel 6 for a sponsorship? Not that I would've wanted to crash there often, but corporate HQ might have dug my thrifty effort and given me free stays in exchange for daily social media plugs.

Anyway, the fact that I was just now brainstorming motel sponsorship possibilities 140 days into this endeavor spoke volumes.

DAY ONE HUNDRED AND FORTY

Wednesday, January 22ⁿᵈ. Redondo Beach, California.

The alarm went off at 7:00, but my eyes were already open; such was my excitement and nervousness for the TV opportunities. Plus, although I tried to ignore them, I couldn't shake my misgivings over abandoning the ice fishing in Brainerd. That decision felt treasonous to Sports Year. Sure, the NBC Sports Network interview could end up saving the whole project, but if the segment fell through for some reason, I'd be officially d-o-n-e.

My mood did not improve any when I started the Saab only to be immediately greeted by the dashboard's warning light: low coolant levels. Probably not how you want to begin a 731-mile drive, the majority of which would cover the deserts of Arizona and Joshua Tree. The last time a car of mine required my adding antifreeze during a road trip occurred in Fall Break of my senior year at Notre Dame. Traveling to Palm Beach, Florida, in the creaky Oldsmobile Cutlass Supreme my parents had bought for me, my four buddies and I ignored the driver's manual and subsequently over-filled the coolant tank, causing the Olds to overheat in the Tennessee mountains. (Trying to do the smart thing and still screwing it up; that was the automotive equivalent of hitting an iron off the tee and still losing your golf ball.) I can still feel the engine coughing as 18-wheelers zipped past on our left, horns blaring. We slept in the car, shivering, as the engine cooled throughout the night. This time, however, I made sure to add the coolant exactly as instructed in the owner's manual. And, to be safe, I did 70-MPH from New Mexico to Manhattan Beach.

As I neared Palm Springs at 3:45 in the afternoon, I got this email from the lead producer at NBC Sports Network:

> Just wanted to update you on where we stand here. In

talking with the producers today, I got the impression that this segment, while worthwhile, would be best with a little extra production kick.

We want to get maybe a map of the US and some other elements together to enhance the appearance with you both on the show. That's tough for us to do in 24 hours, so we'd like to postpone until we can do a better job with it.

Hope that's OK and apologies for the late abort. We'll keep you posted on the next best date with a little better notice, but we're definitely still interested and want to tackle this when we get the next chance.

#RecordScratch. Seemingly every nerve ending in my body flared with pain. In my gut I knew that SportsDash wasn't going to get me on the air before the Super Bowl. The Sports Year game clock had officially begun ticking down.

I got off "the Ten" and took the famed Route 66 through Joshua Tree. During an hour-long stretch I only saw four other cars, so it felt like the road was my own. The sun began to set and I thought back to the loneliest times of my life: June 1990, my first week in basic training at Fort Knox, when, with my self-confidence shot, I questioned whether I could successfully do a left face; December 25th, 1994 in Japan, the first time I hadn't been home for Christmas; April 2008, when I was the best man at my brother's wedding but didn't have a date. This moment was worse than all of them.

And I still had to find an event for today. Twice, I got off the road when I saw light stanchions illuminating ball fields off the freeway, but neither park featured an actual game in progress. Finally, I arrived at the same gym where I'd seen Walton & Leinart exactly seven days ago. No pros this time, just a bunch of regular dudes.

What a difference a week made.

DAY ONE HUNDRED AND FORTY TWO

Friday, January 24th. Hermosa Beach, California.

I filmed a dating TV episode today, words I never expected to type. Unfortunately, I'm contractually prohibited from writing about what a shit show it was behind the scenes of *The Doctors*. But I wish I could file a lawsuit for television malpractice.

There were two other contestants: Mark, a cool lawyer and Krav Maga instructor, and Grant, a standoffish actor who looked like a hipper version of Ross from *Friends*. Reminiscent of *The Dating Game*, we sat on stools next to each other. The studio audience could see us, but the soon-to-be-lucky-lady Dr. Jennifer Berman and her romance coach – Patti Stanger "The Millionaire Matchmaker" – could not. The announcer read brief descriptions of us, based on info we'd emailed the producer yesterday.

Imagine my surprise when I was presented as "a former male sexual dysfunction sales rep." (Can you even sell sexual dysfunction?) WTF? In my email to the producer I had described myself as a writer who published the book that served as the basis for the movie *Love and Other Drugs*. Apparently, though, that description would not have made the studio audience groan loudly enough or made Dr. Berman cringe in horror sufficiently. Need I tell you that I did not get chosen? (She picked Grant, the actor. Mark and I are still Facebook friends.) The episode was scheduled to air three weeks later on Valentine's Day. Quite an experience, to say the least. But, at least I'd have a story I could tell forever.

And the taping ran way late, taking my planned sporting event out of play. Fortunately, a public gym in Hermosa Beach hosted basketball games every night. After arriving, my first stop was the men's room – to make sure I had washed off all the makeup from the show. Then, I caught seventh grade boys' hoops.

I wonder if anybody watching the game noticed the somber man siting in the bleachers barely watching the action on the court. My forgoing the ice fishing in Brainerd turned out to be a total waste of time and effort. Instead of experiencing a sport and culture for the first time, I got embarrassed on one national television program and lost the chance to shine on another.

I got drunk tonight. By myself. Just the third time in my life I'd done so; the other two occurred after particularly painful breakups. But today felt worse than a breakup. It felt like a terminal diagnosis.

Dead man walking, er, driving.

DAY ONE HUNDRED AND FORTY FIVE

Monday, January 27ᵗʰ. Torrance, California.

Kinda surprising that it took me so long to hit a junior college sporting event. Today I thoroughly enjoyed the El Camino College softball team's Opening Day game. The host Warriors easily beat the L.A. Valley College Monarchs 7-2.

After I started Little League, my father demanded that I sprint to first base after drawing a base on balls, as opposed to merely jogging. Rich Reidy got that, of course, from Pete Rose's playing style, which "Charlie Hustle" got from *his* old man. Throughout my athletic career, regardless of the sport, I continued hustling during practices and games, a trait that delighted coaches and annoyed teammates. "Jamie Reidy's hustling. Why aren't *you*?" I always appreciated coaches who established standards and then held their athletes accountable if they failed to meet them.

With that background, it will not surprise you to learn that one of my favorite Sports Year moments occurred *after* today's softball game had ended.

While the losers huddled up for a lecture from their coach, the *winners* lined up in the outfield to run seven wind sprints; one for every mental error they'd made.

Now *that's* coaching!

DAY ONE HUNDRED AND FORTY SEVEN

Compton, California. Wednesday, January 29th.

Today marked my first ever visit to Compton. As I rolled east on the 105, this momentous occasion prompted me to mentally catalog the number of rap songs to which I knew at least half the lyrics.

But I stopped the exercise once I realized that the first five were by Will Smith, Tone Loc and Young MC. Could I *be* any whiter? Jesus, even Mormon guys my age probably had more street cred than me. Scrambling to recover, I found Dr. Dre's "G-Thang" on my iPhone and put it on repeat.

Centennial High's girls' soccer team hosted El Segundo High, a school just ten minutes from my apartment in Manhattan Beach. What was up with my traveling to predominantly minority-attended schools to unwittingly catch white teams in action?

It embarrasses me to admit that I had doubts about my personal safety in this neighborhood. Those concerns were only exacerbated when I couldn't figure out how to get into the school's parking lot. Seriously. I circled the large block several times without finding the damn entrance. I felt like I was losing my mind. Finally, I gave up, driving to the back of school property, which had a view of the soccer field. I parked there.

As I exited the car in gorgeous sunlight, I pondered if this was the dumbest and most dangerous thing I'd done during Sports Year, let alone my entire life. Wasn't hard to imagine word spreading quickly through the neighborhood that an idiot was just begging to be separated from his wallet and car. I stood outside the heavily fortified fence and began watching the sparsely attended contest, which was played on the football field. Forgetting my fears for a moment, I thought, "No head football coach I've ever met would be cool with letting the soccer team use his field."

I moved as fast as I could without actually sprinting, probably resembling a jeans-clad race walker in the Special Olympics. Once inside school grounds, I used yoga breathing techniques to get my heart rate under control. Eventually, I spotted cars pulling into and out of the parking lot. WTF? After a moment, I realized that I'd missed the entrance because the visiting team's bus had parked right at the edge of it, obscuring the opening from my view.

I watched the soccer game from the track. A kick sailed out of bounds, a few yards away from me. In a Sports Year first, I got to throw the ball back to the referee, who handed it to an El Segundo player. Seven seconds after her inbound pass, the visitors scored a goal. Sorry for the jinx, Centennial High!

After the match, I walked back to my car, my head on a constant swivel looking for bad guys who, of course, never appeared. None of my racist fears came to fruition; I didn't get jumped and my car wasn't up on blocks, missing four tires.

Driving home, I realized that the only time I'd been victimized during my journey was in a *wealthy* neighborhood in freaking Indiana.

DAY ONE HUNDRED AND FORTY EIGHT

Thursday, January 30th. *New York City.*

Today I flew to NYC for Super Bowl weekend. I felt incredibly fortunate to have gotten a *free* ticket to the big game from a friend with connections.

My schedule called for me to attend a girls' basketball game at 4:00. So, after landing at JFK, I schlepped my luggage straight to High School of the Performing Arts. *"Remember my name – FAME!"*

But when I arrived at the, uh, renowned school, a security guard told me I could not enter the gymnasium. He explained that New York City's legendary Public School Athletic League (PSAL) had recently instituted new rules governing spectators. Only the home team's family and students could attend a game; no visitors allowed. In other words, parents could never see their children compete on the road. This seemed crazy to me. What a shame that security concerns forced such a drastic move.

More important to me than the collapse of civil society, however, was the fact that now I had no game to watch. Standing on the corner of 46th and 6th, I Googled *private* high schools in midtown Manhattan. Bingo – the Xavier HS frosh boys' basketball team had a game. This actually marked the second time I'd caught a game there; in December I watched the varsity boys' hoopers. When I get myself out of debt, I will be sending Xavier High a donation.

Tonight I met three buddies – John, Terry and David – for dinner and drinks in Times Square. Normally, we would have avoided NYC's biggest tourist trap, but we picked it expressly for the primo people-watching at the "Super Bowl Boulevard," an exposition and experiential area set up by the NFL on Broadway between 34th and 47th Streets. Predictably, thousands of fans flocked there. No question,

Seattle fans outnumbered Denver fans. "It'll be interesting to see how that plays out on Sunday," one of my buddies commented.

After dinner, we hit a dive bar before dropping into an upscale place (the name of which, none of us can recall). At the coat check, Terry looked at me and cracked up. "At one of the hippest joints in all of Manhattan, you're clearly the guy from out of town!" Apparently, among the array of expensive winter coats, my bulky red, white and black ski jacket stood out. My protests that it was 16-degrees out did nothing to stem the tide of insults.

Each of these guys is a married father; two of them long ago ceded control of their weekends to travel soccer or travel hockey schedules. The entire concept – and conceit – of Sports Year left them shaking their heads in wonder. At different points during the night, each of them looked at me with envy. *I wish I could get in the car and just leave it all behind for a while.* They encouraged me to share stories: highlights, lowlights, funny fiascos. Late in the evening, I admitted that the Super Bowl would be Sports Year's last event. When I began mocking myself for only completing 151 days, my friends instantly objected.

"Are you even serious?!"

"Dude. You made it *five months*!"

"That's unreal, regardless. You should be proud of yourself."

John, Terry and David toasted me again and again. Their efforts worked a little; I didn't feel like as much of a total fucking loser as I had when the night began.

Hopefully, I thought, with some distance I'll be able to see that Sports Year wasn't a complete failure. Hopefully I'll be able to see this all wasn't a waste of time.

DAY ONE HUNDRED AND FORTY NINE

Friday, January 31ˢᵗ. New York City.

After a laaaaaate night, I didn't wake up until 2:30. On my Facebook page, I posted, "The main problem with sleeping so late is that it throws off your eating schedule for the rest of the day." This drew the following response from my friend Mark in Colorado: "For anyone who is a parent, I say 'fuck you.'" *That* got my day off to a good start.

Having learned my PSAL lesson yesterday, I only searched online for private school games this afternoon. And I found a winner! A renowned singing institution – St. Thomas Choir School – had a 7th grade boys' hoops game.

Not hard to see that music takes a high priority here:

(Basketball court next to orchestra room at St. Thomas Choir School.)

You know how theaters and opera houses have those balconies along the sides? This gym was so small that it had no fan seating courtside; instead, I caught the basketball action from a balcony, where adoring younger students actively cheered.

One boy stood out from his peers for his especially supportive exhortations. After a missed layup, he yelled, "You'll get 'em next time!"

C'mon, dude, are you ASKING to get wedgied?! Not even my mother ever yelled anything so ridiculous, and she used to count out loud along with my steps as I ran the high hurdles in high school, "One, two, three – JUMP! One, two, three – JUMP!" But this wasn't a middle-aged woman unconsciously rooting on her son. This was a middle school boy sounding a lot like a girl with a major crush.

"You'll get 'em next time!" Instinctively, I cringed and turned away from the tsunami of scorn that was undoubtedly about to swamp that sweet and stupid youngster. Even anti-bullying advocates would have to agree, "He kinda had it coming to him."

Yet, nobody mocked or punched him. His underwear remained intact.

Nice kids? That might have been my best game souvenir.

DAY ONE HUNDRED AND FIFTY

Saturday, February 1st. Tappan, New York.

My brother Pat drove up from south Jersey to meet me at our folks' house. So I took the bus from the city to join everybody. Well, really I just wanted to see my nephew Danny, whose vocabulary was increasing daily.

Fortunately, the Rockland County wrestling championships were being held today. (Haven't heard of Rockland? You've likely heard of Westchester County. Rockland is the redheaded stepchild across the Hudson River on the New Jersey side. But we don't have a chip on our shoulders or anything.) My father picked me up at the bus stop and drove me over to Tappan Zee High School. I asked him if he remembered the last time he'd been in a gymnasium. After some memory searching, he decided it had been twenty years ago to watch Pat wrestle during his freshman year. Wow.

In the gym, I ran into Jimmy Kelly, a high school buddy, whose son James was the top seed at 99-pounds. Jimmy hadn't wrestled in school; he played soccer and scored beers from a deli that served underage kids. Naturally, he became NYPD. I got to see his son pin his semifinals opponent in less than a minute. I spent most of that brief match watching Jimmy watch James.

At that point, I realized that one of my favorite parts of Sports Year had been getting to witness my friends cheering on their children, seeing the parental potpourri of nervousness and enthusiasm, dread and encouragement, satisfaction and resignation. But it was their helplessness that always resonated with me the most. Mothers and fathers could only look on, powerless to aid their kids. I'd never noticed that before I started the trip. Now, I always look for it.

I experienced my own feeling of helplessness as my father and I tried to leave. The doors out of the gym sat between two big sets of bleachers on the wall opposite where we'd been sitting. It was impossible to miss these doors. Or so I thought. On our way out, Dad walked right past them. I chuckled a bit before calling to him. But he couldn't hear me over all the cheering. I watched in panic as Rich Reidy continued walking into a corner of the gym. No doors. But he didn't immediately notice his mistake. Instead, he searched for a bit before the mental tumblers finally clicked. He turned around, shaking his head before making eye contact with me and grinning sheepishly.

Why had I panicked? Mental illness runs in the paternal side of our family (along with, in no particular order, diabetes, hypertension, heart disease, alcoholism, pancreatic cancer, colon cancer, and male pattern baldness. #GeneticLotteryWinner). So, I am hypersensitive to any signs of dementia. Of course, simply walking past the exit doors was not in and of itself symptomatic of mental illness. The gym, crowded and noisy, could have disoriented lots of people. Plus, Dad had never even been there before.

But, still, seeing him struggle, even if ever so briefly, hit me with the force of a body slam. In the car, I started nervously babbling about my high school wrestling career; specifically, winning in the district semifinals to guarantee my first trip to the regionals. My father instantly beamed at the memory. "I was sitting in the front row. And after you won I stood up and yelled, 'YEAH! YEAH!'"

I gaped at him. That was exactly what had happened on a Saturday morning in late February of 1988. Faint sunshine lit the sleepy gym, which had yet to fill to capacity. Dad sat in the front row close to my mat. I took an early lead in my 145-pound match and hung on for a close win. "YEAH! YEAH!"

Rich Reidy's outburst echoed throughout the quiet space. Good Lord, did that embarrass me. But then I looked over at him and saw how irrepressibly goddamn proud he was. That made me so goddamn proud.

Today, sitting in his passenger seat, I felt that pride again. "You yelled so damn loud, Dad!" He simply nodded with a modest smile. *Of course I did.*

Same guy: within ten minutes he both got lost in a gymnasium and made his son's day. I reminded myself that I was lucky that I get to observe my parents as they age; a lot of people don't have that luxury.

We drove home and played with Danny for a few hours. My brother Pat is a tremendous father, relaxed yet attentive, forceful yet patient. I watched him parent and I watched *Dad* watch *him.*

I saw that same irrepressible pride on my father's face.

DAY ONE HUNDRED AND FIFTY ONE

Sunday, February 2$^{nd.}$ East Rutherford, NJ.

During my original Sports Year planning, I assumed my Super Bowl ticket would be both the most difficult and most expensive to acquire. I was wrong on both counts, thanks to that fact that I invited myself to the game.

Leading up to the NFC Championship between the 49ers and Seahawks, my group of buddies at the beach got a kick out of the fact that two of us – Dave and Jim – hailed from San Francisco and Seattle, respectively. There was no chance they'd be watching the game together. On the Monday before the clash, I met some of the guys out for drinks in Hermosa Beach. At some point in the revelry, our friend "Adam" began telling a story just as I excused myself to use the bathroom.

When I returned, I noticed that Jim glowed, happier than I'd ever seen him. And Adam had a "Who's a better friend than me?!" grin. *Uh, so, guys, what'd I miss?* Jim explained that Adam had just shared a big treat for either Dave or Jim: whichever guy's team won the NFC got a *free* pair of tickets to the Super Bowl! As an executive at his company, Adam had the perk of receiving two free tickets to the big game at Met Life Stadium in New Jersey. But he actually had a spot in a luxury box, too, meaning he could give up the extra tickets. We all knew that if San Fran won, Dave would no doubt take his father as his guest. But Jim didn't have anybody in mind to bring with him.

At least, he hadn't mentioned any names in the three seconds that elapsed between the story and my blurting out, "Jimmy, you'll give me your extra ticket, right?!"

Jim, the hoopster responsible for the Luke Walton-Matt Leinart scoop, is one of the nicer people on the planet. If one of my friends had pulled my stunt on *me*, I'd have directed that rude, self-centered cheapskate to stubfuckinghub.com. Instead, Jim graciously offered me his extra ticket to America's premier sporting event. Instantly, I became a big Seahawk fan.

Two weeks later, we found ourselves in NYC on Super Bowl Sunday. Unfortunately, both of us were listed as Questionable on the Injury Report with, as Al Michaels might've said, "stomachs." Jim had caught a flu so debilitating that he nearly didn't get on his Friday night redeye flight from LAX. In fact, after arriving at his midtown hotel, he stayed in bed for twenty-four hours. My tummy trouble had less of an innocent history, traced directly to the late night cocktails forced on me by my evil cousin Brian. I crashed on his couch until 11:00 a.m., which would have made me late to meet Jim, except he wasn't in a hurry to hang out at Met Life Stadium for six hours. Of course, we wouldn't have been allowed in, anyway.

Due to concerns about terrorist attacks, the first "New York" Super Bowl (which was being played in New Jersey) was also the first to ban tailgating in the parking lots. In fact, only a very few special guests were even allowed to drive their personal cars to the game. Taxis and limos were prohibited. You want to walk to the stadium? Take a hike. NFL and civic officials urged attendees to utilize mass transit and to arrive early, hopefully preventing a logjam at the stadium's gates as kickoff approached.

Jim and I rendezvoused at Penn Station, underneath Madison Square Garden, to catch the train. It was tough to tell which of us looked worse. Fifty people stood in line ahead of us for the train ticket machine, every one of them sporting blue and orange or green, blue, and gray (aside from me in my red and black ski jacket, of course). I spoke with a lucky Seahawk fan wearing a vintage #10 jersey, made famous in the 1970s and early 80s by Jim Zorn, the quarterback for the expansion franchise's first eight years of existence. This guy in Penn Station explained that last night he just happened to see the lefty legend walking on a street in midtown. Jim Zorn actually signed the back of the jersey. How cool is that?

After buying our train tickets, we headed down the escalators to the track. But before we could board, NJ Transit workers checked to make sure every passenger had an official Super Bowl ticket. Security was clearly a top priority. The journey required a transfer at Secaucus Station, just across the Hudson River in New Jersey.

While attempting to transfer train lines inside *that* station, we ran into a dreaded logjam. The sticklers at NJ Transit required every passenger to insert his train ticket through the teeny slot in the turnstile. On normal days, this wasn't a big time suck, since regulars had the whole process down pat. But on Super Bowl Sunday, the overwhelming majority of passengers were from out of town, unfamiliar with the turnstile process. You can probably picture the people fumbling for the train tickets beneath their winter coats. *Is it in this pocket? That pocket?* The fact that many fans had already had already begun their pre-partying did not aid the ticket insertion process. We stood in line without moving for forty-five minutes. Forty-five *sweaty* minutes.

Outside of a terrorist attack, the NFL's biggest concern in holding its tent pole event near New York City during the first week of February was a blizzard. You know, like the one predicted in the *2014 Farmer's Almanac*. A snowstorm would have been disastrous on three levels: fans getting to the game late due to traffic, fans freezing their wealthy asses off at the game, and fans at home tuning out due to a sloppy, low scoring contest. Oh, did I mention that MetLife Stadium is an *outdoor* facility, i.e. not a dome? Yeah, so the NFL brass woke up nervous today. Miraculously, though, Mother Nature giftwrapped a flurry-free and unseasonably warm day: 50-degrees at lunchtime. But very few people had dressed for the, relatively speaking, balmy conditions. Maybe, like me, they distrusted the meteorologists and expected the weather to suddenly turn cold after kickoff. Hence, the preponderance of parkas I mentioned earlier.

The hundreds of us packed together inside Secaucus Junction station would've gladly sniffed a nose guard's jockstrap in exchange for 50-degrees. Having planned for typical winter conditions, the building's manager had set the thermostat to combat cold. In addition, the room temperature rose sharply thanks to the hordes of people and their winter clothes. Despite the fact that some passengers fainted and required medical attention, the building's staff apparently could not turn on the air conditioning because they did not have access to the thermostat. So, we all roasted. I worried about Jim, who had begun looking flu-ier than before. His black hair glistened with sweat. Everybody in the station took off their coats, and many people disrobed down to their shirtsleeves. In a classic New Jersey move, one guido stripped all the way down to a white tank T-shirt.

The heat, however, could not scorch the fans' enthusiasm for their teams. Seattle supporters broke into what I learned was their standard chant, where one fan yells, "Sea!" and everybody else screams "Hawks!" For a mind-numbingly simple cheer, it proved surprisingly rousing. Denver devotees then responded with a straight-from-third-grade, "Here we go Broncos, here we go!" clap-clap. Based on that routine, alone, I should have called my bookie and placed Sports Year's first and only bet, a large wager on the NFC champs.

Since nobody had anticipated a nearly hour-long delay in getting to the stadium, very few people had beers with them. One Broncos fan with a Bud Light "tall boy" could have starred in a TV commercial, as restless riders drooled in envious thirst. I asked him how much money it would take for him to part with his can of beer. "$250," he quickly replied, as if he had already asked himself that question. Under the circumstances, I wouldn't have been surprised if somebody paid up.

Finally, a smart NJ Transit employee made the command decision to let every passenger through the turnstiles without having to insert her train ticket first. For a brief time, we were all happy again, staggering into the fresh air on the platform like Tim Robbins into the rain at the end of *Shawshank*. Alas, unlike Andy Dufresne's exhilaration, ours was short-lived.

Remember all that emphasis on security? Various police agencies ran us through a gantlet to get into the stadium. In a waiting area the size of an airplane hangar, we stood in a line that snaked back and forth until we reached the frisking zone thirty minutes later. The powers that be did kindly blast music to keep us entertained. Interestingly, all of the artists that I heard – Billy Joel, Lady Gaga, Beastie Boys – hailed from New York City. *Psst! NFL! Your Super Bowl was being played in New freaking Jersey. No Springsteen or Bon Jovi?!* Lastly, we passed through a TSA-style metal detector. Finally free to do whatever we wanted, Jim and I headed for a beverage stand. Standard operating procedure called for an immediate beer purchase. Not today; my first job was finding my ailing buddy several bottles of water. *Then* we got me a $16 Super Bowl draft beer.

Our seats were in the upper deck directly behind the Seahawks end zone. Did you know that Super Bowl attendees got a swag bag? Neither did we. It contained ear muffs, Kleenex and other stuff we did not need, thanks to the temperature that never dipped below 40-degrees. The gift bag doubled, however, as a much appreciated seat cushion.

We sat next to a Denver fan with a shaved head that displayed a Bronco tattoo. Like, the team logo *was inked into* his scalp. That was the most team spirit I'd seen during Sports Year. A Seattle fan sitting across the aisle from us looked like Mr. T, only with a Mohawk dyed blue and green and a costume designed by Ziggy Stardust.

MetLife Stadium seats 82,500 people. The NFL allocates 17.5-percent of those tickets for each team, meaning at least 14,500 Seattle and 14,500 Denver fans would be at the game. (The rest of the tickets go to corporations, friends of the league, etc.) Obviously, there is a big after-market for scalped tickets. I don't know how Seahawk fans managed it, but they were nearly as loud as the 80,000 LSU fans at the game I saw in Death Valley.

Seattle kicked off toward the end zone right below us. On the game's first play, the Denver center snapped the football before Peyton Manning was ready, leading to a safety, which led to Jim's jumping higher than any flu-stricken person really should have been able to jump. From that point on, the Super Bowl was a super bash for Seahawk fans. My highlight, however, occurred at halftime. It's not like I developed a Man Crush on Bruno Mars or anything. But I may have downloaded six of his songs the next day.

Perhaps buoyed by Mr. Mars's sensational singing and dynamic dancing, Denver fans appeared still hopeful for their team's chances. Then the Seahawks returned the 2nd half kickoff for a touchdown. Poof! Any sense of optimism vanished like orange smoke. Jim just kept shaking his head in disbelief at his team's good fortune. And the poor guy couldn't even enjoy a celebratory beer. I struggled to decipher if he was delirious from the football or the flu, but his smile may have caused new permanent dimples. As we prepared to exit after the 43-8 romp, he quipped, "This reminds me of the preseason game when we beat them 40-10." Jim *had* placed a pre-game call to his sports investment counselor. Ka-ching!

Our grins vanished post-game, once the Public Address announcer spoke some ominous words: "Do not leave the stadium." Thanks to tens of thousands of fans attempting to take the train (as the authorities had f'ing instructed everybody to do), the system bogged down. Hence, NJ Transit suspended train service. *You mean, we had significant delays getting into the stadium and now we will have significant delays getting home???* Many people were hoping the suspensions resulted from the chief of NJ Transit committing suicide by jumping in front of one of his trains. Stuck, Jim and I hung out at a food court-type area inside the stadium. Fortunately, Verizon had installed a charging station, so we waited in line to juice up our iPhones. Unfortunately, the concession stands were not allowed to reopen; that hurt their bottom lines, as the hundreds of us sitting around would've gladly purchased over-priced food and beers, either celebrating or grieving.

My third favorite moment of the day, behind Jim's happiness and Bruno's set, happened on our walk out. We spotted a guy wearing a vintage #55 Brian freaking Bosworth jersey. For the unfamiliar, The Boz had an infamously poor talk:walk ratio. Yet, nearly twenty years after the middle linebacker exited the NFL with his mullet between his legs, here was this fan rocking a Boz jersey on the biggest day in Seattle sports history. I just *had* to catch up to him. When I did, I asked him why he was repping a nadir in team history. "You gotta remember the bad times to appreciate the good," he explained. I felt so grateful for that unexpected insight. SEA... HAWKS!

The iconic American sporting event proved to be as exhilarating as I'd expected, but equally as exhausting. I recommend everybody attend the Super Bowl once; but, unless your team is playing, do not spend your own money – it's just not worth a ticket that costs $900 or more, plus food and drink.

Three hours after the final whistle, Jim and I boarded our train. By the time we got to the city at 1:30 a.m., he declared himself ready for a victory drink. I immediately alerted Adam, our ticket fairy.

At a midtown saloon, my two buddies called for a bourbon toast. "To Sports Year... 151 days... It was a helluva run, Reidy!"

I clinked glasses, made eye contact with them and drank. But I couldn't help wondering, Was it, really?

HE SHOOTS… HE MISSES?

(The following was my final entry in the Sports Year's Tumblr page. Some of this information you, dear reader, already know.)

Wednesday, February 26th. Manhattan Beach, California.

I can't believe it's been more than three weeks since I attended my last sporting event: the Super Bowl.

How is it possible that in all that time I have yet to explain why I shut down Sports Year on Day 151? Please accept my apologies for the delay. I've written several drafts of this, but I haven't been able to bring myself to actually post it. Basically, I've been struggling with embarrassment.

I didn't even get halfway through the year. #Fail. Six months would've been okay; I coulda lived with that. But 151 days? (I don't even drink rum.) 151 days just seems lame. But I've discovered that living with crushing debt is lamer.

I've got unshakable faith in myself. Well, maybe I should say that I *used to* have unshakable faith in myself. My failure to complete this journey has left me a bit rattled. But when I began, I was absolutely certain that a corporate sponsor would swoop down and support me. I didn't need big money; just enough to keep me going. Sadly, I failed to crack the social media code, and as a result, failed to garner interest from sponsors. Pro-tip: Starting a yearlong journey in debt is a really good way to incur a lot more debt.

Which is why I had to shut down Sports Year and get a job. Both parts of that sentence hit me like liver punches. But there are worse fates in life than working.

Fortunately, on Day 2 of the trip I met the national sales director for a medical device company, and he offered me a gig. Part of me felt like a loser in having to slink back into the sales world, but the majority of me was pretty freaking psyched that someone was willing to give me another shot. After all, I wrote the book that should have led to a lifetime ban from the medical industry. So I'm wearing my sales hat again; it's a little loose – I've lost a lot of hair since 2005 – but it feels good.

Know what feels even better? Looking back on what I experienced during my short-lived 151 days on the road.

On Christmas Eve, I pulled into a bowling alley parking lot caring only about seeing some people knocking down pins so I could keep the streak alive. Forty-five minutes later, I left with a better understanding of determination. That's what happens when you meet a pair of teenage brothers who bowl in their wheelchairs.

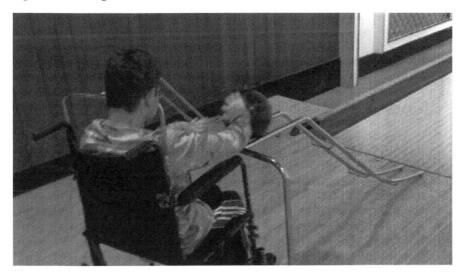

Despite their degenerative muscle disease, they compete for their high school team. Talk about an early Christmas present to me.

If you get the chance, go watch the Wounded Warrior Amputee Softball team enjoy their time on the field like they don't have any problems at all.

You'll leave marveling at the resiliency of the human spirit and a renewed appreciation for how good you've got it.

During my 151 days I discovered women's sports. Yes, I realize how stupid that sounds. But I'd previously hardly seen any, so I'm thrilled to say that I met my pre-trip goal of attending 45% female events. *A goal! I actually achieved one of my goals!!!* If not for Sports Year, I would remain oblivious to the fun and bon homie found at women's games, not to mention the competitiveness and physicality on the fields and courts. Plus, I found a new favorite sport: women's indoor volleyball.

I took five wounded veterans to games on their sports Bucket Lists. Statistically, this was a ginormous fail; I had hoped to average one per week, yet I barely mustered one per month. On the plus side, I made new friends and I helped some men forget their troubles for a few hours. Specifically, one soldier and his grandfather – lifelong Packer fans – attended their first game at Lambeau Field.

In another case, spending the day with me resulted in LSU baseball honoring an ex-soldier for his service and sacrifice prior to a home game on Sunday February 23, 2014. I wish I could've been there in person to see his face when the crowd – the fans with whom he has seen countless games over the years – gave him a standing ovation.

On a less tangible level, I learned that my story inspired people. Very few adults can drop everything and try something as crazy (foolish? Stupid?) as attending a different sporting event every day for a year in all fifty states. Even those who questioned my sanity and/or intelligence shared their envy or expressed their admiration for my breaking the pattern and chasing a dream.

Worst case? I had a freaking blast watching sports every day for 151 days, making new friends and reconnecting with old ones all across the country. Watching my buddies watch their kids play proved to be both more mind bending and more fun than I had anticipated.

Best case? I learned some important things about myself, things I probably should've discovered a long time ago. #SlowLearner. What are they? Well, you'll have to wait for the book to find out. Yep, despite my inability to come close to completing Sports Year, a literary agent is still very interested in working with me on the book. Apparently, trying and failing but landing on my feet makes for a more compelling story than merely succeeding would have done. So, I've got that going for me, which is nice. (RIP Harold Ramis)

Being off the road, it's strange to have uninterrupted quiet all day long. In this age of Twitter, I find myself missing tweets of a different variety: those from a referee's whistle.

Thank you to everyone who hosted and fed me and gave me tickets; I'm forever indebted to you. Thanks also to those who followed along on my journey on Facebook and Twitter.

I hope I gave you all something to cheer about.

- Jamie

EPILOGUE

Friday, November 25, 2016. Hermosa Beach, California.

Jeez. I guess taking three weeks to write a "Sorry I had to quit" Tumblr post seems Usain Bolt-fast in comparison to taking nearly three years to write the Sports Year book.

Can't blame that gap on a rainout or a car problem. I've simply been busy with real life: working my sales job and working on myself. Real life, as you undoubtedly know, sometimes requires the shifting of priorities. My writing got a DNP-Coach's Decision for a few seasons.

Ironically, Sports Year – my desperate escape from adulthood – expedited my return to reality. My "problems" were all self-inflicted, and they had an easy solution: get a fucking job. Pretty much every other adult on earth has to have a regular gig, but somehow that was beneath me? I have no idea where that came from. Rich and Loretta Reidy certainly didn't raise me to think that way.

Eight days after Sports Year's premature conclusion, I found myself in Lincoln, Nebraska, at sales training for Scott's medical device company. One week later I put on a suit and tie for something other than a wedding or funeral for the first time in nine years. Then I did something I swore in 2005 that I'd never do again: entered a doctor's office carrying a pleather bag full of marketing materials that touted a product's effectiveness.

And, you know what? I was okay with that.

When I climbed into the Saab on September 3, 2013, I was operating under the assumption that lightning would strike again for me, just as it had in the form of *Love and Other Drugs,* because, well, I was Jamie Reidy! Yeah, no. That didn't happen.

Failing at Sports Year dislodged me from my longtime perch atop the Hubris Tree. On the way down, I hit every branch face-first, knocking the cataracts of conceit from my eyes. Thank God. Now, I can see clearly the many opportunities I squandered due to arrogance. I recognize that I took success for granted. I expected people to help me, even though I hadn't respected the craft of writing and hadn't put in the necessary work. I'd call myself the world's oldest Millennial, but that would unfairly insult a lot of younger people.

I'm still in debt, but I'm steadily chipping away at the mountain. And I'm still driving the Saab (and still annoying the people behind me in parking garages).

In another example of winning from losing, my failing at Sports Year also led to my falling in love! Scott's company gave me a sales territory covering all of California. The CEO couldn't understand why I was spending so much time in the Bay Area, when the data suggested doctors in SoCal were more likely to buy our medical device. Uh, Amy lived in San Francisco. Those extra trips north may not have resulted in sales, but they did land me a life partner. Had I been driving around the country attending a different game every day, Amy never would have taken me seriously. Today, we share a bungalow at the beach. Someday, we're gonna buy a house. I'm not lacking in motivations to close sales deals.

Hopefully, I'll also sell a creative project. Yep, I started writing again, working on another nonfiction book and a TV sitcom pilot. With all due respect to LL Cool J, you can call this a comeback.

My writing career lends itself to sports parlance like a 6-4-3 double play. As a rookie, I put up surprisingly good numbers. But following an off-season spent reading – and believing – my press clippings, I arrived at spring training out of shape. The big league club cut me, but my pride prevented me from accepting my assignment to the minors. Nevertheless, I still received an invitation to try out the next season. Inexplicably, I showed up even heavier and slower, a cardinal sin for a player who owed his early success more to hustle and grit than talent. I repeated that behavior for many years. Eventually, teams stopped returning my calls altogether. My agent dropped me. Somehow, I still viewed myself as an All-Star, when in reality many people had stopped caring that I'd ever been a has-been.

As the 2017 season looms, though, I'm in the best shape of my life, thanks to sessions on my therapist's couch. I'm trying a new approach at the plate. No longer will I be content to let decent offerings pass by as I wait for that perfect pitch to take deep. Now, I want to get on base however I can: draw a walk, lay down a bunt, lean into a heater. Whatever the ball club needs, I'll be happy to do. My uniform will get dirty from doing the little things that don't show up in a box score. I just need one GM/publisher/producer to give a hungry veteran a chance.

This time, I'll be sure to appreciate it.

December 23, 2016
Hermosa Beach, California

Acknowledgements

Without the encouragement and generosity of the following folks, Sports Year would have been more like Sports Week. I am eternally grateful to these people who believed in me.

$100
Angie and Jeremy Akers
Angela and Chris Akers
Ernie Altbacker
Katie Anthony
Helen and Al Bourne
Murray Brush
Jay Burke
Tony Dill
Billy Goldberg
Trinda Gregoire
Daryl Hodgkinson
Denis Klein ($126)
John Lamarche
Suzanne LeFevre
Maureen Lynch
The Kolodny Family
Bryan Marvis
Fran McCan
Julie Morgan
Terry Redican
Mike Rooney
Kath Salvaty
Sidney Sherman
Pat Stack
Kay and Doug Stanley
Greg Stross
Jen Sullivan
John Westermeier

$200
Jeff Berthold
Robert Chiappetta
Allan Flowers
Greg Hendry
Max Heppelmann
The Mannings
Kevin McGee
Charlotte and Chris Moscardelli
Kim and Peter Mourani
Brian Reidy
Clare and Patrick Reidy
Gerald Reidy
David Spath
Patrick Sweeney
Liz and Steve Walters ($250)

$500
Deb Fisher (I still owe you a game/day!)
Mary Harder and Wes Mark
Tim Herron
Ryan Hilbelink (See: above comment to Debbie!)
Mike Pearl
Jenny and Mike Rooney
Jenn and Phil Sheridan
Trip Tierney
Mike Zeliger

$1000
David LeFevre
Loretta and Rich Reidy
Matt Smith
Bob Terbrueggen

Jamie Reidy

During Sports Year, I spent 112 nights on the road. To my hosts, I thank you for the bed, the food and the Wi-Fi.

Several people either paid for my tickets or pulled strings for me to get into games where nothing memorable happened. I didn't write about those events, but those omissions belie my gratitude to David Spath (Houston Astros), Mike Barton (Cincinnati Reds), Jaime Maggio (Philadelphia 76ers), Jaime Keating (Duke-UCLA hoops), and Chris Nelson (Boston Celtics).

I am a better person due to the five wounded veterans who gave me the privilege of taking them to games. Oscar, Aaron, Justin, Lamar, and Tom – thank you for your service and your sacrifices. You gentlemen are heroes. Please don't ever forget that.

The debt I owe my editors Steve Egan and Maureen Lynch for their keen eyes and insightful suggestions is huge, but will likely be repaid with cheeseburgers, fries and pitchers of Harp. Angela Lewis-Akers, you are one kickass graphic designer; your book cover nailed my vision better than I had imagined it. Donna and Ed Cavanaugh, my publishers at Humor Outcasts Press and Shorehouse Books, thank you for your tireless enthusiasm and support.

Lastly, Amy Lloyd and I moved in together, and, shortly thereafter, I began writing this book. Cohabitation presents enough challenges and stressors of its own – a partner doesn't need the added joys of learning how to deal with a writer's temperament and "schedule." Thank you, baby, for loving, not killing, me.

About The Author

Jamie Reidy is a University of Notre Dame graduate and a U.S. Army veteran. His first book Hard Sell: The Evolution of a Viagra Salesman served as the basis for the feature film Love and Other Drugs, starring Jake Gyllenhaal as "Jamie." Real-life Jamie really likes typing that sentence. He has published two other books, but nobody wanted to turn them into movies.

Acknowledgements

Without the encouragement and generosity of the following folks, Sports Year would have been more like Sports Week. I am eternally grateful to these people who backed me.

$100
Angie and Jeremy Akers, Angela and Chris Akers, Ernie .Altbacker, Katie Anthony, Helen and Al Bourne, Murray Brush, Jay Burke, Tony Dill, Billy Goldberg, Trinda Gregoire, Daryl Hodgkinson, Denis Klein ($126), John Lamarche, Suzanne LeFevre, Maureen Lynch, The Kolodny Family, Bryan Marvis, Fran McCann, Julie Morgan, Terry Redican, Kath Salvaty, Sidney Sherman, Pat Stack, Kay and Doug Stanley, Greg Stross, Jen Sullivan, and John Westermeier

$200
Jeff Berthold, Robert Chiappetta, Allan Flowers, Greg Hendry, Max Heppelmann, The Mannings, Kevin McGee, Charlotte and Chris Moscardelli, The Mouranis, Brian Reidy, Clare and Patrick Reidy, Gerald Reidy, David Spath, Patrick Sweeney, and Liz and Steve Walters ($250)

$500
Deb Fisher (I still owe you a game/day!), Mary Harder and Wes Mark, Tim Herron, Ryan Hilbelink (See: above comment to Debbie!), Mike Pearl, Jenny and Mike Rooney, Jenn and Phil Sheridan, Trip Tierney, and Mike Zeliger

$1000
David LeFevre, Loretta and Rich Reidy, Matt Smith, Bob Terbrueggen